D0713094

Climate Leviathan

Climate Leviathan

A Political Theory of Our Planetary Future

Joel Wainwright and Geoff Mann

VERSO

London • New York

First published by Verso 2018
© Joel Wainwright and Geoff Mann 2018

1 3 5 7 9 10 8 6 4 2

Verso
UK: 6 Meard Street, London W1F 0EG
US: 20 Jay Street, Suite 1010, Brooklyn, NY 11201
versobooks.com

Verso is the imprint of New Left Books

ISBN-13: 978-1-78663-429-0
ISBN-13: 978-1-78663-430-6 (US EBK)
ISBN-13: 978-1-78663-431-3 (UK EBK)

British Library Cataloguing in Publication Data
A catalogue record for this book is available from the British Library

Library of Congress Cataloging-in-Publication Data
A catalog record for this book is available from the Library of Congress

Typeset in Minion Pro by Hewer Text UK Ltd, Edinburgh
Printed in the UK by CPI Group (UK) Ltd, Croydon CR0 4YY

Contents

Figures

Preface

For most of our lives, we have thought of climate change as a threat looming on the horizon, a challenge that would, perhaps soon, need to be faced. Those days are past. Today, all around the world, the menace we worried about is no longer merely potential, but has rapidly materialized. Record-breaking temperatures on every continent. Rates of extinction so high that the only relevant comparisons are to planetary cataclysms far beyond human memory. Species and ecosystems scrambling to change their geographical range and—where they cannot move quickly, as with coral reefs—perishing altogether. Rising seas, forests ablaze, glaciers disappearing, superstorms. The underlying cause is well known. The increasing proportion of certain trace gases in the Earth's atmosphere (in round numbers, carbon dioxide [CO_2] has risen from 250 to 400 parts per million, methane [CH_4] from 700 to 1700 parts per billion) means a larger proportion of the sun's energy remains in the Earth's seas, land masses, and atmosphere, changing the movement of heat energy through the world's climatic system.[1] As global temperatures rise, the weather changes too. Not just the unbearable summer days that now plague cities across the planet, but highly variable precipitation bringing flood or drought, volatile temperature changes, and more intense storms. This is already taking a toll on everyone, but the heaviest weight of all has fallen on relatively poor and powerless people, as well as the other living things with whom we share this planet. The troubles caused by climate change are accelerating so quickly that we have no ledger capable of measuring them.

We have long known what we need to do to tackle climate change: stop taking carbon (the "C" in CO_2 and CH_4) from the Earth's crust and pumping it into the atmosphere. This means no more extracting and burning coal, oil, and gas. We need to leave fossil fuels in the Earth's crust, where they were formed. It would also make a big difference if we stocked far fewer cows and stopped cutting forests. Had such measures been taken by those who had the capacity to do so, we probably could have averted the terrible implications of climate change. But they were not. The vast proportion of historical greenhouse gases have been emitted as byproducts of the choices and activities, not of the masses of ordinary people, but rather of a wealthy minority of the world's people. Why

---

1   These are simplifications. For details, see Intergovernmental Panel on Climate Change, *Fifth Assessment Report*, Working Group I, 2013.

that wealthy minority did nothing, and what that means for our political futures, are crucial questions we address in this book.

Though we contend with climate change now, its most significant ecological and political consequences are still to come. The challenge of analyzing and anticipating those consequences is enormous. This is partly because both the planet's ecologies and its politics are extraordinarily complex and subject to an almost infinite variety of influences, and partly because climate change is changing what it means to be human on Earth.[2] In this sense the term "Anthropocene" is a useful marker for where we stand: at a transition or break within and into a new era of natural history in which human actions are the decisive force ecologically and geologically.[3] But, in another sense, the term "Anthropocene" is unhelpful, because climate change also makes it clear that there is no such thing as a universal "human" agent that precipitated this new era in planetary history, and no such thing as a common vantage point from which "we all" understand and experience it. There are, rather, only different human communities and ways of reasoning our way through our time.

This book offers a political theory of our planetary future. Our work on these ideas began in the heady days before the 2009 Copenhagen climate summit, a time when we each spoke publicly on these matters. This project emerged as an attempt at self-critique and clarification from within the climate justice movement. We draw upon a robust tradition of political philosophy and critique of capitalist political economy to explain why capitalist societies created our planetary emergency and have failed to mitigate climate change. It is not, however, just another Marxist critique of capitalism's ecological consequences (valuable as those contributions have been). Rather, we are interested in the political effects of these consequences. Rapid climate change will transform global political economy and alter our world's basic political arrangements, processes we call the "adaptation of the political." Our point is not that global warming will simply cause everything to change or collapse. Instead, we argue that under pressure from climate change, the intensification of existing challenges to the extant global order will push existing forms of sovereignty toward one we call "planetary." To advance these arguments, we engage with a wide range of both "classical" sources and more "recent" philosophical attempts to grasp nature, political economy, and sovereignty. The result is a contribution to a political philosophy of planetary climate change, one we hope is adequate to our conjuncture. In Part I, we survey the horizon of our project, outlining the potential political-economic paths we anticipate unfolding in a rapidly warming world. In Part II, we examine in closer detail the path we regard as most likely, which we call "Climate Leviathan." In Part III, we sketch the outlines of a radical alternative.

---

2   We write from North America, in English. The book's provenance cannot be separated from the social formation causing the planetary crisis.

3   The suffix "-cene" (Pleistocene, Holocene, Anthropocene) comes from the Greek *kainos*, "new." See C. Bonneuil and J. Fressoz. *The Shock of the Anthropocene: The Earth, History and Us*, New York: Verso, 2016.

While this is fundamentally a theoretical project, we hope its underlying political stakes are clear and concrete. To date, there has been little substantive carbon mitigation by the leading capitalist states. Global carbon emissions continued to climb each year we worked on this book, and show little sign of slowing down. We are not even close to the scale of change needed to realize the 1.5°C mean temperature increase limit to which the world's leading states agreed at Paris in December 2015. Indeed, the Paris Agreement does not place any substantive limits on the carbon emissions that drive warming (and, of course, Trump pulled the US "out of Paris", weakening the agreement's prospects).[4] The world is getting hotter fast, and the rapid, large-scale carbon mitigation the world needs is impossible without radical change in the existing political-economic structure.

While we struggle, as we must, to limit rapid climate change by mitigations great and small, we also have to think carefully about its likely political consequences, because a world environment as radically changed as climate science suggests will have massive impacts on the way human life on Earth is organized. These questions are on the minds of many, from novelists to physical scientists, from military strategists to organic intellectuals of subaltern social groups. Yet political theory on these questions lags far behind atmospheric chemistry and the physics of ocean heat. This is a major gap. A stable concept of the political can only hold in a relatively stable world environment; when the world is in upheaval, so too are the definition and content of the realm of human life we call "political." Political theory thus has a place in natural history and finds its meaning through critical reflection upon it. Whether we know it or not, all our thinking is environmental, even when it rebels against nature.

Unfortunately, the prospect of rapid environmental change has generally produced an insufficient theoretical response among mainstream "progressive" thinkers. Most of it is pious utopianism ("ten simple ways to save the planet"), an appeal to market solutions ("cap and trade"), or nihilism ("we're fucked").[5] These are false solutions. Lamentably, the Left has rarely done much better, too often treating the climate as peripheral to struggles for democracy, liberty, equality, and justice, when it is precisely these ideals that make the climate struggle so

---

4   The year the Paris Agreement came into effect, 2016, was the warmest on record: "a remarkable 1.1° C above the pre-industrial period, which is 0.06° C above the previous record set in 2015"; World Meteorological Association, "WMO Statement on the State of the Global Climate in 2016," WMO No. 1189, 3, available at library.wmo.int.

5   Of these, only the latter requires citations. The expression "we're fucked" appears not infrequently in political writing on climate change. See, for example, Roy Scranton's *Learning to Die in the Anthropocene*, New York, City Lights, 2015, 16; Wen Stephenson, *What We Are Fighting for Now Is Each Other: Dispatches from the Front Lines of Climate Justice*, Boston, Beacon Press, 2015, 35. Oxford scientist Stephen Emmott uses the same words ("we're fucked") in the documentary *Ten Billion* (2015). The political despondency reflected by the repetition of this phrase is a symptom of the limits of our political imagination. If "we" really are "fucked", then we had better organize for a struggle—to which end we need a stronger political analysis than doom-saying.

fundamental. They are the core goals of the struggle for justice in a world that will be radically transformed by climate change. Consequently, our goal is to make climate *more* political. That requires a theory—a way to conceptualize our conjuncture and understand the relationship between the categories we use to make sense of it—that can help us navigate a hotter planet and the inevitable political-economic changes it will elicit. That kind of theory should embrace science's analysis of environmental change but not expect too much of it politically; it should try to understand the world's possible political-ecological futures without lapsing into environmental determinism; and it should anticipate the coming socio-ecological transformations as a moment of transition in natural history. We offer this book as a contribution toward that theory and the struggles it might inform. Even if our theory turns out to be wrong, it will be worthwhile if it offers a vision of alternatives without appealing to false hopes.

We have been thinking about climate politics for a long time and had help from a lot of people along the way. It is not possible to name them all. After so many informal conversations, and a string of detailed readings and critique, we can no longer distinguish between our own ideas and those of others with whom we've engaged.

The ideas this book originates with first appeared in our paper "Climate Leviathan," *Antipode* 45, no. 1, 1–22, and we would like to thank the journal for supporting its publication. we followed up in "Climate Change and the Adaptation of the Political," *Annals of the Association of American Geographers* 105, no. 2, 313–21. Much of these two papers is scatterd in bits and pieces throughout this book, and we appreciate Wiley-Blackwell's and Routledge's permission to put those thoughts to further work. Other papers we have written that have provided more limited material we draw upon are cited in the text.

We have benefitted from energetic discussion of earlier versions of these arguments at Bucknell, Penn State, University of British Columbia, University of California-Berkeley, Ohio State, Clark, Simon Fraser, University of Victoria, Kentucky, Harvard, Arizona, Uppsala, and West Virginia and the Vancouver Institute of Social Research. We would like to express our deepest appreciation to a few people who made this book not only possible, but also far better than it would have been without them: the folks at Verso (Sebastian Budgen, Duncan Ranslem and Ida Audeh in particular), Dan Adleman, Kiran Asher, Josh Barkan, Patrick Biggar, Michelle Bonner, Jason Box, Bruce Braun, Brad Bryan, Emilie Cameron, Brett Chrstophers, Rosemary Collard, Glen Coulthard, Selena Couture, Deb Curran, Peter Curtis, Jessica Dempsey, Nicolle Etchart, John Foran, Vinay Gidwani, Jim Glassman, Jesse Goldstein, Marcus Green, Matt Hern, Nik Heynen, Am Johal, Will Jones, Kojin Karatani, Mark Kear, Indy Kent, Brian King, Paul Kingsbury, Jake Kosek, Mazen Labban, Philippe LeBillon, Larry Lohmann, Seung-Ook Lee, Bernhard Malkmus, James McCarthy, Kristin Mercer, Sanjay Narayan, Marianna Nicolson, Shiri Pasternak, Shalini

Satkunanandan, Janet Sturgeon, Stephanie Wakefield and Maria Wallstam. All royalties will be donated to Grassroots International's Climate Justice Initiative (grassrootsonline.org).

Anyone who spends some of their time thinking about climate change and about the politics of the world it is producing (and there are a lot of people like that) knows that the going is often tough, the future looks very bleak, and the nights are sometimes sleepless. At times, it is hard not to want to hide away. The more one knows and the longer one stares into the abyss, the more one may be tempted to abandon all hope. Fortunately for us, every day we wake to good reasons not to do that, and it is to them this book is dedicated: Inés, Seamus, and Finn.

Part I

1

Hobbes in Our Time

Auctoritas non veritas facit legem (Authority, not truth, makes law).

Hobbes

I

Carl Schmitt once wrote that "state and revolution, leviathan and behemoth, are actually or potentially always present"—that "the leviathan can unfold in unexpected historical situations and move in directions other than those plotted by its conjurer."[1] For Schmitt, the modern thinker most closely associated with Thomas Hobbes and his *Leviathan*, this was no minor point of order. Leviathan, whether in the Old Testament or in even older myths, was never a captive of its conjurer's will and remains at large today, prowling between nature and the supernatural, sovereign and subject. Yet Leviathan no longer signals the many-headed serpent of the eastern Mediterranean, but Melville's whale and Hobbes's sovereign, the "Multitude so united in one Person" to form the "Common-wealth":

> This is the Generation of that great Leviathan, or rather (to speak more reverently) of that *Mortall God*, to which wee owe under the *Immortall God*, our peace and defense. For by this Authoritie, given him by every particular man in the Common-Wealth, he hath the use of so much power and strength conferred on him, that by terror thereof, he is enabled to forme the wills of them all, to Peace at home, and mutuall ayd against their enemies abroad . . . And he that carryeth this person is called Soveraigne, and said to have Soveraigne Power; and every one besides, his Subject.[2]

How did this figure of sovereign power come to be called Leviathan? Hobbes does not say, but the reference is certainly to the Book of Job. Job, abused by misfortunes cast upon him by Satan, cries out against the injustices visited upon the faithful. God's reply is neither kind nor comforting: he reminds Job not only of His justice, but of His might. God taunts Job with the Leviathan, proof of His worldly authority and of Job's powerlessness:

---

1 Carl Schmitt, *The Leviathan in the State Theory of Thomas Hobbes: Meaning and Failure of a Political Symbol*, Chicago, IL: University of Chicago Press, 2008 [1938], 53.

2 Thomas Hobbes, *Leviathan*, New York: Penguin, 1968, 227–28, emphasis in original.

Can you pull in the leviathan with a fishhook or tie down his tongue with a rope?
Can you put a cord through his nose or pierce his jaw with a hook?
Will he keep begging you for mercy? Will he speak to you with gentle words? . . .
Any hope of subduing him is false; the mere sight of him is overpowering.
No one is fierce enough to rouse him. Who then is able to stand against me?
Who has a claim against me that I must pay?
Everything under heaven belongs to me. [. . .]
On earth [leviathan] has no equal, a creature without fear.
He looks down on all that are haughty; he is king over all that are proud.[3]

Although this reference to a worldly king suggested the metaphor of Leviathan to Hobbes, it was very roughly transposed.[4] As Schmitt is at pains to explain, Hobbes's personification of the emerging form of state sovereignty as Leviathan "has obviously not been derived from mythical speculations."[5] Rather, in the text that bears its name, Leviathan is put to work for different purposes. Leviathan, a sea monster who seems the very embodiment of nature's ferocity, is figured by Hobbes as the means to *escape* the state of nature. As Schmitt indicates, Hobbes's sovereign is a machinic antimonster. And, unlike God's taunts to Job, its sovereignty is not rooted in mere terror, but grounded in a social contract.

Schmitt claimed his 1938 philology of Leviathan was a response to Walter Benjamin that has "remained unnoticed"—specifically, to Benjamin's "Critique of Violence" of 1921. The real point of contention is crystallized in what Giorgio Agamben calls the "decisive document in the Benjamin–Schmitt dossier," that is, Benjamin's thesis VIII on history:[6]

> The tradition of the oppressed classes teaches us that the "state of emergency" in which we live is the rule. We must attain to a concept of history that is in keeping with this insight. Then we shall clearly realize that it is our task to bring about the real state of emergency.[7]

Since the United States inaugurated its most recent states of emergency through wars on terror and economic crisis, Benjamin's eighth thesis has received a lot of attention, and rightly so. Much of this work has been inspired by Agamben's claim that "the declaration of the state of exception has gradually been replaced by an unprecedented generalization of the paradigm of security as the normal technique of government."[8] The ecological crisis has been largely excluded from this discussion. This is a pity because the regulation of security under

---

3   Job 41: 1–34. Biblical quotations are taken from the Ndew Internataional Version.

4   This also holds true if Hobbes was inspired by the reference to the covenant at Job 41: 4.

5   Schmitt, *The Leviathan in the State Theory of Thomas Hobbes*, 21; Gopal Balakrishnan, *The Enemy: An Intellectual Portrait of Carl Schmitt*, London: Verso, 2000, 209–11.

6   Schmitt, quoted in Giorgio Agamben, *State of Exception*, Stanford, CA: Stanford University Press, 2005, 52.

7   Walter Benjamin, *Illuminations*, New York: Schocken Books, 1969, 258.

8   Agamben, *State of Exception*, 14.

exceptional conditions is increasingly a planetary matter. Even more than economic crisis, it is global climate change that has produced the conditions in which "the paradigm of security as the normal technique of government" is being solicited at a scale and scope hitherto unimaginable. What will become of sovereign security under conditions of planetary crisis? Is a warming planet "fierce enough to rouse" Leviathan? Or will Leviathan "beg for mercy"?

Perhaps this seems hyperbolic—perhaps the genie of carbon emissions can be stuffed back in the bottle. But where is the push to mitigate carbon? The long-term trends, which provide the clearest signal, are obvious: since the birth of fossil-fueled capitalism in England, carbon emissions have risen steadily. As that social formation has spread and reformed the world, emissions have grown exponentially. The graph of the quantity of CO_2 in the atmosphere since the emergence of humans approximately 200,000 years ago looks relatively flat until the early nineteenth century. In only the most recent 0.01 percent of human history, everything has changed (see Figure 1.1.) The World must somehow break this so-called hockey stick. We are nowhere near doing so.

Figure 1.1. Atmospheric CO_2, past 10,000 years, the infamous 'hockey stick'

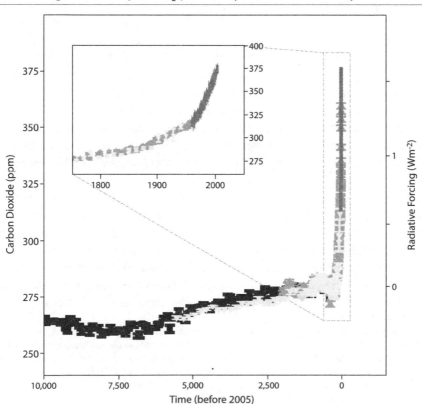

Source: Intergovernmental Panel on Climate Change, Fifth Assessment Report, Working Group I, 2013, available at ipcc.ch.

Figure 1.2. Monthly mean atmospheric CO_2 at Mauna Loa Observatory, 1958 – 2017

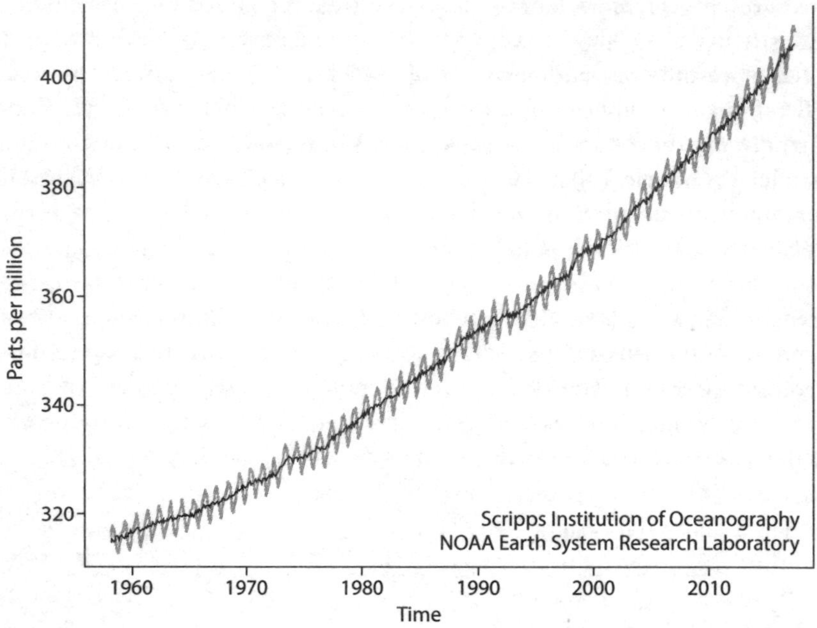

Source: Earth System Research Laboratory, Global Monitoring Division, National Oceanic and Atmospheric Administration, July 2017, available at esrl.noaa.gov.

Even with very slow economic growth after 2007, global carbon emissions jumped by 2.2 percent between 2000 and 2010 (see Figure 1.2).[9] This was the fastest decadal increase in emissions ever recorded, but it is likely to be surpassed in 2010–2020 as global CO_2-equivalent emissions continue to climb, driven by increasing emissions in East Asia, the world's center of commodity production.[10] Capital's drive for profit locks in policies for growth, whatever the cost. One clear signal since 2007–2008 is that elites everywhere, faced with prospects of slow economic growth, are prepared to act swiftly and commit bottomless public funding to prime the pump. The need for profit also locks in infrastructure with devastating climatic implications. In 2012 the International Energy Agency, hardly a revolutionary outfit, warned that without a change of direction, by 2017 the world would have energy infrastructure that "locked in" emissions at a scale that closed "the door" on the possibility of

9   Intergovernmental Panel on Climate Change, Working Group III, Summary for Policymakers, 2014, 7; see also Justin Gillis, "Carbon Emissions Show Biggest Jump Ever Recorded," *New York Times*, December 4, 2011; Glen Peters, Gregg Marland, Corinne Le Quéré, Thomas Boden, Josep G. Canadell, and Michael Raupach, "Rapid growth in CO_2 emissions after the 2008-2009 global financial crisis," *Nature Climate Change* 2, no. 1, 2012, 2–4. We elaborate on these trends in this chapter and the next.

10   James H. Butler and Stephen A. Montzka, "The NOAA Annual Greenhouse Gas Index (AGGI)," 2016, Earth System Research Laboratory, esrl.noaa.gov.

limiting global warming to non-disastrous levels. That infrastructure has since been built.[11] Consistent with the agency's warning, reports from science have grown ever more fantastic as the climatic and ecological implications intensify.

We presume our audience knows the basics, and to avoid hyperbole we will refrain from appealing to frightening headlines from scientific reports. Furthermore, beyond an appreciation of the scientific consensus on climate change, it is not clear that scientific literacy is necessary to grasp the political-economic transformations required, and many who understand the science are not on our side. The political problems we face cannot be fixed by simply delivering science to the masses. If good climate data and models were all that were needed to address climate change, we would have seen a political response in the 1980s. Our challenge is closer to a crisis of imagination and ideology; people do not change their conception of the world just because they are presented with new data. Despite the many dire signals, most people in the global North still find comfort in the belief that the worst consequences—scarcity of food and water, political unrest, inundations and other so-called "natural disasters"—are far enough away or far enough in the future that they will not live to experience them.

That reaction, although ethically unjustifiable, is nevertheless understandable, because the negative consequences of climate change sound out in two rhythms that are not synchronized.[12] There is, on one hand, the almost imperceptible background noise of rising seas and upward ticking of food prices, punctuated, on the other hand, by the occasional pounding of stochastic events. When we started this book in 2010, the northern hemisphere cooked through the hottest summer on record; when we finished it in 2017, those records, already beaten, were surpassed again, month after month. There is no part of the world that has not changed dramatically. Yet as soon as unheralded events occur—wildfires in Russia and Canada, floods in Pakistan and England, coral bleaching in Australia and Belize, species declining everywhere—they are rinsed and lost by the quotidian wash of whatever comes next. The biggest events have a sound of their own, the high-pitched scream of emergency. But because the background noise ultimately *is* this emergency in latent form, the true tone of climate change is not yet properly heard. Neither is Benjamin's call for a "real state of emergency," to which we return in Chapter 8.

---

11   International Energy Agency, *World Energy Outlook 2012*, Paris: International Energy Agency, 2012, 3. At the end of 2015 we spoke with IEA policy analysts in Paris. Right on schedule, they warned that without massive investment in carbon capture-and-storage, we will be locked in to rapid climate change.

12   On historical sensibility and climate change, see Dipesh Chakrabarty, "The Climate of History: Four Theses," *Critical Inquiry* 35, no. 2, 2009, 197–222; also Dale Jamieson, *Reason in a Dark Time: Why the Struggle Against Climate Change Failed—and What it Means for Our Future*, Oxford: Oxford University Press, 2014.

Meanwhile, the ongoing wars for the world's energy supplies are waged on multiplying fronts. Consider the Arctic, which concentrates all the contradictions of our conjuncture into one geographical region. Warming has reduced the polar ice cap so rapidly that we can expect ice-free ship passage by 2030.[13] Rather than spark a rush to cut off fossil fuel exploitation, this terrible manifestation of our planetary emergency has provoked a new geopolitical struggle—led by Russia, China, the United States, and Canada—to control the flow of resources from and through the north, especially fossil fuel energy. The leading capitalist states thus address the problems they have created by deepening the same problems.[14]

In the face of these trends it is difficult to contemplate the future calmly. Merely to confront our perils can paralyze us with fear. As Mike Davis says, "on the basis of the evidence before us, taking a 'realist' view of the human prospect, like seeing Medusa's head, would simply turn us into stone."[15] We have done our best to suppress that dread and wrote *Climate Leviathan* to think through the political-economic futures that climate change seems to us most likely to induce. The mandate for that undertaking, for all its limitations and guesswork, stems from the looming political-economic formations that are no small part of our peril. Above all, we must not be afraid to ask hard questions.

II

To begin, consider two very difficult clusters of questions. First, if the world is to achieve the massive reductions in global carbon emissions we know are necessary, how might we do so? What political processes or strategies could make that happen in anything resembling a just manner? In other words, can we conceive of revolution(s) in the name of *climate justice*, and if so, what do they look like? Second, if carbon emissions do not decline adequately (as seems highly likely to us, for reasons explained below), and climate change reaches some threshold or tipping point at which it is globally impossible to ignore or reverse, then what are the likely political-economic outcomes? What processes, strategies, and social formations will emerge and become hegemonic? Can the defining political-economic formation of the modern world—the capitalist nation-state—survive catastrophic climate change? If so, how, and in what

---

13   And "unprecedented new optimal navigation routes for PC6 vessels through the central Arctic Ocean and Northwest Passage (NWP) ... plainly evident by 2040–2059": Laurence C. Smith and Scott R. Stephenson, "New Trans-Arctic Shipping Routes Navigable by Midcentury," *PNAS* 110, no. 13, 2013, 1191–95.

14   Compare to Charles Ebinger and Evie Zambetakis, "The Geopolitics of Arctic Melt," *International Affairs* 85, 2009, 1215–32; Richard Sale and Eugene Potapov, *The Scramble for the Arctic: Ownership, Exploitation and Conflict in the Far North*, London: Frances Lincoln, 2010. More generally, see Sanjay Chaturvedi and Timothy Doyle, *Climate Terror: A Critical Geopolitics of Climate Change*, London: Palgrave Macmillan, 2015.

15   Mike Davis, "Who Will Build the Ark?" *New Left Review* II/61, January–February 2010, 46.

form? Do we have a theory of how capitalist nation-states are transforming as a consequence of *planetary* change?

We posit that presently, we have few if any answers to these questions. Our challenge, to develop a politics adequate to the current conjuncture, calls for all of us who identify with the emerging global movement for climate justice to elaborate responses to these problems. This will not be easy of course. Coherent answers are not only a matter of theory, but also of forms of political struggle that sound out the barriers to and prospects for social and ecological transformation.

Many are thinking through these questions. There is a raft of recent scholarship on climate change and the prospects for political change, with especially significant contributions from environmental sociology, critical human geography, and international relations.[16] Yet given that climate change is a complex, antidisciplinary problem, it is perhaps unsurprising that much of the most exciting work on the prospects for radical change has been written outside of academia. For example, Naomi Klein's *This Changes Everything: Capitalism Versus the Climate* answers our first question—can we conceive of revolution(s) in the name of *climate justice*, and if so, what do they look like?— affirmatively, arguing that we can overcome the deadlock in the struggle between capitalism and climate justice by building a global movement from "Blockadia":

> Blockadia is not a specific location on a map but rather a roving transnational conflict zone that is cropping up with increasing frequency and intensity wherever extractive projects are attempting to dig and drill, whether for open-pit mines, or gas fracking, or tar sands oil pipelines. What unites these increasingly interconnected pockets of resistance is the sheer ambition of the mining and fossil fuel companies: the fact that in their quest for high-priced commodities and higher-risk "unconventional" fuels, they are pushing relentlessly into countless new territories, regardless of the impact on the local ecology . . . What unites Blockadia too is the fact the people at the forefront—packing local council meetings, marching in capital cities, being hauled off in police vans, even putting their bodies between the earth-movers and earth—do not look much like your typical activist, nor do the people in one Blockadia site resemble those in another. Rather, they each look like the places where they live, and they look like everyone: the local shop owners, the university professors, the high school students, the grandmothers . . . Resistance to high-risk extreme extraction is building a global, grassroots, and broad-based network . . . driven by a desire for a deeper form of democracy, one that provides communities with real control over those resources that are most critical to collective survival—the health of the water, air, and soil. In the process, these place-based stands are stopping real climate crimes in

---

16   Even a selective summary of these fields would result in an unwieldy (and rather arbitrary) list.

progress. Seeing those successes, as well as the failures of top-down environmentalism, many young people concerned about climate change are taking a pass on the slick green groups and the big UN summits. Instead, they are flocking to the barricades of Blockadia.[17]

Although we do not agree with everything in *This Changes Everything* (we quibble with Klein's approach to capitalism and its history), we strongly endorse this utopian vision of a movement from Blockadia, one that overturns fossil fuels and capitalist political economy in the name of a new relationship to community and the environment. Klein's vision of a prefigurative politics—reworking democracy through the collective act of placing our "bodies between the earth-movers and earth"—provides a vibrant and compelling answer to the question of what climate justice revolution looks like. For good reason, therefore, Klein has been at the forefront of the international climate justice movement.

Another critical stream of recent literature takes a darker view of the prospects for social and ecological transformation. In marked contrast to Klein, philosopher Dale Jamieson argues that the window of time for Blockadia-driven changes has already closed; the world is firmly committed to climate change. If we are to generate an ethical response to the Anthropocene, he claims, we must learn to accept where we stand historically, which is at the end of a period when climate science generated insights that could have led to dramatic political-economic change, but did not.

> In 1992 the largest gathering of heads of state ever assembled met at the Rio Earth Summit and more than 17,000 attended the alternative NGO forum. This marked the beginning of a truly global environmental movement . . . The Rio dream was that the countries of North and South would join hands to protect the global environment and lift up the world's poor. After nearly two decades of struggle, it was clear by the 2009 Copenhagen Climate Change Conference [COP15] that the [Rio] dream was over. The hope that the people of the world would solve the problem of climate change through a transformation in global values had come to an end. What I want to understand is what happened in those years to bring us to where we are today. In that understanding is a key to surviving the future.[18]

The strength of Jamieson's argument is its resolute realism. He brackets the debate on whether meaningful mitigation (emissions reductions that could avoid calamity) is still possible; instead, he seeks to explain why we failed. His

---

17   Naomi Klein, *This Changes Everything: Capitalism Versus the Climate*, New York: Simon and Schuster, 2014, 253–54.

18   Dale Jamieson, *Reason in a Dark Time: Why the Struggle against Climate Change Failed—and What It Means for Our Future*, Oxford: Oxford University Press, 2014, 3. On political philosophy and climate change see also Steve Vanderheiden (ed.), *Political Theory and Global Climate Change*, Cambridge, MA: MIT Press, 2008.

explanation centers on important elements: the challenge of communicating the complexities of climate science for political and economic policy; the lack of attention to the issues in the United States; the failure of successive US administrations to commit to international agreements; and so on. Yet his account is lacking in some respects we consider crucial. It provides no analysis of capitalism or its relation with nature. Even though it relies at key points on the concept of "ideology," there is little analysis of the substance of ideology in climate politics. And, while his detailed historical chapter is largely persuasive on its terms, we see little justification for beginning the narrative in the late nineteenth century, with the development of climate science.[19] Even if humanity only began to *understand* climate change in the late nineteenth century, we began to *cause* it earlier. To grasp the philosophical roots of our climate politics predicament, we must dig deeper.

Roy Scranton's *Learning to Die in the Anthropocene* provides another history of the failure to address climate change, one that pushes the narrative farther back to the origins of "Western civilization". It is a vivid manifesto for those who believe "civilization" is doomed:

> [W]e have failed to prevent unmanageable global warming and . . . global capitalist civilization as we know it is already over . . . [H]umanity can survive and adapt to the new world of the Anthropocene if we accept human limits and transience as fundamental truths, and work to nurture the variety and richness of our collective cultural heritage. Learning to die as an individual means letting go of our predispositions and fear. Learning to die as a civilization means letting go of this particular way of life and its ideas of identity, freedom, success, and progress.[20]

In the face of all the world's challenges, we can appreciate the urge to "let go" of an entire way of life. But Scranton's call for us to "learn to die" offers no political direction, only misanthropy. At a time when the Left everywhere must reinvent means to live together, we cannot make acceptance of death our aspiration. And while we too think that climate change will intensify liberal capitalism's challenges, Scranton is wrong that "nobody has real answers" and that "the problem is *us*."[21] The coming crisis is not "unmanageable"; it is already here, already being managed by liberal capitalism (if rather badly). Indeed, the very "manageability" of the crisis is part of the problem we face. To address it, we do not need to learn to die, but to think, live, and rebel. Moreover, the problem is hardly "us" in the abstract, as if that catastrophe was built into human nature. The problem

---

19   On ideology, see Jamieson, *Reason in a Dark Time*, 37, 47; on history, see Chapter 2. These differences notwithstanding, we reiterate our appreciation for Jamieson's unflinching realism and strongly agree with him that historicizing the failure to address climate change is essential.

20   Ibid., 24.

21   Roy Scranton, *Learning to Die in the Anthropocene*, New York: City Lights, 2015, 68, emphasis added.

is largely associated with a specific minority of "us," and the way that minority's "civilization" have determined the fate of the entire planet. Rather than accept that "civilization" is dead, we need to struggle to create one that is truly civilized.

At the core of all these contributions—and many others in a literature too vast to review here—are arguments regarding history and nature: How shall we study history and learn its lessons? Any hope of overcoming the planetary crisis requires that we understand that crisis, and this effort must be self-consciously historicist, that is, it must analyze that crisis as an historical moment, to understand, as far as possible, the forces that have helped shape it. The always-fraught politics of historical interpretation is further complicated by the question of nature, human and nonhuman. To what can or should human life aspire? How far back should we go in trying to relay the story of climate change? Many, like Klein, date the crisis to the failure to address climate change during the 1970s. Jamieson focuses on the science of climate change and its encounter with elite policy-makers in the capitalist core, which takes him to the late nineteenth century. The so-called "ecological Marxist" literature offers a much deeper appreciation of our historical trajectory. One lesson it teaches is that natural history underwent a decisive shift during the eighteenth century in England, when a metabolic rift opened between the city and the country, society (the masses) and nature (the Earth's material flows).[22] Some of the richest work examines the political side of these processes, to provide a theory of the emergence of the modern capitalist nation-state system as an event in the Earth's natural history. These works provide a framework for a critical natural history of the planetary crisis; ours attempts to theorize its likely political consequences.

To be sure, we too take Marx's analysis of capitalism as fundamental, and ecological Marxism as a crucial contribution. But these readings also impose limitations for our project. They often simply posit the inevitable "natural limits" to capital's growth tendency as the basis for a political analysis—the so-called "second contradiction" of capital (the "first contradiction" being that between the forces and social relations of production). But the distinctive, complex qualities of climate change as a political problem—such as the centrality of science for diagnosing our future, the spatial unevenness of causes and effects, the paradoxical temporality of a "tomorrow" that must be addressed today—can be neither explained nor overcome with an analysis limited to Marx's critique of capitalism. Indeed, even its critics must acknowledge capitalism's distinctive dynamism and robustness; it has deferred a long list of supposedly "inevitable" crises far past the immanent deadlines so often pronounced. To our knowledge, no ecological Marxists have elaborated a theory of the likely political

22   Andreas Malm, *Fossil Capital: The Rise of Steam Power and the Roots of Global Warming*, London: Verso, 2015; John Bellamy Foster, Brett Clark, and Richard York, *The Ecological Rift: Capitalism's War on the Earth*, New York: Monthly Review Press, 2010.

consequences of climate change. Indeed, in some works, the thorny question of the political is almost entirely evaded, except to say that capitalism must be transcended. But what if it isn't?

III

It will be useful to begin to lay the ground for our theoretical framework by identifying four core propositions upon which we build our argument.

1. There is no legitimate basis for debating climate change as such. The climate is changing because of anthropogenic modification of the chemical composition of our atmosphere. The knowledge we have of these changes, distilled from scientific research, is crucial for calibrating our understanding of the future, and we should support further scientific analysis. At the same time, we must beware of expecting too much from science politically.[23]
2. Rapid climate change is sure to have dreadful and often deadly consequences, particularly for the relatively weak and the marginalized (both human and nonhuman). A political or ethical analysis is therefore of the utmost urgency.[24]

The authors cited in the past few pages all agree with these first two points. Important divergences stem from the third and fourth.

3. The political-ecological conditions within which decisions about climate change are being (and will be) made are marked fundamentally by uncertainty and fear; there are no real climate *decisions*, only reactions. Humanity may or may not have time to drastically mitigate carbon and, therefore, slow climate change. Given the complexity of the world's climatic system, however, we can only ever know this retrospectively. We assume that we may not yet be past the point where rapid climate change is unstoppable; however, as we will elaborate, there are strong political-economic reasons to believe that we are not going to avoid this fate. In other words, we agree with Jamieson and Scranton—and others, like Alyssa Battistoni and Andreas Malm—that the time has come for an analysis that anticipates (even as it fights against) a rapidly warming world.[25]

---

23 Intergovernmental Panel on Climate Change, *Fifth Assessment Report*, Working Group I; Lonnie G. Thompson, "Climate Change: The Evidence and Our Options," *The Behavior Analyst* 33, no. 2, 2010, 153–70. The only hold-outs from recognizing this point, so-called "hard-core climate deniers," will find little of use in *Climate Leviathan*: nonetheless, we will try to recuperate one important element of their political position in Chapter 2. We return to Thompson and the politics of climate science in Chapter 3.

24 Intergovernmental Panel on Climate Change, *Fifth Assessment Report*, Working Group II.

25 Alyssa Battistoni, "Back to No Future," *Jacobin* 10; Malm, *Fossil Capital*.

4. The elite transnational social groups that dominate the world's capitalist nation-states certainly desire to moderate and adapt to climate change—not least to stabilize the conditions that produce their privileges. And yet, to date, they have failed to coordinate a response.[26] Thus climate change poses direct and indirect challenges to their hegemony, processes of accumulation, and modes of governance. In light of this, we must expect that elites will increasingly attempt to coordinate their reactions, all while sailing seas of uncertainty and incredulity.

Whether or not Mike Davis is correct that "growing environmental and socio-economic turbulence may simply drive elite publics into more frenzied attempts to wall themselves off from the rest of humanity,"[27] we must consider the means by which such power might be exercised. And we must think these possibilities through beyond the increasingly common "collapse" narratives.[28] It is not enough to forecast doom, however justified it might sometimes seem, in the hope that the mere fear of it will help us find an emergency exit. Only an analysis of the political forces that produce the potentiality of collapse, and the ways in which those forces might themselves be transformed by that potentiality, will lead to an understanding of emerging "relations of force."[29] These relations of force will take a limited number of forms. Examining the possibilities is urgent if we are to produce an effective counterresponse.

To this end, *Climate Leviathan* elaborates a framework by which to understand the range of political possibilities, taking into consideration their attendant theoretical resources, social class bases, contradictions, and so on. Our aim is to grasp how the world is moving in the face of a *necessary* conjuncture, which is nothing but a product of *contingency*. This "necessity" has absolutely nothing to do with inviolable laws of historical development; neither does it translate to "inevitability." Rather, it is a "necessity" in the full Hegelian sense, one that describes the conditions, dynamics, qualities, and forces that make our conjuncture what it is and not something else. The immanent logic of planetary sovereignty, whether it ever realizes itself, is already at work, already shaping our world.[30] The necessity of the precarious world in which we live lies not in what nature has wrought, but in the determinant features of what Nicos Poulantzas called the "current situation." We must debate the state of the planet, how power

26   Davis, "Who Will Build the Ark?" 2010; Patrick Bond, "Climate Capitalism Won at Cancun," *Links: International Journal of Socialist Renewal*, December 12, 2010.

27   Davis, "Who Will Build the Ark?" 38.

28   For example, Gwynne Dyer, *Climate Wars: The Fight for Survival as the World Overheats*, Oxford: Oneworld, 2010; Cleo Paskal, *Global Warring: How Environmental, Economic, and Political Crises Will Redraw the Map of the World*, London: Palgrave, 2010.

29   Antonio Gramsci, [Q13§17] *Selections from the Prison Notebook*, translated and edited by Quintin Hoare and Geoffrey Nowell Smith, New York: International Publishers, 1971, 180.

30   See, for example, Kennedy Graham (ed.), *The Planetary Interest: A New Concept for the Global Age*, London: UCL, 1999.

operates, our political opportunities, and more. But we must also take those conclusions, tentative and partial as they will be, as a description of the *necessary* conditions in which we work, and thereby attempt to anticipate what futures they might bring.[31] To put this in methodological terms, we offer a conjunctural analysis, not a teleology, to describe an array of existing social forces and the paths along which they are likely to unfold. Such analyses are inherently limited yet necessary if we seek a different political and ecological arrangement.[32]

To execute this project, we join two broad philosophical traditions. First, we extend the critique of political economy, drawing principally from Marx-Gramsci-Poulantzas, to examine the likely responses of capitalist societies (and their states) to the challenge of planetary climate change. To this end, we present a concise explanation of capital as a form of organizing social and natural life and examine how this form shapes the conception of "adaptation" in the bourgeois imagination. This is by no means to argue that capitalist societies cannot adapt to climate change—they are already doing so. Rather, we contend that the drive to defend capitalist social relations will push the world toward "Climate Leviathan," namely, adaptation projects to allow capitalist elites to stabilize their position amidst planetary crises. This scenario, we posit, implies a shift in the character and form of sovereignty: the likely emergence of *planetary sovereignty*, defined by an exception proclaimed in the name of preserving life on Earth. We are not suggesting that sovereignty will be characterized by the quasi-monarchical rule of a single person, but rather we recognize—as some suggest Hobbes himself and even Carl Schmitt, at least after 1932, also recognized—that it is almost certainly to be exercised by a collection of powers coordinated to "save the planet," and to determine what measures are necessary and what and who must be sacrificed in the interests of life on Earth.

Elaborating these concepts requires a critical if selective engagement with theories of sovereignty since Hobbes. Our guiding thread is the conviction that only a theory capable of radically examining capitalism *and* sovereignty holds any hope of orienting us today. If we are to become capable of enacting revolutionary climate justice, we need a stronger conception of that being, that politics, that world, for which we act.[33] Fighting for climate justice will require a critique of false

---

31   On Hegel's conception of necessity, see Geoff Mann, "A Negative Geography of Necessity," *Antipode* 40, no. 5, 920–33.

32   As Merleau-Ponty once wrote: "It was said long ago that politics is the art of the possible. That does not suppress our initiative: since we do not *know* the future, we have only, after carefully weighing everything, to push in our own direction. But that reminds us of the gravity of politics; it obliges us, instead of simply forcing our will, to look hard among the facts for the shape they should take." (*Humanism and Terror: An Essay on the Communist Problem,* Boston: Beacon Press, 1947, *xxxv*).

33   Many of our colleagues in the climate justice movement have said this before. Consider, for instance, this statement from the Building Bridges Collective:

It is clear . . . that much more work is required if climate justice is to become an effective concept for linking up and expanding the social struggles we desperately require . . . [A]t the very least,

solutions but also much more. Hence, we conclude by offering our prognosis for change. Our mandate here comes from a conviction that only in a world that has defeated the emerging Climate Leviathan and its planetary sovereignty while also transcending capitalism is it possible to imagine a just response to climate change. In Chapter 7 we speculate upon a revolutionary political strategy, a possible means through which elite reactions may be thwarted, which—to avoid suggesting we know or can yet determine the form it will take—we call "Climate X." So, if Climate X is our dénouement, why title the book *Climate Leviathan*?

IV

Thomas Hobbes's *Leviathan, or, The Matter, Forme & Power of a Common-Wealth Ecclesiaticall and Civil*, is a massive, sprawling and often enigmatic work, an account of everything from the nature of sovereignty and law to England and the immanent Kingdom of God. Hobbes's arguments remain a subject of heated debate. Some read *Leviathan* as an argument for absolutism as the only protection against the chaos of the state of nature; some find in it the outlines of bourgeois liberalism's property-based social order or even "radical democracy."[34] Others read it as nothing less than the "philosophical correlative of the inherent instability of a community founded on power."[35]

Published in 1651, *Leviathan* reflects the tumultuous political times of Hobbes's England. Conflict between Parliament and Charles I had been brewing for years, the king even going so far as to dissolve Parliament for eleven years (1629–1640). Parliamentary recall in 1640 led quickly to further struggle, and civil war broke out in 1642. Hobbes was by then living in self-imposed exile in Paris, having fled in 1640 in fear that the circulation of his pro-royalist writings made him a target for retribution. *Leviathan* thus eventually appeared in print near the end of nine years of civil war, from which (as Hobbes expected) the Parliamentarian "Roundheads" would emerge victorious, having only two years earlier beheaded Charles I. But, as Hobbes would also have anticipated, the victory did not mean an end to political instability. By 1653, Parliament was dissolved again and Oliver Cromwell had assumed a dictatorial "Protectorship" over all of

---

[the concept of climate justice] can help us to move beyond ideas that climate change is somehow separate from the rest of our lives [and] re-politicise the crisis in a way that refocuses attention back on the way our societies are organised . . . However, this can only be done by opposing the more problematic and contradictory uses of the term . . . Climate justice . . . can be part of opening up these many answers . . . in its ability to bring people into an antagonistic relation with capital . . . through the active creation of different ways of organising existence.

Building Bridges Collective, *Space for Movement? Reflections from Bolivia on Climate Justice, Social Movements and the State*, 2010, 82–83, available at spaceformovement.files.wordpress.com.

34   Quentin Skinner, *Hobbes and Republican Liberty*, Cambridge: Cambridge University Press, 2008; James R. Martel, *Subverting the Leviathan: Reading Thomas Hobbes as a Radical Democrat*, New York: Columbia University Press, 2007.

35   Hannah Arendt, *The Origins of Totalitarianism*, New York: Harcourt, Brace, 1951, 139–43.

England. He lasted only five years, and in the upheaval following his death, royalist opposition managed to arrange Charles II's restoration to the throne in 1660.

All of which is to say that when Hobbes was writing in Paris in the late 1640s and early 1650s, his world was extraordinarily uncertain, saturated with violence and volatility. Prospects seemed dire. There was little reason to expect the emergence of a new and lasting social order. *Leviathan* was Hobbes's response to this almost ungraspable conjuncture. In it, he takes up a mode of exposition that Hegel, writing a century and a half later, would call "speculative." In the section called "Common-wealth," Hobbes describes and justifies the fundamental political and social structures of a world that (unlike his own) would be adequate to the challenge of his conjuncture—in other words, one that could have subdued the political unrest without descending into civil war. His analysis is speculative insofar as it serves as a basis for judging worlds (like his own) not yet equal to that task. Arguably, Hobbes had no choice but to embrace speculation: theorizing something that did not yet exist would have been the only way to understand his world in a manner that did not entail abandoning his hopes for what it might yet become.[36]

Therefore, we should refrain from dismissing *Leviathan* as either utopian—however different Hobbes's vision looks from our own utopias—or teleological, that is, predicated upon an inevitable endpoint. These are standard criticisms of Hegel and Marx, too, and in all three cases they are unfounded. Hobbes's hopes were rooted in what we now recognize as a proto-capitalist, market-based society, ruled by a pre-modern form of absolutism that few would endorse today.[37] Like Kant's *Perpetual Peace*, Hegel's *Philosophy of Right*, and Marx's *Capital*[38]— and other speculative efforts before and since—it was an attempt to understand existing conditions by showing their underlying tendencies and their direction as well as an analysis that sought to explain what was coming by helping to bring

---

36 This is surely part of the reason it is among the first major works of political philosophy written in vernacular English (not Latin, the language of European scholarship at the time).

37 Reinhart Koselleck, *Critique and Crisis: Enlightenment and the Pathogenesis of Modern Society*, Boston: MIT Press, 1988, 40: "Hobbes raised the issues that characterized the seventeenth century. What proves the strength of his thinking is its inherent prognosticative element."

38 We discuss Kant and Hegel below. Apropos this element of Marx's thought, it is worth revisiting the important claim from *The German Ideology*:

[S]imple categories [may] represent relations or conditions which may reflect the immature concrete situation without as yet positing the more complex relation or condition which is conceptually expressed in the more concrete category . . . Money . . . existed in historical time before capital, banks, wage-labour, etc. came into being. In this respect it can be said, therefore, that the simpler category expresses relations predominating in an immature entity or subordinate relations in a more advanced entity; relations which already existed historically before the entity had developed the aspects expressed in a more concrete category. The procedure of abstract reasoning which advances from the simplest to more complex concepts to that extent conforms to actual historical development.

Karl Marx and Friedrich Engels, *The German Ideology*, Amherst, MA: Prometheus Books, 1967 [1846], 142.

a new order into being. That effort required an assessment of the conjuncture "without despondency but also without pretence."[39]

Hobbes was a seventeenth-century Christian: he never doubted history's ultimate destination in the Kingdom of God. But he was more than aware that natural history does not follow a track and makes no promises. He knew well that worldly things will not take care of themselves and could go terribly wrong: this is obvious enough from someone who tells us that in the "state of nature" human life is "nasty, brutish, and short."[40] This is why he felt compelled to speculate on forces that might emerge and on worlds that did not yet exist. Marx struggled similarly, in fact. He and Engels acknowledge on the first page of the *Manifesto of the Communist Party* that in the ongoing historical opposition between "oppressor and oppressed," revolutionary social transformation is not guaranteed. Instead, it is only one of two likely outcomes: the other is "the common ruin of the contending classes." For them, rather like Leviathan's Common-Wealth, the proletarian revolution becomes the object of "speculation"—a theory that might help realize itself.

This book takes up the speculative mode in a way that is indebted to both Hobbes and Marx. We are emphatically not Hobbesian in the colloquial, "war of all against all" sense of the term. Rather, we follow Hobbes's efforts to understand a form of power or government that is not yet consolidated but which exists *in potentia*: hence we call it "Climate Leviathan." Like Hobbes, we believe that even though it is not yet realized, power is gathering to make it so, and insofar as its possible emergence already organizes expectations of the future, it indelibly shapes the present. Yet, unlike Hobbes, we are not hopeful at the prospect of this Leviathan. Hence we seek also to understand a global movement that is emergent but is not yet realized, and to contribute in a minor way toward its realization: a global climate justice revolution. Whereas Marx characterized the proletariat as capital's gravediggers, we will not specify any particular social group or class as *the* revolutionary subject (or the "anti-Leviathan")[41] While

---

39   Lucio Magri, *The Tailor of Ulm*, London: Verso, 2011, 54.

40   Hobbes's famous depiction of the state of nature has been internalized by some in the modern environmental movement. One of the many recent books published by a left-wing climate activist, J. Brecher's *Against Doom* (Oakland, CA: PM Press, 2017), concludes by sketching "two scenarios" of possible futures. One is eco-utopian; the other is simply called "Doom" (95–96). In the latter scenario, "Life will be nasty, brutish, and short" (96). Brecher does not cite Hobbes.

41   Marx's claim about capital creating its own gravediggers comes from Chapter 1 of the *Manifesto of the Communist Party*, written with Engels:

The essential conditions for the existence and for the sway of the bourgeois class is the formation and augmentation of capital; the condition for capital is wage-labour. Wage-labour rests exclusively on competition between the labourers. The advance of industry, whose involuntary promoter is the bourgeoisie, replaces the isolation of the labourers, due to competition, by the revolutionary combination, due to association. The development of Modern Industry, therefore, cuts from under its feet the very foundation on which the bourgeoisie produces and appropriates products. What the bourgeoisie therefore produces, above all, are its own grave-diggers.

Karl Marx and Friedrich Engels, "The Manifesto of the Communist Party" (1848), Chapter 1, accessed at marxists.org.

diverse kinds and forms of power constitute the current conjuncture, we hope to identify a basis to confront what lies ahead: a mode of capitalist planetary governance, an unstable Climate Leviathan that arrogates to itself sovereign authority to act in the interests of life on Earth. The present demands a theory of a movement still in formation, to oppose a power still inchoate. The specters of both are already taking shape.

We conceive of this speculative demand, and our effort to respond to it, as paradigmatically political. This may seem an unnecessary qualification: if you are talking about a potential Climate Leviathan and a global climate justice struggle, then it hardly needs saying that it is political. If we may define "the political" as the arena of the social in which the relations between the dominant and the dominated are worked out, then it is true that some forms of specula-tion are inherently depoliticizing insofar as they either elide the gap between paradise and the current situation (utopianism) or imply that history will take us there on its own (teleology).[42] Indeed, these are the bases upon which many have dismissed Marx as a hopeless utopian and Hegel as the philosopher of the Prussian restoration. Both accusations are entirely wrong-headed, and the history of speculative political thought—at least the thread we follow, running from Hobbes, Kant, and Hegel to Marx—cannot be written off as merely utopian or reactionary.

V

This brings us back to the political thought associated with Carl Schmitt and his influential reading of Hobbes. Schmitt defines the political not by a specific domain of action (legislative or juridical, for example) but as the realm of pure sovereign decision (always executed in the context of actual or potential violence) and the identification of friend and enemy. The determination of the friend/enemy distinction is irreducibly existential and ultimately constrained only by the strategic self-interests of the sovereign. Outside the sovereign's single obligation—the protection of its subjects, which grants the decision its existen-tial character—no ethical or legal frameworks can hamper the decision, or chal-lenge it once made. In this sense, the sovereign's actions are exempted from the weight of culture, obligation, tradition, honour and history. The only ground is that provided by the irremediable possibility of violent death: war, civil or foreign. Consequently, the political as sovereign decision describes the inescap-able acts of identification of and confrontation with the enemy, and its only law is no law at all: a sovereign variation on what Kant called *Ius necessitatis*, the law of necessity, and (as Kant himself put it) *necessitas non habet legem*—necessity has no law.[43] This is the basis upon which Schmitt prioritizes legitimacy over

---

42   A provisional definition. On "the political," see Chapter 4.

43   Immanuel Kant, "The Metaphysics of Morals," in *Practical Philosophy*, Cambridge: Cambridge University Press, 1996 [1797], 392.

legality, since the law is not the source but the product of legitimate sovereign power: as Hobbes said, *auctoritas non veritas facit legem*—authority or power, not truth, makes law.[44]

Sovereignty is thus inherently and paradoxically contextual and noncontingent, historically specific yet seemingly transhistorical. It is exercised unconditionally, *in situ*, hinging only upon itself. In a stylized history of European modernity underwritten by Hobbes and Schmitt, the state *qua* sovereign (product of the necessary friend–enemy distinction, rooted in the human–nature distinction) operates a political theater that advances the general interests through sovereign power and domestic order: the precondition for the flourishing of private freedom in civil society (mediated by money, protected by property). The protection of this bourgeois civil society by an absolutist state, through its total domination of the political, is a crucial step on the road to modernity. On this account, what we call today "civil society" emerged because the state proscribed private morality, including religion, from the political realm, in which decisions were made not on the basis of justice but force: life versus death. For Schmitt, politics is only authentically political when political society *qua* state actors advance the interests of the sovereign, unconstrained by a civil society that (in return for stability and protection) willingly offers up its obedience.

Taking a leaf from Hegel, Schmitt's student Reinhart Koselleck elaborated this argument in the historical realm. The dynamic established by this conception and practice of politics, he said, germinated the seeds of sovereignty's undoing.[45] In the soil of ordered stability that absolutism allowed, where civil society developed relatively freely, it nurtured appropriately "nonpolitical," moral conceptions of political life that judged the sovereign by abstract and "unrealistic" standards which took no account of the messy pragmatics of real-world political constraints. Koselleck argues that this attack on the absolutist state on merely speculative bases undermined the legitimacy of the tough, decisive, and violent realm of *raison d'état* in which ethics was always subordinate to politics—or, more precisely, in which any difference between ethics and politics is "thematically pointless," since the "need to found a state transforms the moral alternative of good and evil into the political alternative of peace and war."[46] An increasingly autonomous private realm, elaborated under the protection that obedience secured, cultivated Enlightenment and "critique," ultimately throwing into crisis the very state order that made it possible: "Bourgeois man [*sic*], condemned to a non-political role, sought refuge in Utopia. It gave him power

---

44   Carl Schmitt, *Legality and Legitimacy*, Durham, NC: Duke University Press, 2004. The phrase is from the Latin edition of *Leviathan* Hobbes published in 1668, part II, 133.

45   Koselleck, *Critique and Crisis*, 15; see also Schmitt, *The Leviathan in the State Theory of Thomas Hobbes*; Jürgen Habermas, *The Structural Transformation of the Public Sphere: An Inquiry into a Category of Bourgeois Society*, Cambridge, MA: MIT Press, 1991, 90–91.

46   Koselleck, *Critique and Crisis*, 25.

and security. It was the indirect political power *par excellence* in whose name the Absolutist order was overthrown."[47]

Seen from sovereign heights, then, speculation is not so much nonpolitical but evidence of an antipolitical politics, meaning that speculation fails to grasp the essence of the political. It is threatening because it rejects the concrete conjuncture in favor of an abstract principle as its basis. According to Koselleck, in contrast to liberal or radical histories of the consolidation of critique in popular political life—crystallized in figures like Rousseau, Kant, and Marx, and leading to revolution and democracy—the revolutionary end of absolutism and the flourishing of the public sphere, with which so many have associated Rousseau, was *not* emancipatory. On the contrary, by rejecting the existential priority of the sovereign as defining the political, it opened the historical door to all manner of speculative political instability and ideological fanaticism, including Nazism and Stalinism. Thus some conservative social thinkers, again like Koselleck, have found unexpected fellows in certain Marxists, like Adorno and Horkheimer, who see in Nazism the disastrous apotheosis of the Enlightenment. This finding is neither accidental nor the result of an elite contempt for populism (even if Adorno and Koselleck shared that contempt). The idea that the ultimate source of evil and its demagogues is the virus of private morality and "ideology" circulating in place of politics reflects the persistent grip of Hobbesian common sense, at least in the liberal capitalist heart of Europe and North America, especially but not only among elites.

Notwithstanding the reconstitution of the political terrain in the twentieth century—the result of tireless struggles like those of the labor, anticolonial, civil rights, and feminist movements, among others—this fundamentally absolutist conception of politics remains powerful, if not dominant. Hobbes's Leviathan is widely presumed to be what sovereign power really is, or how it actually works, when the chips are down; it alone reflects properly *political* politics. Any attempt to propose or construct an alternative, however compelling, is seen as more or less quixotic insofar as it proposes to reorient history's "natural" trajectory. The critique of radical democracy or communism, for instance, is rarely that Left politics are ethically unjustifiable. It is that they are fundamentally naive, utopian, unrealistic, and so on. This unspoken absolutism remains persuasive to many. It shapes the right-Hobbesian lineage running through Schmitt and Koselleck to the so-called "realists" of international relations scholarship. This is how, for example, Schmitt (not entirely unfairly) recruits Hegel—who joyfully toasted the fall of the Bastille every fourteenth of July—to the defense of Leviathan when Hobbes fails. The result seems paradoxical: Schmitt the defender of the sovereign exception announces himself as the

---

47   Ibid., 182.

savior of true freedom from liberalism's "neutralizations and depoliticizations."[48]

But it is not only in the reactionary theoretical tradition that background levels of absolutism radiate (Schmitt traced his own lineage through Bodin, de Maistre, Bonald, and Donoso Cortés).[49] We can find a more specific instance in Hannah Arendt's seemingly common-sense assessment of the origins of totalitarianism. With the geopolitical fallout of World War I, she reasoned,

> [the] last remnants of solidarity between the non-emancipated nationalities in the "belt of mixed populations" [central Europe] evaporated with the disappearance of a central despotic bureaucracy which also served to gather together and divert from each other the diffuse hatreds and conflicting national claims. Now *everybody was against everybody else*, and most of all against his closest neighbors.[50]

Arendt presciently recognized that this condition—which she characterized as the "denationalization" of the "stateless people"—would become "a powerful weapon of totalitarian politics," a weapon forged in the "power vacuum" left by the dismantling of the Austro-Hungarian empire and the dissolution of the Czarist regime.[51] Arendt's analysis repeats Hobbes differently ("now everybody was against everybody else"), while also foreshadowing the political reaction we should expect to a world with hundreds of millions of climate refugees who are not recognized as such—but only as denationalized or stateless peoples, and perhaps as victims of "natural disasters."

Even when we manage to construct institutions and social relations that keep it at bay, Leviathan is, if tacitly, posited as inevitable. And this inevitability seems irrefutable because in one form or other it always returns: state of emergency, exception, crisis, "everybody against everybody"—these are synonyms for a force that pulls the political compass toward its magnetic North, Leviathan. Hence Schmitt's conception of the political ("sovereign is he who makes the decision") cannot be written off as the ranting of a proto-fascist or nostalgic monarchist. Schmitt, regrettably, was onto something, something very similar to Hobbes (authority not truth makes law). The act of deciding the exception—determining what is crisis and what is not—is the sovereign backstop to modernity, even in its national-popular, democratic forms.[52] So Leviathan is never dead; it merely hibernates.

---

48   Carl Schmitt, *The Concept of the Political*, Chicago, IL: University of Chicago Press, 2007, 80–96; Carl Schmitt, *Political Theology II: The Myth of the Closure of Any Political Theology*, Cambridge: Polity, 2008, 129–30.

49   Carl Schmitt, *Political Theology: Four Chapters on the Concept of Sovereignty*, translated by G. Schwab, Chicago, IL : University of Chicago Press, 2005, 8–9, 53–66.

50   Arendt, *Origins of Totalitarianism*, 276-70, emphasis added.

51   Ibid.

52   Agamben, *State of Exception*.

VI

If our current conjuncture seems especially unstable, terrifying, or even apocalyptic, it is helpful (and a little heartening) to remember that this is not the first time in history that feeling has been widespread. Indeed, what Arendt called the "awareness of the possibility of doomsday" is common enough that it has a history of its own:[53]

> The tragedy of our time has been that only the emergence of crimes unknown in quantity and proportion and not foreseen by the Ten Commandments made us realize what the mob has known since the beginning of the century: that not only this or that form of government has become antiquated or that certain values and traditions need to be reconsidered, but that the whole of nearly three thousand years of Western civilization, as we have known it in a comparatively uninterrupted stream of tradition, has broken down; the whole structure of Western culture with all its implied beliefs, traditions, standards of judgment, has come toppling down over our heads ... Nothing, certainly, is more understandable than reluctance to admit this situation. For it means that, though we may have many traditions and know them more intimately than any generation before us, we can fall back on none, and that, though we are saturated with experience and more competent at interpreting it than any century before, we cannot use any of it.[54]

Arendt wrote these words in 1951, after three decades of total war and catastrophic depression, the genocide of the Holocaust and the razing of Hiroshima and Nagasaki—an era that only found closure through technologies of annihilation so powerful they seemed biblical in scale. These technologies would loom over her thought, and that of many others, from then on.

Leviathan was Hobbes's response to a similar challenge and constructed in a time of war. As Koselleck puts it:

> for Hobbes there could be no other goal than to prevent the civil war he saw impending in England, or, once it had broken out, to bring it to an end ... To Hobbes, history was a continuous alternation from civil war to the State and from the State to civil war. *Homo homini lupus, homo homini Deus.*[55]

Ending civil war is the desperate hope that drove Hobbes, but part of what distinguishes his contribution—what makes it speculative as opposed to merely utopian—is his recognition that hope was insufficient. As long as the task of avoiding partisan civil war is deemed a problem of morality, it is impossible. The Leviathan posited by Hobbes, or the sovereign *qua* state power, defers this

---

53   Hannah Arendt, *Crises of the Republic*, New York: Harcourt Brace, 1972, 119.
54   Arendt, *The Origins of Totalitarianism*, 434.
55   Koselleck, *Critique and Crisis*, 23, 34. [Man is wolf to man, man is God to man.]

problem by standing above all parties, drawing them into a unity: substituting its particularity for the complex whole, ending civil war, and fusing politics with morality. Thus hegemony is won, and politics becomes the "public conscience" in which all have an interest:

> It is only in respect of civil war, and of reason's supreme commandment to put an end to this war, that Hobbes's system becomes logically conclusive. Morality bids men submit to the ruler; the rule puts an end to civil war; in doing so he fulfills morality's supreme commandment. The sovereign's moral qualification consists in his political function: to make and maintain order.[56]

By Hobbes's logic, in civil war, the sovereign's moral qualification is therefore both renewed (by its reassertion) and challenged (since war could destroy the polity).

As with some civil wars, climate change poses political problems for which the current order has no answer. Like Hobbes, we are living through a period where the immanent, hegemonic conception of the world requires and presumes the emergence of a new kind of sovereign, a new order—albeit one that cannot yet be realized.[57] This may seem paradoxical, but history is replete with illustrations of highly unequal and apparently contradictory social-political orders ruled by elites who remained hegemonic for a considerable duration (typically with violent consequences), despite lacking answers to fundamental problems. As Gramsci, writing between the world wars, once put it: "The crisis consists precisely in the fact that the old is dying and the new cannot be born; in this interregnum a great variety of morbid symptoms appear."[58]

---

56   Ibid., 33; see also Habermas, *Structural Transformation of the Public Sphere*, 103.

57   We restate here a core argument that Gramsci takes from Hegel. See Gramsci, [Q11§12], *Selections from the Prison Notebooks*, 323–43.

58   Gramsci, [Q3§34]; *Selections from the Prison Notebooks*, 276.

2

Climate Leviathan

Human beings are now carrying out a large scale geophysical experiment of a kind that could not have happened in the past nor be reproduced in the future.

Revelle and Seuss, 1957[1]

I

The International Energy Agency opened its 2012 World Energy Outlook with the following warning:

> The global energy map is changing, with potentially far-reaching consequences for energy markets and trade. It is being redrawn by the resurgence in oil and gas production in the United States . . . By around 2020, the United States is projected to become the largest global oil producer . . . The result is a continued fall in US oil imports, to the extent that North America becomes a net oil exporter around 2030 . . . [T]he climate goal of limiting warming to 2°C is becoming more difficult . . . [A]lmost four-fifths of the CO_2 emissions allowable by 2035 are already locked-in by existing power plants, factories, buildings, etc. If action to reduce CO_2 emissions is not taken before 2017, all the allowable CO_2 emissions would be locked-in by energy infrastructure existing at that time . . . No more than one-third of proven reserves of fossil fuels can be consumed prior to 2050 if the world is to achieve the 2°C goal, unless carbon capture and storage (CCS) technology is widely deployed . . . Geographically, two-thirds [of proven reserves] are held by North America, the Middle East, China and Russia. These findings underline the importance of CCS as a key option to mitigate CO_2 emissions, but its pace of deployment remains highly uncertain.[2]

A rapid and massive change in the geographies of energy production and consumption is presently underway. In a bid for energy security and a repatriated stream of profits, some of the world's largest consumers of energy are turning to "friendlier," ideally domestic, suppliers. Big oil's gaze has turned north (to the Arctic), deeper (offshore), and dirtier (tar sands). While the Middle East still

---

1   Roger Revelle and Hans Suess, "Carbon Dioxide Exchange Between Atmosphere and Ocean and the Question of an Increase of Atmospheric CO_2 during the Past Decades," *Tellus* 9, no. 1, 1957, 19–20.

2   International Energy Agency, *World Energy Outlook*, 2012. The Organisation for Economic Co-Operation and Development founded the International Energy Agency in 1974 (at the behest of the United States) to coordinate wealthy countries' response to dependence on Middle Eastern oil.

holds most of the world's oil reserves, it accounts for only about a third of current global oil production.[3] Meanwhile, hydraulic fracturing ("fracking") has generated a massive push into "unconventional" hydrocarbon resources. Despite persistent talk of "peak oil," the world is awash in fossil fuels. For the major energy corporations, demand is a bigger problem than supply.

These centripetal forces are reconfiguring the world's political geography, and at least two profoundly significant developments can be identified. First, the "winners" of this geopolitical game, already the world's most powerful states, are likely to become even more dominant through a concentration of political-economic power, military force, and energy resources. The United States and China have developed two of the largest fracking industries, and both have potentially enormous reserves of shale gas. Second, this shift signals the end of any hope for meaningful carbon mitigation. Fracking and related extractive processes are much more carbon-intensive than drilling Saudi oil, and the explosion in unconventional hydrocarbons guarantees increased greenhouse gas emissions.[4] In addition, the geographic and political-economic distribution of these resources deepens the global division of wealth and power, exacerbating geopolitical inequalities and further destabilizing what little ground international negotiations have cleared for cooperation on climate-related concerns.

The International Energy Agency does not say mitigation is no longer possible, and, to be sure, some sectors, firms, and localities have reduced emissions. "Green energy" has expanded in many places—there are new solar panels in China and Europe, more dams on tropical rivers, and so on. Putting aside the environmental costs of these forms of energy, global demand for electricity has soared (and shows little sign of slowing). There is as yet no green energy boom (see Figure 2.1).[5] Yet carbon emissions continue to accelerate.[6] The International Energy Agency explains:

---

3 Gavin Bridge and Philippe Le Billon, *Oil*, London, Polity Press, 2013, 15.

4 Ibid., 9. Hence the new geography of energy demands increasing amounts of energy in the process of extraction relative to the energy of that extracted. During the last century, the global average fell from 1:100 to 1:30, and as low as 1:5 in some unconventional operations. In other words, whereas an average extraction project once produced 100 times the amount of energy invested, it now produces only 30, and often less.

5 In the Organisation for Economic Co-Operation and Development, total renewable electricity production doubled (from ~1200 to ~2400 TWh) between 1988 and 2014: International Energy Agency, "Recent Energy Trends in OECD," 2015, excerpt from International Energy Agency, *Energy Balances of OECD Countries: 2015 Edition*. As of 2015, roughly half of this renewable production comes from hydropower, which is not without environmental consequences.

6 The best scientific review of evidence on emissions is Intergovernmental Panel on Climate Change, *Working Group II: Impacts, Adaptation, and Vulnerability. Fifth Assessment Report Technical Summary*, March 31, 2014, Yokohama, Japan. Between February 2012 and February 2013, Mauna Loa recorded 3.26 parts per million rise in CO_2, registering 400 parts per million for the first time in May 2013, relative to preindustrial levels of approximately 280 parts per million. John Vidal, "Large Rise in CO_2 Emissions Sounds Climate Change Alarm," *The Guardian*, March 8, 2013. Kirsten Zickfeld, Michael Eby, H. Damon Matthews, and Andrew J. Weaver, "Setting Cumulative Emissions Targets to Reduce the Risk of Dangerous Climate Change," *Proceedings of the National Academy of Sciences* 106, 2009, 16129–34.

Despite the growth of non-fossil energy (such as nuclear, hydropower and other renewable sources . . . the share of fossil fuels within the world energy supply is relatively unchanged over the past four decades. In 2014, fossil sources accounted for 82% of the global [energy supply].[7]

As we detail below, there has been little substantive progress in international carbon *mitigation*. Without radical change, the world's atmosphere will not fall below 400 parts per million CO_2 until after the Anthropocene. The International Energy Agency's emphasis on the desperate need for carbon capture and storage surely means that it recognizes the insurmountable obstacles to CO_2-emissions reductions on the necessary timelines (that is, "before 2017").[8]

Figure 2.1. Global energy consumption, fossil and non-fossil fuels, 1971 and 2014

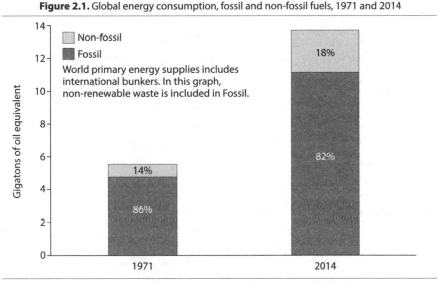

Source: International Energy Agency, "CO_2 Emissions from Fuel Combustion," 2016, 10.

7   International Energy Agency, "CO_2 Emissions from Fuel Combustion: Highlights," 2016, 10.

8   In 2011 global CO_2 emissions reached a record high of 31.6 gigatons (Gt), a 1.0 Gt (3.2 percent) increase over 2010 (International Energy Agency, 2012). The world is on track to emit ~58 Gt in 2020, the year the Durban agreement commitments are supposed to begin, ~14 Gt more than can be emitted if we are to limit warming to 2°C: United Nations Environment Programme, The Emissions Gap Report, Nairobi, 2012. From 2004 to 2013, atmospheric greenhouse gas concentrations measured at Mauna Loa increased 2.13 percent, the fastest decadal increase yet. Concentrations of CO_2 in the Earth's atmosphere (parts per million) derived from in situ air measurements at the Mauna Loa observatory in Hawaii are given at www.co2.earth.

The possibility of rapid, global carbon mitigation as a climate change abatement strategy has passed. The world's elites, at least, appear to have abandoned it—if they ever took it seriously. In 2010, Mike Davis imagined a "not improbable scenario" in which mitigation "would be tacitly abandoned . . . in favour of accelerated investment in selective adaptation for Earth's first-class passengers." His prediction may prove prescient.

> The goal would be the creation of green and gated oases of permanent affluence on an otherwise stricken planet. Of course, there would still be treaties, carbon credits, famine relief, humanitarian acrobatics, and perhaps the full-scale conversion of some European cities and small countries to alternative energy. But worldwide adaptation to climate change, which presupposes trillions of dollars of investment in the urban and rural infrastructures of poor and medium income countries, as well as the assisted migration of tens of millions of people from Africa and Asia, would necessarily command a revolution of almost mythic magnitude in the redistribution of income and power.[9]

What does the plausibility of such a terrible future scenario mean for politics today? This question is the focus of what follows. The momentous socio-ecological transformations to which Davis refers—and against which a global climate justice movement might enact a "revolution of almost mythic magnitude"—is best grasped as a dangerous, conjunctural moment of transition in the planet's natural history. This is in no way to suggest it is beyond politics. On the contrary, in the midst of these changes the urgent questions concern not merely a transformation *in* politics—more representative proceduralism, for example, or more precautionary environmental policy-making—but a transformation *of* the political. To ask by what paths we might undertake political transformations required for something like a just and livable planet is necessarily to ask not only what political tools, strategies, and tactics might achieve a revolution of "mythic magnitude," but also what conception of the realm of the political might render such tools, strategies, and tactics imaginable. What conceptions of the political legitimate the warming norm, and what alternatives can provide grounds for genuine alternatives?

II

We posit that two conditions will fundamentally shape the coming political-economic order. The first is whether the prevailing economic formation will continue to be capitalist or not. While a great deal of diversity can be found within and between capitalist societies, they all are shaped by what Marx called the general formula of capital: M-C-M'.[10] Whether this circuit of

---

9   Mike Davis, "Who Will Build the Ark?" 39.
10   Karl Marx, *Capital*, Vol. I, New York: Penguin Random House, 1992 [1867].

capital continues to expand—that is, whether the value-form will continue to shape social life—is a fundamental determinant of the emerging order. The second condition is whether a coherent planetary sovereign will emerge, that is, whether sovereignty will be reconstituted for the purposes of planetary management. What we call Climate Leviathan exists to the extent that some sovereign exists who can invoke the exception, declare an emergency, and decide who may emit carbon and who cannot. This sovereign must be planetary in a dual sense: capable of acting both at the planetary scale (since climate change is understood as a massive collective action problem) and in the name of planetary management—for the sake of life on Earth. A task of biblical proportions, amounting to an impossible global accounting of everything, like determining "a weight for the wind and apportion[ing] the waters by measure."[11]

Figure 2.2. Four potential social formations

	Planetary sovereignty	Anti-planetary sovereignty
Capitalist	Climate Leviathan	Climate Behemoth
Non-capitalist	Climate Mao	Climate X

This pair of dichotomies produces four potential global political responses to climate change, each of which is distinguished by the hegemony of a particular bloc, a mode of appropriation and distribution through which that hegemony is exercised: a capitalist Climate Leviathan; an anticapitalist, state-centered Climate Mao; a reactionary capitalist Behemoth; and an anticapitalist, anti-sovereign Climate X (see Figure 2.2). The top half of the box reflects capitalist

---

11   Job 28: 25.

futures. The left column represents scenarios where planetary sovereignty is affirmed and constructed.

Our thesis is that the future of the world will be defined by Leviathan, Behemoth, Mao, and X and the conflicts between them. This is not to say that all future politics will be determined by climate alone, but rather that the challenge of climate change is so fundamental to the global order that the complex and manifold reactions to climate change will restructure the world along one of these four paths. To say the least, the continuing hegemony of existing capitalist liberal democracy cannot be safely assumed.

To reiterate, our aim is not to develop a taxonomy of the world's futures, whence to decide where to place our bets. Rather it is to capture the significance of these crucial dimensions of the future in these broad trajectories, in an effort to grasp how the world is moving in the face of a necessary conjuncture which is nothing but a product of contingency (since the course of history is not prede-termined). These political futures are "ideal types" in the Weberian sense: not "ideal" in the "best possible" sense, but roughly sketched yet identifiable types produced by the interplay of historical and political economic forces. Our accounts of each potential path for climate politics are not detailed forecasts of the empirical form they might take in any particular geography, but descrip-tions of the principal features we argue are likely to determine their general dynamics, and the political implications of those dynamics for attempts to construct a world of climate justice.

Among the possible paths we can imagine, Climate Leviathan is presently leading but is neither consolidated nor certain to succeed. Because of its likely dominance in the near term, the possible futures that exist outside Climate Leviathan may largely be seen as responses to it. Behemoth is Leviathan's great-est immediate threat, and, while unlikely to become hegemonic, may well remain disruptive enough to prevent Leviathan from achieving a new hegem-onic order. If Leviathan essentially reflects the dream of a sustainable capitalist status quo and Behemoth a conservative reaction to it, Mao and X are compet-ing revolutionary figures in the worldly drama. X is in our view ethically and politically superior, but Mao is more likely to enter the scene from stage left. In the rest of this chapter, we consider each in turn.

III

Climate Leviathan is defined by the dream of a planetary sovereign. It is a regu-latory authority armed with democratic legitimacy, binding technical authority on scientific issues, and a panopticon-like capacity to monitor the vital granular elements of our emerging world: fresh water, carbon emissions, climate refu-gees, and so on. Notwithstanding their failure to reduce global carbon emis-sions, the annual meetings of the United Nations Conference of the Parties (COP) to advance the United Nations Framework Convention on Climate

Change (UNFCCC) represent the first institutional manifestation of this dream of planetary regulation, a process that the dominant capitalist nation-states will consolidate as climate-induced disruptions of accumulation and political stability become more urgent. Although binding consensus could not be reached in Copenhagen or Cancún, the 2015 Paris Agreement clarifies the present conditions of any possible global agreement.[12] To begin, capitalism is treated not as a question, but as the solution to climate change. Indeed, filtered through the COP lens, climate change appears to capital as an opportunity: trade in emissions permits ("cap-and-trade"), "green" business, nuclear power, corporate leadership, carbon capture and storage, green finance, and ultimately, geoengineering: these are Leviathan's lifeblood.

Why call this "Leviathan"? Climate Leviathan is a direct descendant from Hobbes's original to Schmitt's sovereign: when it comes to climate, Leviathan will decide and is constituted precisely in the act of decision. It expresses a desire for, and the recognition of, the necessity of a planetary sovereign to seize command, declare an emergency, and bring order to the Earth, all in the name of saving life. If Agamben is correct that "the declaration of the state of exception has gradually been replaced by an unprecedented generalization of the paradigm of security as the normal technique of government," then the consolidation of Climate Leviathan represents the rescaling of the "normal technique[s]" to encompass planetary security, or the making-secure of planetary life.[13] With this achievement, the state of nature and the nature of the state would form a self-authorizing union.

Geographically at least, Climate Leviathan exceeds its lineage, for it must somehow transcend the state-based, territorial container fundamental to Hobbes and Schmitt.[14] Even for those states most committed to national autonomy, it is increasingly clear that independent regulatory regimes are inadequate to the global challenge of sharply reducing carbon emissions. This contradiction—rending deep fissures in the UNFCCC process—may lead, as with other "public good" collective action problems, to the construction of a nominally "global" frame that is in fact a political and geographical extension of the rule of the extant hegemonic bloc: the capitalist global North (working with its allies and, sometimes, China). But this is by no means certain. Any realizable planetary Climate Leviathan must be constructed with the approval of a range of actors formerly excluded from global governance—China and India most notably, but the list could go on. Ensuring China's support for any binding climate

---

12   On the diplomatic failure prior to the Paris meeting in 2015, see, for example, David G. Victor, *The Collapse of the Kyoto Protocol and the Struggle to Slow Global Warming*, Princeton, NJ: Princeton University Press, 2004; Elmar Altvater and Achim Brunnengräber (eds), *After Cancún: Climate Governance or Climate Conflicts*, Berlin, Germany: Verlag für Sozialwissenschaften and Springer, 2011. We discuss Paris more below.

13   Agamben, *State of Exception*, 14.

14   A planetary sovereign is a *non sequitur* for Schmitt, but we are not faithful Schmittians. We also part ways á propos capital, which Schmitt saw as epiphenomenal to sovereignty.

regulation complicates the role of capital in Leviathan. (We return to this in Chapter 5.)

We conjecture that Leviathan could take one of two broad forms. On one hand, a variety of authoritarian territorial sovereignty, arguably truer to Hobbes's own vision, could emerge in nations or regions where political economic conditions prove amenable to transcending capital. We name this possibility "Climate Mao." On the other hand, we could see Leviathan emerge as the means by which to perpetuate the extant rule of northern liberal, democratic capitalist states. We think the most likely scenario (elaborated in Chapters 5 and 6) is that, through the coming decades, the waning, US-led, liberal capitalist bloc will collaborate with China to create a planetary regime that, in light of political and ecological crisis, will brook no opposition in defense of a human future for which it volunteers itself as the first and last line of defense.[15] The pattern of mobilization will likely be familiar, in which the United Nations or other international fora serve as a means of legitimizing aggressive means of surveillance and discipline. This could make the construction of Climate Leviathan a key means by which to salvage US hegemony—a prospect that only increases the likelihood of its consolidation.[16]

How might a potential capitalist Climate Leviathan press for its diplomatic resolution? One might find an argument for this effort in a book coauthored by John Holdren, former Harvard physicist and senior advisor to President Barack Obama.[17] After his 2008 appointment, right-wing media derided Holdren as the harbinger of a climate police state. One website claims he has called for "forced abortions and mass sterilization" to "save the planet."[18] Paranoid hyperbole, certainly, but the underlying critique is not entirely misplaced. Holdren was an early visionary of Climate Leviathan. In the conclusion of Holdren's 1977

---

15   We emphasize *most likely*. There are no certainties. We hasten to remind our readers of a point made repeatedly by Nicos Poulantzas, that neither capital as such nor the capitalist state includes an automatic or teleological mechanism for resolving crises: "neither within capital as a whole nor within monopoly capital itself, is there an instance capable of laying down who should make sacrifices so that others may continue to prosper"; *State, Power, Socialism*, London: Verso, 1979, 182–83.

16   The UN Security Council has considered the establishment of an "environmental peacekeeping force," "green helmets" who will manage the coming climate-induced unrest: "UN Security Council to Consider Climate Change Peacekeeping," *The Guardian*, July 20, 2011. In the United States, the military arguably marks the cutting edge of climate adaptation. The US Navy has rolled out its "great green fleet," an environmentally friendly arsenal powered entirely by biofuels. See "US Navy to Launch Great Green Fleet," *The Guardian*, April 20, 2010; see also National Research Council, "National Security Implications of Climate Change for US Naval Forces," 2011, available at nap.edu.

17   Formal titles: Teresa and John Heinz Professor of Environmental Policy at Harvard University and Assistant to the President for Science and Technology and Director of the White House Office of Science and Technology Policy.

18   "John Holdren, Obama's Science Czar, Says: Forced Abortions and Sterilization Needed to Save the Planet", at zombietime.com/john_holdren.

textbook on resource management, for example, he outlined a new sovereignty he called a "Planetary Regime":

> *Toward a Planetary Regime*: . . . Perhaps those agencies, combined with [the United Nations Environment Programme] and the United Nations population agencies, might eventually be developed into a Planetary Regime—sort of an international superagency for population, resources, and environment. Such a comprehensive Planetary Regime could control the development, administration, conservation, and distribution of all natural resources . . . Thus the Regime could have the power to control pollution not only in the atmosphere and oceans, but also in such fresh-water bodies as rivers and lakes that cross international boundaries or that discharge into the oceans. The Regime might also be a logical central agency for regulating all international trade, perhaps including assistance from [developed countries] to [less developed countries], and including all food on the international market. The Planetary Regime might be given responsibility for determining the optimum population for the world and for each region and for arbitrating various countries' shares within their regional limits. Control of population size might remain the responsibility of each government, but the Regime would have some power to enforce the agreed limits.[19]

Holdren's coauthors, the Ehrlichs, are well-known neo-Malthusians. But this proposed Regime owes more to Schmitt than Malthus.

We emphasize the specifically *capitalist* character of the Climate Leviathan to whom this call appeals. In contrast to the sovereign Leviathan conceived by Schmitt—for whom capital was at best an epiphenomenon—capitalist Climate Leviathan emerges in a manner reminiscent less of National Socialism than of the disparate efforts to save capitalist civilization after 1929, retrospectively collected under the umbrella term "Keynesianism": a concentration of political power at the national scale in combination with international coordinating institutions that attempt to render liberal hegemony immutable—allowing, as with the United Nations, for specific constraints on capital's dominion. The notion of "green-washing" hardly does justice to the pretentions of the current transition to globalized green capitalism. As Edward Barbier describes in his outline of a "Global Green New Deal"—only one of several sophisticated schemes for a "green Keynesianism" (see Chapter 5)—it will require both an institutional-juridical structure of planetary sovereignty and the construction of sophisticated and liquid global markets in a series of novel enviro-financial instruments whose status as functioning "securities" is by no means clear.[20]

---

19   Paul Ehrlich, Anne Ehrlich, and John Holdren, *Ecoscience: Population, Resources, Environment*, San Francisco: W.H. Freeman, 1977, 942–43.

20   Edward B. Barbier, *A Global Green New Deal: Rethinking the Economic Recovery*, Cambridge: Cambridge University Press, 2010; Larry Lohmann, "Regulatory Challenges for Financial and Carbon Markets," *Carbon and Climate Law Review* 2, 2009, 161–71; Larry Lohmann,

Nevertheless, Climate Leviathan will be the fundamental regulatory ideal motivating elites in the near future. Still, it is neither inevitable nor invincible; it is strong and coherent but not uncontested. It is threatened within by the usual burdens of any state-capitalist project divided by multiple accumulation strategies, and it is almost impossible to imagine that it will actually reverse climate change. Given the drive for incessantly expanded accumulation without which capital ceases to be, the constant conversion of the planet into means of production, and the material throughput and energy-intensity through which it is operated, capitalism is (as the ecologican Marxists tell us) effectively running up against its planetary limits. If there is a "spatial fix" for this contradiction, it is as yet unavailable.[21]

Moreover, capitalism's tendency to deepen inequalities of wealth and power is tightly linked to the challenge of confronting climate change.[22] Any attempt to reduce planetary carbon emissions will require sacrifices and transnational alliances. Deep inequalities within and between nations are fatal to such efforts: intranationally because inequalities make it difficult to build trans-class coalitions around shared sacrifice and entrench the capacity of the wealthy to prevent the conversion of carbon-intensive economies into more sustainable alternatives, and internationally because the world's stupefying inequalities of wealth and power prevent the transnational coordination that will be necessary for Leviathan to rule effectively. Thus, even if Climate Leviathan can come into being—through a global consolidation of ecological

---

"Financialization, Commodification and Carbon: The Contradictions of Neoliberal Climate Policy," *Socialist Register* 48, 2012, 85–107. Climate finance lies at the center of the debates surrounding the Paris Agreement today. Pablo Solón, former ambassador to the United Nations Conference of the Parties from Bolivia, explains regarding the Paris Agreement: "developed countries in a very clever way replaced the word 'provide' with 'mobilize' [in the section on climate finance]. Article 9 of the agreement states that 'developed country Parties should *continue to take the lead in mobilizing climate finance* from a wide variety of sources, instruments and channels,' such as public funding, private investment, loans, carbon markets and even developing countries" [emphasis added]. The phrase "continue to take the lead" implies that they are already doing something worthy; "mobilizing" implies that private finance will continue to be about the only sort available. Even when public finance is provided, it could be mediated by, e.g., the World Bank. Imagine a loan granted to Jamaica to build a seawall; it surely will be counted toward the $100 billion [pledged in Paris], since the North would be "mobilizing climate finance" and the loan must be paid back with interest.

21　On the spatial fix, see David Harvey, *The Limits to Capital*, Chicago IL: University of Chicago Press, 1982; on the socioecological fix, see James McCarthy, "A Socioecological Fix to Capitalist Crisis and Climate Change? The Possibilities and Limits of Renewable Energy," *Environment and Planning A* 47, no. 12, 2015, 2485–2502.

22　Marx, *Capital*, Vol. 1; Richard Walker and David Large, "The Economics of Energy Extravagance," *Ecology Law Quarterly* 4, 1975, 963–85; Harvey, *The Limits to Capital*; Neil Smith, *Uneven Development: Nature, Capital and the Production of Space*, London, Oxford: Blackwell, 1984; Leigh Johnson, "Geographies of Securitized Catastrophe Risk and the Implications of Climage Change," *Economic Geography* 90, 2014, 155–85. John Bellamy Foster, Brett Clark, and Richard York, *The Ecological Rift: Capitalism's War on the Earth*, New York: Monthly Review Press, 2010; Joel Wainwright, "Climate Change, Capitalism, and the Challenge of Transdisciplinarity," *Annals of the Association of American Geographers* 100, 2010, 983–91.

and economic sovereignty and some combination of coercion and consent—it is unlikely to secure confident hegemony. But we should not assume it will die an early or quiet death. Today its advocates desperately seek a containment strategy for its foes.

The Paris Agreement of December 2015 is a legal and political foreshadowing of Climate Leviathan's form. The first thing to note about the meetings of the 21st Conference of the Parties (COP21) is that they were not actually in Paris, but at Le Bourget, an old airfield in the northern suburbs.[23] It was a strange space on the margins of the city. The landscape looked like a cheap movie set, or better, a refugee camp: richly made, but a camp nonetheless; a temporary city of plywood walls and police lines, secured for diplomacy. Inside Le Bourget were separate buildings for "accredited persons," and "enterprises"—"civil society" also had its own building, walled off from the others by a security barrier. The space for "accredited persons" stood at the center: the state, mediating between capital and society, presumably.

To what end this diplomacy? "To save the planet," it was said again and again, and not without reason. The world turned to Paris for lack of alternatives. All sides say the COP process is flawed. Nevertheless, most parties acknowledge it as the international diplomatic process for climate change, so we must work with it. This is an understandable position, but insufficient for the Left. The UNFCCC/COP process is the central nexus of international negotiations, an unavoidable passage point for climate politics. Yet this should not prevent us from analyzing what it represents: Climate Leviathan in formation.

In a sense, the diplomats succeeded in Paris. The agreement signed mid-day on December 12, 2015, is the new international law on climate change. French president at the time François Hollande called the Paris Agreement "a major leap for mankind"; for his part, then British prime minister David Cameron claimed the elites had "secured our planet for many, many generations to come."[24] The major news media followed suit. The *New York Times* called the agreement "a vindication of Mr. Obama's decision to make tackling climate change a center-piece of his second term," and *The Guardian* called the Paris Agreement the "first universal climate deal [to] see an accelerated phase-out of fossil fuels, the growth of renewable energy streams and powerful new carbon markets to enable countries to trade emissions and protect forests."[25]

---

23   Le Bourget is the same spot Charles Lindberg landed after his 1927 trans-atlantic flight. We were privileged to engage the Paris meetings from the ramparts.

24   "World Leaders Hail Paris Climate Deal as 'Major Leap for Mankind,'" *The Guardian*, December 12, 2015.

25   Julie Hirschfeld Davis, "Obama, Once a Guest, Is now a Leader in World Talks," *New York Times*, December 12, 2015. In fairness, *The Guardian* "balanced" this one-sided front-page story with a photo essay showing different forms of protest in and around Paris/COP21; see Eric Hilaire, "Thousands Defy Paris Protest Ban to Call for Climate Action—in Pictures," *The Guardian*, December 10, 2015. However, the photo essay lacked any text that would allow the reader to understand the ideological, social, and spatial differences on display in the protests.

This is hyperbole. George Monbiot (also writing in the *Guardian*) provided a more balanced evaluation: "by comparison to what it could have been, [COP21 was] a miracle. [But] by comparison to what it should have been, it's a disaster."[26] The "miracle" in this view is the existence of the first global agreement on climate change. The "disaster" is the tragic failure the agreement represents: no binding limits on carbon emissions and no commitment to do the one thing absolutely necessary: keep fossil fuels in the Earth's crust. Here is, arguably, the fundamental statement in the 31-page Paris Agreement, paragraph 1 of Article 4:

> In order to achieve the long-term temperature goal set out in Article 2 [i.e., to keep the global mean temperature increase only 1.5 or 2°C relative to pre-industrial levels], Parties [i.e., practically all the world's governments] aim to reach global peaking of greenhouse gas emissions as soon as possible, recognizing that peaking will take longer for developing country Parties, and to undertake rapid reductions thereafter in accordance with best available science, so as to achieve a balance between anthropogenic emissions by sources and removals by sinks of greenhouse gases in the second half of this century, on the basis of equity, and in the context of sustainable development and efforts to eradicate poverty.[27]

The Paris Agreement does not separate party-states into groups with different commitments based on wealth or income, unlike the Kyoto Protocol of 1997, in which so-called Annex II parties (members of the Organization for Economic Cooperation and Development) "are expected to provide financial resources to assist developing countries to comply with their obligations" in addition to meeting their own targets and abetting technology transfer.[28] The language in Article 4 of the Paris Agreement indicates a compromise between core capitalist states (led by the United States and the European Union) and developing countries (effectively represented by China and India). Every country promises cuts—"to reach global peaking of greenhouse gas emissions as soon as possible"—but levels and timelines are left undefined, and the inclusion of language about equity, poverty, and delayed peaking of developing country emissions reflect the success of China, India, and their bloc in defending their "carbon space" or "right to emit."

The critical element here is the goal of the agreement: to "achieve a balance between anthropogenic emissions by sources and removals by sinks . . . in the second half of this century." This seems to suggest the world will be carbon neutral some time between 2050 and 2100. This is improbable at best, at odds

---

The representation of the protests therefore flattened and homogenized disparate and divided groups.

26   George Monbiot writing in *The Guardian*, December 12, 2015.

27   United Nations, Conference of the Parties, "Adoption of the Paris Agreement," Twenty-first Session, 30 November–11 December 2015, Article 4, para 1, 21, available at unfccc.int.

28   Kyoto Protocol, Article 11, available at unfccc.int.

with the present trajectory and impossible to square with the lack of language on fossil fuels.[29] Pablo Solón, former Bolivian ambassador to the UNFCCC, ridiculed the gap between rhetoric and action:

> [T]hanks to the "contributions" of emission reductions presented in Paris, global emissions of greenhouse gases that in 2012 were 53 Gt CO_2e, will continue to climb up to around 60 Gt CO_2e by 2030. If governments really want to limit the temperature increase to less than 2°C they should commit to reduce global emissions to 35 Gt of CO_2e by 2030. Governments know this and yet do the opposite and even shout: "Victory! The planet is saved!" Is [this] not a particular type of schizophrenia?[30]

Naomi Klein offers a more colorful metaphor:

> It's like going: "I acknowledge that I will die of a heart attack if I don't radically lower my blood pressure ... I therefore will exercise once a week, eat four hamburgers instead of five ... and you have to call me a hero because I've never done this before and you have no idea how lazy I used to be."[31]

Radical critic Niclas Hällström said the global North's refusal to commit to emissions reductions or finance for adaption "means we are sleep walking into climate chaos."[32] In climatologist Jim Hansen's words, the Paris Agreement is a "fraud."[33]

There is truth to each of these criticisms, and the outrage that underwrites them is more than justified. But something is missing too, because the Agreement is not actually the result of schizophrenia or weak will. The world's elites are not really "sleepwalking" into chaos, and it is not all some elaborate scam. However ineffective, it constitutes a new international law, created by elite representatives of the world's nation-states (and strong enough to survive Donald Trump's

---

29   John Foran, "The Paris Agreement: Paper Heroes Widen the Climate Justice Gap," System Change Not Climate Change, December 17, 2015, parisclimatejustice.org.

30   Pablo Solón, "From Paris with Love for Lake Poopó," Observatorio Boliviano de Cambio Climático y "Desarrollo," December 21, 2015.

31   David Beers, "Naomi Klein, Bill McKibben Knock Paris Climate Deal," The Tyee, December 14, 2015, thetyee.ca. In a subsequent, excellent essay ("Let Them Drown," London Review of Books, June 2, 2016), Klein writes that the Paris target—keeping warming below 2°C—is

beyond reckless. When it was unveiled in Copenhagen in 2009, the African delegates called it "a death sentence" . . . At the last minute, a clause was added to the Paris Agreement that says countries will pursue "efforts to limit the temperature increase to 1.5°C." Not only is this non-binding but it is a lie: we are making no such efforts. The governments that are making this promise are now pushing for more fracking and more tar sands development—which are utterly incompatible with 2°C, let alone 1.5°C.

32   Megan Darby, "COP21: NGOs React to UN Paris Climate Deal," Climate Home, December 12, 2015.

33   Oliver Milman, "James Hansen, Father of Climate Change Awareness, Calls Paris Talks 'a Fraud'," The Guardian, December 12, 2015.

decision to pull the United States out). Its ineffectiveness—is not a result of the whole thing being staged to fool the world, however duplicitous this or that party to the agreement. Rather it is the result of the fundamentally contradictory character of political-economic responses to climate change in liberal, capitalist societies, which produces an inadequacy the agreement (amazingly) acknowledges:

> [The Conference of the Parties] notes with concern that the estimated aggregate greenhouse gas emission levels in 2025 and 2030 resulting from the intended nationally determined contributions do not fall within least-cost 2°C scenarios but rather lead to a projected level of 55 gigatonnes in 2030, and also notes that much greater emission reduction efforts will be required than those associated with the intended nationally determined contributions in order to hold the increase in the global average temperature to below 2°C above pre-industrial levels . . .[34]

The Paris Agreement admits its own failures.

So, it would be more accurate to say (as Hegel might have) that the Paris Agreement is an entirely "rational" manifestation of the world's reason—a world and reason wrought by deep contradictions. The world's elites recognize these contradictions and—although they are by no means agreed on what to do—are trying to address them within limiting conditions, conditions that cause them to "fail." The principle failure is that the Paris Agreement does not keep fossil fuels in the ground, but this does not mean it will not set the foundation for adaptation on a burning planet. On the contrary, the so-called "failures" of Paris are enabling, and part of, a crucial adaptation, the adaptation of the political. Notwithstanding inadequacies on the carbon question, the Paris Agreement constitutes an important step toward the emergence of planetary sovereignty— the left half of Figure 2.2. This sovereignty, as we said, could take two distinct forms, depending on whether the emerging sovereign acts to defend or overthrow capitalism. Let us consider the latter.

IV

Of the two incarnations of Climate Leviathan, one lies at the end of the red thread running from Robespierre to Lenin to Mao. Climate Mao is marked by the emergence of a noncapitalist authority along Maoist lines. If capitalist Climate Leviathan stands ready to embrace carbon governance in an evolving Euro-American liberal hegemony, Climate Mao expresses the necessity of a just terror in the interests of the future of the collective, which is to say that it represents the necessity of a planetary sovereign but wields this power *against* capital. The state of exception determines who may and may not emit carbon—at the

---

34   Paris Agreement, p. 3, para 17, available at unfccc.int.

expense of unjust wastefulness, unnecessary emissions, and conspicuous consumption.

Relative to the institutional means currently available to capitalist liberal democracy and its sorry attempts at "consensus," this trajectory has some distinct advantages with respect to atmospheric carbon concentration, notably in terms of the capacity to coordinate massive political-economic reconfiguration quickly and comprehensively. In light of our earlier question—how can we possibly realize the necessary emissions reductions?—it is this feature of Climate Mao that most recommends it. As the climate justice movement struggles to be heard, most campaigns in the global North are premised on an unspoken faith in a lop-sided, elite-biased, liberal proceduralism doomed to failure given the scale and scope of the changes required. If climate science is even half-right in its forecasts, the liberal model of democracy is at best too slow, at worst a devastating distraction. Climate Mao reflects the demand for rapid, revolutionary, state-led transformation today.

Indeed, calls for variations on just such a regime abound on the Left. Mike Davis and Giovanni Arrighi have more or less sided with Climate Mao, sketching it as an alternative to capitalist Climate Leviathan.[35] We might even interpret the renewal of enthusiasm for Maoist theory (including Alain Badiou's version) as part of the prevailing crisis of ecological-political imagination.[36] Minqi Li's is arguably the best developed of this line of thought, and like Arrighi he locates the fulcrum of global climate history in China, arguing that Climate Mao offers the only way forward:

> [U]nless China takes serious and meaningful actions to fulfill its obligation of emissions reduction, there is little hope that global climate stabilization can be achieved. However, it is very unlikely that the [present] Chinese government will voluntarily take the necessary actions to reduce emissions. The sharp fall of economic growth that would be required is something that the Chinese government will not accept and cannot afford politically. Does this mean that humanity is doomed? That depends on the political struggle within China and in the world as a whole.[37]

Taking inspiration from Mao, Li says a new revolution in the Chinese revolution—a re-energization of the Maoist political tradition—could transform China and save humanity from doom. He does not claim this is likely; one need only consider China's massive highway expansions, accelerated

---

35   Davis, "'Who Will Build the Ark?'"; Giovanni Arrighi, *Adam Smith in Beijing: Lineages of the Twenty-first Century*, London: Verso, 2007, part IV; see also Patrick Bigger, "Red Terror on the Atmosphere," *Antipode*, July 2012, radicalantipode.files.wordpress.com.

36   Alain Badiou, *The Communist Hypothesis*, London: Verso, 2010, 262–79.

37   Minqi Li, "Capitalism, Climate Change, and the Transition to Sustainability: Alternative Scenarios for the US, China and the World," *Development and Change* 40, 2009, 1055–57.

automobile consumption, and subsidized urban sprawl.[38] But he is right that if an anticapitalist, planetary sovereign is to emerge that could change the world's climate trajectory, it is most likely to emerge in China.

Even today, when an increasingly non-Maoist Chinese state invokes its full regulatory authority, it can achieve political feats unimaginable in liberal democracy. Perhaps the most notable instance of state-coordinated climate authority is the manner in which Beijing's air quality was re-engineered during the 2008 Olympics—flowers potted all over the city, traffic barred, trees planted in the desert, and factories and power plants closed—all to successfully blue the skies for the Games.[39] Another effect of this power is the way in which the Chinese state effectively killed General Motors's gas-guzzling Hummer in early 2010, when it blocked the division's sale to Sichuan Tenzhong Heavy Industrial Machinery due to the vehicle's emissions levels.[40] One might also point to the "Great Green Wall" against desertification, which, if successfully completed, will cross 4,480 kilometers of northern China, and various tree-planting programs that will purportedly give the country 42 percent forest cover by 2050.[41] And since vowing in the summer of 2010 to apply an "iron hand" to the task of reducing emissions, the Communist Party closed more than 2,000 steel mills and other carbon-emitting factories by March 2011.[42] In mid-2016, the government announced new dietary guidelines, encouraging people to consume no more than 75 grams of meat per day.[43] Reducing meat consumption was justified on health and environmental grounds and hailed by climate activists. Such policies foretell the possibility of a Climate Mao, were China to become a global hegemon and also change under revolutionary pressures. To be clear, that is a very big "if." Though Chairman Mao's face looms over Tiananmen Square and decorates every *yuan* note, China is emphatically not on the path toward Climate Mao. The Communist Party of China appears committed, at least today,

---

38   Compare Dale Wen, "Climate Change, Energy, and China," in Kolya Abramsky (ed.), *Sparking a Worldwide Energy Revolution*, Baltimore, MD, and Oakland, CA: AK Press, 2010, 130–54.

39   Y. Wang, J. Hao, M. McElroy, J. W. Munger, H. Ma, D. Chen, and C. P. Nielsen, "Ozone Air Quality during the 2008 Beijing Olympics: Effectiveness of Emission Restrictions," *Atmospheric Chemistry and Physics* 9, 2009, 5237–5.

40   "Hummer: China isn't Buying it Either" [Editorial], *Los Angeles Times*, February 25, 2010.

41   "China's Great Green Wall Grows in Climate Fight," *The Guardian*, September 23, 2010. "Ordinary citizens have planted some 56 billion trees across China in the last decade, according to government statistics. In 2009 alone, China planted 5.88 million hectares of forest."

42   Andrew Jacobs, "China Issues Warning on Climate and Growth," *New York Times*, February 28, 2011.

43   Oliver Milman and Stuart Leavenworth, "China's Plan to Cut Meat Consumption by 50% Cheered by Climate Campaigners," *The Guardian*, June 20, 2016:

The average Chinese person now eats 63kg of meat a year, with a further 30kg of meat per person expected to be added by 2030 if nothing is done to disrupt this trend. The new guidelines would reduce this to 14kg to 27kg a year.

to building a capitalist Climate Leviathan.[44] The centrality of China to the Paris Agreement only proves the point.

Still, we must speak of Climate Mao, not Climate Robespierre or Lenin, for both theoretical and geographical reasons. Mao was a Leninist who insisted on combining a faith in the masses with a vanguard party. Yet his great theoretical contributions to the Marxist tradition were to analyze the distinct class fractions within the Chinese peasantries and to argue for recentering revolutionary practice around the poor and (some of the) middle peasants, together with the urban proletariat (a relatively marginal class in 1930s China). Mao emphatically denied that only a fully proletarianized class could serve as the basis of a revolution, and argued that even "poor peasants" and the "semi-proletariat" could achieve revolutionary class consciousness in Marx's sense.[45] In an era with large and growing social groups that, to put it mildly, do not fit neatly into the bourgeois-proletariat distinction, Mao's general insight is crucial to reconsider.

Climate Mao is, in the near future, a specifically Asian path, a global path which can only be cut from Asia. In contrast to sub-Saharan Africa or Latin America, only in Asia—and only with some revolutionary leadership from China—do we find the combination of factors that make Climate Mao realizable: massive and marginalized peasantries and proletariats, historical experience and revolutionary ideology, and powerful states governing large economies. The key comparison here is with Evo Morales of Bolivia, once the most powerful voice on the Left in the UNFCCC/COP, who facilitated the Cochabamba accord (initially written in counterpoint to the Copenhagen framework). While the view from Cochabamba is definitely and admirably radical—it calls for a 50 percent reduction in greenhouse gas emissions by 2017 while rejecting carbon credits and "the consumption patterns of developed countries"—it is difficult to see how it could translate into global

---

44   Consider China's recent voluntary "border tax adjustment" program, aimed at reducing exports of energy-intensive products (Wen, "Climate Change, Energy, and China," 143–46); in contrast, compare Jonathan Watts, "Chinese Villagers Driven Off Land Fear Food May Run Out," *The Guardian*, May 19, 2011.

45   Mao Tse-Tung, "Analysis of Classes in Chinese Society," in *Selected Works of Mao Tse-Tung*, vol. I, Peking: Foreign Languages Press, 1926. To say the least, the works of Mao (and Maoism more generally) are not mainstream sources in contemporary, Anglophone Marxist scholarship. In a well-known passage from her essay, "Can the Subaltern Speak?" where Gayatri Spivak criticizes Foucault and Deleuze for failing to address their Eurocentric "implication in intellectual and economic history," she emphasizes, as an illustration, their vague references to "A Maoist" (Spivak, "Can the Subaltern Speak?" in Cary Nelson and Lawrence Grossberg (eds), *Marxism and the Interpretation of Culture*, Urbana: University of Illinois Press, 1988, 272). Spivak claims their "Maoism" "simply creates an aura of narrative specificity," which would be "a harmless rhetorical banality" except that that it "renders 'Asia' transparent." Anyone working from the Western Marxist tradition who seeks to engage the prospects of change from a (still-vibrant) Maoist tradition will run the risk of such errors. But ignoring Maoism is worse. Notwithstanding their limitations, our references to and discussions of Mao and Maoism are intended as a correction to a Eurocentric tendency to downplay the importance of Maoism for Marxism as a world-historical phenomenon.

transformation.[46] By contrast, Climate Mao is not impossible in Asia because of the confrontation between millions of increasingly climate-stressed poor people and the political structures that abet those very stresses, not to mention the living legacies of Maoism. In the imminent confrontation of Asia's historical-geographical conditions with catastrophic climate change, too many people have too much to lose, too quickly—a formula for revolution. Mao writes: "Qualitatively different contradictions can only be resolved by qualitatively different methods . . . [T]he contradiction between society and nature is resolved by the method of developing the productive forces."[47] The logic of Climate Mao is that only revolutionary state power rooted in militant, popular mobilization would be sufficient to transform the world's productive forces and thus resolve our planetary "contradiction between society and nature."

We are not suggesting that Climate Mao will emerge through an ecological awakening on the part of Indian or Chinese peasants. Asian peasants (and recently urbanized former peasants) will respond not to carbon emissions *per se* but to state failures to act in response to material crises (shortages of water, food, shelter, and so on) and elite expropriations certain to come in the face of climate-induced instabilities. However, presently China's state is building the path toward Climate Leviathan. How we get from here to Climate Mao would depend principally on the Chinese proletariat and peasantry. As is commonly noted, China's emissions are growing daily, and the economic growth with which those emissions are associated is the basis of much of the legitimacy enjoyed by the Chinese state and ruling elites.[48] If the Chinese working class responds to massive climate-change-induced disruptions in growth, the possibilities for an energetic Climate Mao are substantial. Moreover, the preconditions for the rise of Climate Mao are extant and in some cases thriving: outside the Maoist tradition in China itself, the Maoist Naxalites of India's "red corridor" are actively engaged in armed conflict with India's coal mafia; Maoists effectively now hold power in Nepal; and North Korea, although not exactly Maoist, is not going away.[49] Certainly the collective embrace of the West's vision of capitalist Leviathan on the part of Asia's peasant and proletariat classes seems unlikely.[50] Rather, the opposite is more plausible: the rapid rise

46   "Final Declaration of the World People's Conference on Climate Change and the Rights of Mother Earth," Cochabamba, Bolivia, April 26, 2010, available at readingfromtheleft.com.

47   Mao, "On Contradiction," in *Selected Works of Mao Tse-Tung*, Vol. I, 321–32.

48   Minqi Li, *The Rise of China and the Demise of the Capitalist World Economy*, New York: Monthly Review, 2008; Stefan Harper, *The Beijing Consensus: How China's Authoritarian Model Will Dominate the Twenty-First Century*, New York: Basic Books, 2010.

49   We recognize that ours is a too concise summation of quite different Mao-influenced movements. See Achin Vanaik, "The New Himalayan Republic," *New Left Review* II/49, 2008, 47–72; S. Giri, "The Maoist 'Problem' and the Democratic Left in India," *Journal of Contemporary Asia* 39, 2009, 463–74; and Bruce Cumings, "The Last Hermit," *New Left Review* II/6, November–December 2000, 150–54.

50   Li, *The Rise of China and the Demise of the Capitalist World Economy*, 187.

of more authoritarian state socialisms, regimes that use their power to deci-
sively reduce global carbon emissions and maintain control during climate-
induced "emergencies."

Figure 2.3. CO$_2$ emissions per capita, 2010, projected on a cartogram distorted to show the
number of people exposed to droughts, floods and extreme temperatures, 2000 – 2009
(using 2010 population data)

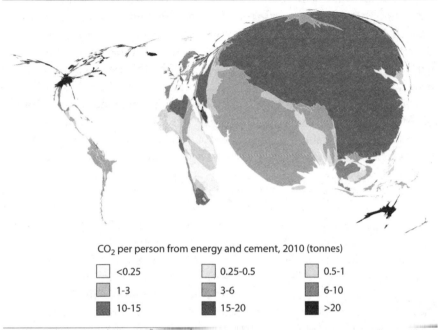

CO$_2$ per person from energy and cement, 2010 (tonnes)

<0.25	0.25-0.5	0.5-1
1-3	3-6	6-10
10-15	15-20	>20

*Sources: Map by Kiln, see: carbonmap.org. Data source for CO$_2$ emmissions: G. Peters, G. Marland, C. Le Quéré, T. Boden, J. Canadell,
and M/ Raupach, "Rapid growth in CO$_2$ emmissions after the 2008-2009 global financial crisis", Nature Climate Change 2, 2012, 2-4.
Data for people at risk: the OFDA/CRED International Disaster Database, a project of the Université Catholique de Louvain and
the World Bank, available at EMDAT.be.*

What, if anything, makes Climate Mao a plausible basis for global transformation? Figure 2.3 makes two points uncomfortably clear. First, most rich
countries (the United States, Canada, Western Europe and some oil-producing
states) are home to very few people who are directly at risk of the negative effects
of climate change. Second, there is an extraordinary geographical unevenness to
the world's at-risk population. They live mainly in South and East Asia, between
Pakistan and North Korea, a belt of potentially revolutionary change. Asia is not
only home to the majority of humanity, but also the center of capital's economic
geography: the world's hub of commodity production and consumption (and
carbon emissions). We might expect, therefore, climate-induced social turbulence to combine in a region with an enormous, growing capacity to reshape the
consumption and distribution of all the world's resources. Consequently, it is a

more interesting thought experiment to ask how radical social movements in Asia could challenge Leviathan than to imagine a would-be Climate Mao emerging in, say, Lagos or La Paz.

V

While Climate Mao looms over Asia, the specter haunting the world's core capitalist states today is that of reactionary conservatism. That reaction takes one of its most important forms as a mode of Climate Behemoth, represented by the upper right of Figure 2.1. Behemoth opposes Leviathan's drive for planetary sovereignty, which is itself not a bad thing in our view. When Schmitt remarked that "state and revolution, leviathan and behemoth" are always potentially present, he cast Behemoth in the revolutionary role. So he should, given its function as the figure of the masses in Hobbes's work (behemoth is the plural of the Aramaic *behema*, ordinary cattle or beast).[51] But while it symbolizes the masses which might stand against Leviathan, revolution is no straightforward historical mechanism. Napoleon is as much a product of the French Revolution as the *sans-culottes*.

Behemoth provides at least two possible, mass-based responses to Leviathan: reactionary populism and revolutionary anti-state democracy. In its reactionary form—where populism rallies to capital (as represented by the upper-right corner)—Climate Behemoth stands in its most stark Schmittian opposition to Climate Leviathan's planetary sovereignty. It is not hard to find evidence of this reactionary tendency today, epitomized in the continued influence of climate change denial in mainstream political discourse, especially in the United States. The millenarian variety of this formation embraces an ideological structure that renders it impervious to reason. Indeed, that is the point. The disproportionate influence of this proudly unreasonable minority, agitated by the ill-gotten riches of a handful, will persist, at least for a while.

What is the class basis for climate Behemoth? Certainly, its leadership (and funding) come from the fraction of the capitalist class with ties to fossil fuels. This fraction plays an outsized role in shaping ideology, but it is far too small, numerically speaking, to consistently win elections in formally

---

51 Patricia Springborg, "Hobbes and Schmitt on the Name and Nature of Leviathan Revisited," *Critical Review of International Social and Political Philosophy* 13, 2010, 297–315. Hobbes's inspiration for Behemoth is said to be Job 40:15 ("Behold now the Behemoth that I have made with you; he eats grass like cattle"), but it is not entirely clear, since this passage is "one of the most extreme *non sequiturs* in literature"; D. Wolfers, "The Lord's Second Speech in the Book of Job," *Vestum Testamentum* 40, 1990, 474–99. Schmitt, at his least insightful, absolved himself of responsibility for thinking it through in any detail; Tomaz Mastnak, "Schmitt's Behemoth," *Critical Review of International Social and Political Philosophy* 13, 2010, 275–96. In the epic clash of the Leviathan and Behemoth, Schmitt says, "Jewish-cabbalistic interpretations" staged "world history . . . as a battle among heathens"; Carl Schmitt, *The Leviathan in the State Theory of Thomas Hobbes: Meaning and Failure of a Political Symbol*, Chicago, IL: University of Chicago Press, 2008 [1938], 8–9.

democratic societies. The elite backers of climate denialism need allies among subaltern social groups. In the capitalist core—particularly where the fossil energy sector is large (the United States, Canada, Australia)—they have found their most willing allies among those segments of the proletariat that perceive climate change not only as a threat to their jobs and cheap energy, but also as a sophisticated means to empower elite experts and hinder the exercise of national(ist) sovereignty. Nevertheless, the variation in class composition within capitalist societies makes generalizations across nation-states challenging, to say nothing of the global scale. Trump voters in Ohio or Michigan, for example, are a mixed lot and differ in important respects from their counterparts in Texas; similar variation exists among supporters of Prime Minister Narendra Modi of India, or Brexit proponents, and so on.

Some broad trends are identifiable, however. Right-wing movements have grown steadily since the 2000s, mobilized around ethno-religious-nationalist (and often hyper-masculinist) ideologies, leading to momentous political victories for authoritarian, neoliberal leadership. From India to Brazil, Turkey to Egypt, Russia to England and the United States, the success-ful transmission of "populist" energies has pulled capitalist states to the right. While the signature issue for many of these movements is immigra-tion and "security" for privileged racial and/or religious groups, in most cases the political shift has been accompanied (as in post-Brexit England) or enabled (in the United States under Trump) by a rejection of international collaboration to address climate change. There may be no social basis for a transnational alliance among these political forces for Climate Behemoth, but simply by virtue of their support for distinct brands of authoritarian, nationalist, right-wing populism, they contribute in parallel to a global political movement that obstructs the realization of Climate Leviathan. In this sense, the variegation of social classes supporting Behemoth is one of its strengths. The Trump and the Modi voter may come from different social groups and classes, and they may be mobilized around particular forms of racial, national and gendered prejudice. But what they oppose almost unani-mously is the legitimacy of a distinctly international political sphere, espe-cially if it has the capacity to discipline (national) capital.

Ultimately, though, Behemoth's constant failure to offer a coherent alter-native to liberal capitalism's crises—witness the political calamities under Donald Trump and British prime minister Theresa May—will limit the medium and long-term political force of Climate Behemoth, as it has hobbled all Behemoths throughout history. Today's Behemoth substitutes free-market, nationalist, and evangelical rhetoric for explanation. It is truly reactionary. Even in its milder manifestation, where the fact of climate change is acknowl-edged but posited as beyond our control because of human or nonhuman nature, reaction dominates the chorus of ridicule aimed at "alarmists" calling for political-economic reorganization to address environmental change. These "rational" Behemoths, though less self-obsessed and misanthropic than their millenarian associates who affirm that if the world is coming to an end it must be God's will, condemn the regulatory hubris of climate science no less vigorously. To put it in our terms, Behemoth hates Mao for its faith in secular revolution, Leviathan for its liberal pretension to rational world government, and both for their willingness to sacrifice "liberty" for lower carbon emissions.

Yet there is a key division within the fear behind this hatred. One one side we find many on the right raging against Leviathan's anticipated assault on the nation-state. For them, it is nationalism, misogyny and racism that lead them to reject any idea of a legitimate transnational (let alone planetary) order. Even though nationalist climate denialism like that of the Republican Party is often couched in the terms of so-called free markets and the use of the climate change "hoax" as a cover for illegitimate state "meddling," the logic of the position is in no way founded in classical liberal arguments regarding efficient resource allocation in *laissez-faire* conditions. Instead, the concept "free market" is code in libertarian grandstanding for individual freedom. But many other powerful actors who oppose Leviathan—including massive segments of the natural resource sector—would welcome transnational cooperation in other spheres, like defense. They dismiss the threat of climate change and international regulation in the name of an unfettered capitalist market.[52] This means Climate Behemoth is founded on two not necessarily commensurable principles. In the United States, the signature affiliations of the reactionary right—market fetishism, cheap energy, white nationalism, firearms, evangelical faith—buttress reactionary Behemoth. The result is an opportunistic, but contradictor and unstable, blend of fundamentalisms: the security of the homeland, the freedom of the market, and the justice of God.

How long that combination will hold sway over the administrative power of the state in the United States remains to be seen. Certainly the climate crisis is one among many reasons for the turmoil in the Republican Party exposed by Trump's election. To the extent that US hegemony will continue to require affordable fossil fuels, the emergence of Leviathan poses threat enough to energize Behemoth and thus to check Leviathan's planetary potential—for now. But barring an act of coordinated political imagination of which it seems incapable, this situation is unlikely to last. Indeed, notwithstanding the Trump presidency, the United States could yet become the heart of Leviathan.

---

52   Behemoth's climate denialism can perhaps be functionally attributed to fossil fuel-based economic interests, but that is hardly a convincing explanation for the problem. First, because capital is heterogeneous and most fractions would prefer Leviathan's planetary solution. Second, because class politics never operate independently of social difference, and capital (let alone one sector) is hardly the sole element behind Behemoth. Thus, it would be a grave mistake to expect to defeat Behemoth by proposing a more rational economic policy.

VI

Part of what Hobbes and Schmitt feared was that "the quintessential nature of the state of nature, or the behemoth, is none other than civil war, which can only be prevented by the overarching might of the state, or leviathan."[53] Yet this is not what we face today in the formations we are calling Climate Behemoth. Instead, we confront something closer to a revolutionary people that, *in extremis*, can realize itself one of two ways. The first is the nightmare outcome of reactionary Behemoth like that described above, the terrifying potential realized in the Nazi state described by Franz Neumann as early as 1942 in his *Behemoth: The Structure and Function of National Socialism*.[54] The second Behemoth is also prefigured by Hobbes, somewhat disdainfully, in the "democratical gentlemen" of Parliament with "horrible designs" of "changing the government from monarchical to popular, which they called liberty"—and, says Hobbes, "no tyrant was ever so cruel as a popular assembly."[55] Hobbes's cynicism regarding these "gentlemen" might well have been justified, as is our own, confronted with their current avatars in the Euro-American political establishment, rich defenders of a "popular liberty" that abets their wealth and power.

As none of the previous trajectories contain the possibility of a just climate revolution, let alone one of "almost mythic magnitude," we are searching for a handhold of nonreactionary opposition to Climate Leviathan. This challenge is daunting enough that much of the Left seems, perhaps understandably, to have concluded that building Climate Leviathan is either the only or the most practical path, even if many recognize it is unlikely to achieve effective hegemony quickly. The chief strength of Leviathan today is that it enjoys the status of liberal common sense regarding the arrangement of the world's future—as the vast popular mobilizations at Copenhagen, New York, and Paris demonstrate—and for that reason alone it seems to present the least impossible, most pragmatic, climate survival strategy. Yet if we look closely those mobilization scenes are uncanny. Many in the crowds carry hopeful banners, but with heavy hearts: optimism of the will (hoping for carbon mitigation plans) and pessimism of the intellect ("knowing" it will fail).[56] This is Gramsci's well-known political formula, and Fredric Jameson has famously captured it in a more doom-laden mode appropriate to our current conjuncture. Today, "it is easier to imagine the end of the world than to imagine the end of capitalism."[57]

---

53   Schmitt, *The Leviathan in the State Theory of Thomas Hobbes*, 21; Robert Kraynak, "Hobbes' Behemoth and the Argument for Absolutism," *American Political Science Review* 76, 1982, 837–47.

54   Franz Neumann, *Behemoth: The Structure and Function of National Socialism*, London: V. Gollancz, 1942.

55   Thomas Hobbes, *Behemoth or the Long Parliament*, London: Simpkin, Marshall and Co., 1889 [1681], 26, 23.

56   For an admirably "realist" example, see Christian Parenti, *Tropic of Chaos: Climate Change and the New Geography of Violence*, New York: Nation Books, 2011.

57   Fredric Jameson, "Future City," *New Left Review* II/21, May–June 2003, 76.

Faced with an overwhelming challenge to which we have as yet no coherent response—the apparent impossibility of which provides Climate Leviathan with no small part of the "pragmatic" legitimacy it enjoys—there are two things that must not be forgotten. First, although imagination is of course not enough on its own, and it is indeed "easier" to imagine the end of the world, it is not only possible but imperative that we imagine the end of capitalism. We must try to assemble effective conceptions of such a world, alternative rallying points and revolutionary strategies for climate justice. Second, despite their novel appearance through atmospheric chemistry and glacial melt rates, the problems posed at present are not new. The basic questions which have tormented the Left for centuries—the relations between sovereignty, democracy, and liberty; the political possibilities of a mode of human life that produces not exchange value but social wealth and dignity for all—are still the ones that matter. The defining characteristic of their present intensity is that they have an ecological deadline. The urgency that global warming imposes does not cut us off from the past, but only reignites the past in the present.

We must remember that we are not without resources with which to derail Leviathan's mystical train and reactionary varieties of Behemoth's general will. In his thesis X on history, Benjamin excoriates the Social Democrats with whom "the opponents of fascism have placed their hopes":

> These observations are intended to disentangle the political worldlings from the snares in which the traitors have entrapped them. Our consideration proceeds from the insight that the politicians' stubborn faith in progress, their confidence in their "mass basis," and, finally, their servile integration in an uncontrollable apparatus have been three aspects of the same thing. It seeks to convey an idea of the high price our accustomed thinking will have to pay for a conception of history that avoids any complicity with the thinking to which these politicians continue to adhere.[58]

Thesis X basically restates the more famous thesis IX (the "angel of history") in an explicitly political form. The politics Benjamin impugns here—faith in progress, confidence in mass basis, servile integration into apparatus—are precisely those of our three opponents in the struggle ahead. Leviathan's ethos is faith in progress; Mao's is confidence in the masses; reactionary Behemoth is the integration into the security apparatus of captial and terror. Barring the realization of alternative rallying points and revolutionary strategies for climate justice—we call our admittedly utopian contribution to this effort "Climate X" (elaborated in Part III)—these are the three alternatives we face, none of which is willing to own up to "the high price our accustomed thinking will have to pay

---

58   Walter Benjamin, *Illuminations*, New York, Schocken Books, 1969, 257.

for a conception of history that avoids any complicity with the thinking to which . . . politicians continue to adhere."[59]

Can we measure the costs of this complicity? Climate Leviathan is emerging and at war with Climate Behemoth and a global war between Leviathan and Mao is hardly unimaginable. The terrifying ecologies and polities these coming conflicts would generate are the price we face for our progress. God ordered Job to "lay your hand on [Leviathan]; remember the battle, don't try again" (Job 41:8), but we have no choice.

59   Ibid. Our analysis of X is indebted to Kojin Karatani, *Transcritique: On Kant and Marx*, Cambridge, MA: MIT Press, 2003 283–306, and Kojin Karatani, "Beyond Capital Nation State," *Rethinking Marxism* 20, 2008, 569–95. On the geographies of X, see Kojin Karatani and Joel Wainwright, "'Critique Is Impossible without Moves': An Interview with Kojin Karatani," *Dialogues in Human Geography* 2, 2012, 30–52.

Part II

3

The Politics of Adaptation

[I]n the interests of science it is necessary over and over again to engage in the critique of [our] fundamental concepts, in order that we may not unconsciously be ruled by them.

Albert Einstein, 1953[1]

I

Science is inescapably social. This is easy to forget because it is often imagined as a project of distinct *individuals*: people, armed with genius and objective data, who make "breakthroughs".[2] In truth, breakthroughs are exceptionally rare, and even when they occur—Darwin's theory of evolution, Einstein's theory of relativity—they are the result of the social labor of many more people who, by learning from the insights of others, exchanging ideas, trying things, comparing results and so on, generate insights that enable creative thought. (Not to mention the many others who have no direct involvement in the "science" but enable the would-be Darwin or Einstein to devote themselves to scientific pursuits.) Even more fundamentally, the scientific process always requires coordination, exchange, and language. Thus, it always exhibits some traces of the underlying social relations that give rise to it. For this reason, science is also always deeply historical; scientific activities and meanings are of their time. This is difficult to grasp for one's own time but obvious in retrospect. What qualified as science for the ancient Maya and Greeks was the result of genuinely scientific social labor (trying things, comparing results, and so on), even if much of it has little "scientific" meaning today.

Like every other scientific discipline, modern climate science is studied and taught by people with strengths and weaknesses, desires and fears, intellectual abilities and constraints, interests and ideologies, and so on. This is not to malign climate scientists, but merely to remind us that no climate scientist can escape the fact that (as Aristotle put it), the human being is *zōon politikon*: a being whose very animality is social and hence political. But what does it mean to be political? And if "being political" determines our common humanity, does that mean it is "natural," biological? If so, then

---

1 Albert Einstein, "Foreword," in Max Jammer, *Concepts of Space: The History of Theories of Space in Physics*, New York: Harper, 1960 [1953], xiii.
2 Stereotypically presented as white men wearing white lab coats.

are humans really just part of nature, the planetary crisis really just the sad fate encoded in human evolution? We take up questions regarding the human–nature distinction below by scrutinizing the concept of the political (in Chapter 4) and the prospects for changing our place in natural history (Chapter 8). In this chapter, we focus on the question of science and its sociality. Recognizing the inherent social and political nature of human affairs is fundamental to an assessment of contemporary climate science, which is both undeniably necessary and animated by politics—or animated by necessity and undeniably political.

To begin, take as an illustration the work of Lonnie G. Thompson. Much of what we know about the material change in the Earth's atmosphere stems from basic research in atmospheric chemistry, and Thompson's widely cited scientific work is central to this achievement. His specialty is reconstructing natural history for the past ~10,000 years with data derived from gases trapped in bubbles in glacial ice (see Figure 1.1). He has spent his life drilling ice cores in glaciers around the world, extracting gases from the bubbles, deriving evidence from their chemistry, and thereby piecing together Earth's atmospheric history. Thompson would be the first to note that his scientific work has been enabled by the social labor of innumerable others—beginning with his partner and scientific collaborator, Ellen Mosley Thompson. And like many other scientists whose insights have forced them to confront the changing global environment, Thompson has spoken out about the need for change, bringing scientific authority to the political realm. In this he exemplifies a more general trend, as the climate science community has tried to alert the world to the immanent, grave dangers indicated by their findings. The process followed by the Intergovernmental Panel on Climate Change is essentially a world-scale version of the same dynamic.[3]

In 2010 Thompson published a remarkable essay entitled "Climate Change: The Evidence and Our Options." It aims to explain society's options for responding to climate change. Discerning these options requires making decisions concerning, first, what we could do, and second, what we ought to do. Obviously, these decisions are inescapably political. Thompson proceeds by laying an empirical foundation (scientific data on the changing environment), upon which he erects "ought" statements (what we should do).

The impulse to move from the facts of climate science to outlining sociopolitical options is commonplace today, inherent to our conjuncture, and the division between the descriptive and prescriptive is increasingly blurry in climate science. This has produced considerable tension for many climate scientists, who have, as a rule, been disciplined against making strong prescriptive statements or drawing out the moral and political implications of their

---

3 For a concise history of the Intergovernmental Panel on Climate Change, see Jamieson, *Reason in a Dark Time*, 32–33.

findings.[4] To accommodate statements that imply moral or political leadership, therefore, many climate scientists adopt (consciously or not) an apologetic tone. Thompson's paper begins with the following sentences:

> Climatologists, like other scientists, tend to be a stolid group. We are not given to theatrical rantings about falling skies. Most of us are far more comfortable in our laboratories or gathering data in the field than we are giving interviews to journalists or speaking before Congressional committees.[5]

Why begin with a qualification? Like all openings, its aim is to legitimate the coming narrative. Thompson expresses a sentiment common among climate scientists who feel uncomfortable that their research compels them to speak politically. Environmental scientists will experience more of this discomfort in years to come, as will other disciplines brought to bear upon the challenge of adaptation (economics especially; see Chapter 5). One of our aims in this chapter is to consider climate science's politics in light of the question of adaptation—a concept that also emerges from science but has become fundamental to contemporary politics.

Thompson's central claims are elegantly summarized in the paper's abstract:

> Ice cores retrieved from shrinking glaciers around the world confirm their continuous existence for periods ranging from hundreds of years to multiple millennia, suggesting that climatological conditions that dominate those regions today are different from those under which these ice fields originally accumulated and have been sustained. The current warming is therefore unusual when viewed from the millennial perspective provided by multiple lines of proxy evidence and the 160-year record of direct temperature measurements. Despite all this evidence, plus the well-documented continual increase in atmospheric greenhouse gas concentrations, societies have taken little action to address this global-scale problem. Hence, the rate of global carbon dioxide emissions continues to accelerate. As a result of our inaction, we have three options: mitigation, adaptation, and suffering.[6]

This is an unusual framing of our options. Almost everyone, including the Intergovernmental Panel on Climate Change (IPCC), speaks in terms of a binary option set. We can choose between "mitigation" (reducing carbon emissions to slow or prevent climate change), or "adaptation" (adjusting ourselves to a warmer world). Thompson adds a third option, "suffering," introducing an explicitly moral element to our decisions. In this chapter, we consider the implications of this move and bring these insights to bear on the IPCC's discussion of adaptation.

---

4   On the interpretation of claims from climate science, see Candis Callison, *How Climate Change Comes to Matter: The Communal Life of Facts*, Durham, NC: Duke University Press, 2014.
5   Thompson, "Climate Change," 153.
6   Ibid.

Given Thompson's insertion of suffering into an apparently value-neutral discussion of "options" in the face of climate change—to some, an unnecessary political digression—we preface our discussion of the politics of adaptation with a few remarks on climatology, politics, and the character of science.

II

Despite the extraordinary urgency of addressing the problem of climate change, the modern university, particularly the social sciences, is only beginning to rise to the challenge.[7] Our technical understanding of the physical processes driving climate change has run far ahead of our explanations of the social and political processes driving these physical processes, and yet it is the social and political processes that must change.

A common response is to argue for more collaboration across the natural science–social science divide, to build interdisciplinary or transdisciplinary models of social and environmental change, but has there been little effective collaboration. A partial explanation lies in important differences between research in the natural sciences and the social sciences concerning fundamental concepts.[8] While climate scientists engage in (often contentious) debates about the meaning of their results, they rarely reestablish the basic building blocks taken for granted in their research.[9] Two scientists may engage in vigorous discussion of the precise role of CO_2 or CH_4 in physical atmospheric processes, but carbon's basic qualities—its atomic number or weight, chemical properties, and so on—will not be called into question.[10] In contrast, when two social scientists discuss, say, the dominance of market-based approaches in climate policy discourse, they are very likely to put a lot of energy into determining the meaning of "hegemony," "markets," "climate policy," "discourse," and so on, because understandings of these and related concepts reflect different conceptions of the

---

7   This subsection includes revised material from Joel Wainwright, "Climate Change and the Challenge of Transdisciplinarity," *Annals of the Association of American Geographers* 100, 2010, 983–91.

8   Scholars of the "social sciences" and "humanities" study much the same things, albeit differently, and usually without much collaboration. In Allen Bloom's words, the fields "represent the two responses to the crisis caused by the definitive ejection of man . . . from nature, and hence from the purview of natural science or natural philosophy, toward the end of the eighteenth century" (Allen Bloom, *The Closing of the American Mind*, New York: Touchstone, 1987, 357). For Bloom, the difference between them "comes down to the fact that social science really wants to be predictive, meaning that man [sic] is predictable, while the humanities say that he is not."

9   Bruno Latour, *Science in Action: How to Follow Scientists and Engineers through Society*, Cambridge, MA: Harvard, 1987, 2.

10   This is emphatically not to deny the necessity of examining scientific practices, or the social quality of knowledge about climate (see Michael Hulme, *Why We Disagree About Climate Change*. Cambridge: Cambridge University, 2009). Rather it is to recognize these substantive (if only relative) differences between the production of knowledge in the sciences and the humanities . Climate science is a complex discipline since its object (climate) is an ensemble of processes without fixed boundaries. Its fundamentals derive mainly from physics and chemistry.

world.[11] Which is to say that social science almost always involves extended reflection on its "basic" units of analysis. This is not to deny that social thinking can be "rigorous", but it is nevertheless true that frequently, one social thinker's rigor is merely ideology to another, because we are always involved in social life and the constant reuse and remaking of social concepts through language. There is no meta-language that operates beyond the social world with which to fix these concepts "objectively". Debates over the meaning of the building-block concepts for social thought are complex, interminable, and necessary. Since we unconsciously inherit our social concepts, as well as our means of calibrating their use, social thinking at its best proceeds by accounting for its conditions of possibility through a kind of recursive process of reflecting on basic concepts. Antonio Gramsci called this approach "absolute historicism," but whatever term we use, it invariably enriches and complicates the task of social analysis.[12]

In 1949, Albert Einstein addressed these challenges in a concise essay written to inaugurate the first issue of the socialist magazine *Monthly Review*. His essay confronts the question of whether and how his status as a natural scientist facilitates his venture into social thinking, and it merits careful reading today, when the relation between science and social knowledge lies at the heart of the debate about climate change.

"It might appear," Einstein begins, "that there are no essential methodological differences between astronomy and economics: scientists in both fields attempt to discover laws of general acceptability." But, he explains, there are two key differences. The first is that the involvement of conscious human

---

11 Antonio Gramsci, [Q11§12] *Selections from the Prison Notebook*, translated and edited by Quintin Hoare and Geoffrey Nowell Smith, New York: International Publishers,1971, 323–25.

12 On Gramsci's "absolute historicism," see ibid., 465 [Q11§27], 417 [Q15§61]. Gramsci also developed an original philosophy of science in his notebooks, highly pertinent to current debates around climate (and which we draw upon in this chapter). He argues that science is an iterative social practice, whereby the body and instruments are connected in new ways to advance humanity's understanding of the world. Gramsci thus rejects the commonsense notion that science is an objective procedure for studying reality. He sees objectivity not as an existing condition but as an ideological disposition: "'Objective' means this and only this: that one asserts to be objective, to be objective reality, that reality which is ascertained by all, which is independent of any merely particular or group standpoint. But basically, this too is a particular conception of the world, an ideology" (Gramsci, [Q11§37] *Further Selections from the Prison Notebooks*, Minneapolis: University of Minnesota Press, 1995, 291). But if objectivity is not the basis for scientific truths, then what is? The answer lies in science's social iterability. "If scientific truths were conclusive," he writes, then "science would have ceased to exist as such, as research . . . [Yet f]ortunately for science this is not true" (ibid., 292). Scientific truths are strong because they remain open: disagreements persist; different schools continue their research in parallel; what is today viewed as correct by scientists may come to be seen otherwise. Gramsci's approach situates scientific practices on the same plane as all other acts involving knowledge-production. This displacement of scientific objectivity opens a way for us to recognize the distinctiveness of scientific practices without separating them from the other elements that constitute hegemony: conflicts between social groups, the integral state, and so on. (See Joel Wainwright and Kristin Mercer, "The Dilemma of Decontamination: A Gramscian Analysis of the Mexican Transgenic Maize Dispute," *Geoforum* 40, 2009, 345–54.)

activity in social relations introduces profound complexities for social analysis. Taking economics as his social science example, Einstein writes, "the discovery of general laws in the field of economics is made difficult by the circumstance that observed economic phenomena are often affected by many factors which are very hard to evaluate separately."[13] These complications make the task of predicting human affairs—such as climate scientists may do by modeling social and economic responses to climate change—extremely complex, if not impossible.

Einstein uses a curious illustration to make this point, one that elegantly foreshadows his core argument and has profound implications for the climate debate. He notes that for the discipline of economics, neither its object of study ("the economy") nor its core concepts ("discounting," for example) can be separated from the history of conquest and empire that facilitated the emergence of global capitalism:

> The discovery of general laws in the field of economics is made difficult by the circumstance that . . . the experience which has accumulated since the beginning of the so-called civilized period of human history has . . . been largely influenced and limited by causes which are by no means exclusively economic in nature. For example, most of the major states of history owed their existence to conquest. The conquering peoples established themselves . . . as the privileged class of the conquered country. They seized for themselves a monopoly of the land ownership and appointed a priesthood from among their own ranks. The priests, in control of education, made the class division of society into a permanent institution and created a system of values by which the people were thenceforth, to a large extent unconsciously, guided in their social behavior.[14]

Einstein underscores the differences between natural science and the study of humanity: the complex imbrication of social knowledge in unequal social relations makes it difficult to discern cause and effect (what Einstein calls "general laws"), and the historical embeddedness of economics in the processes that shape our thought, the "system of values" that "unconsciously . . . guid[e] social behavior."

Einstein could have stopped there, leaving economics to the economists. Instead, he concludes that all scientists have a responsibility to engage with worldly affairs, but one they should embrace with an awareness of science's limitations:

> Science . . . cannot create ends and, even less, instill them in human beings; science, at most, can supply the means by which to attain certain ends. But the ends

---

13   Albert Einstein, *Why Socialism?* New York: Monthly Review Press, 1951, 4.
14   Ibid., 4–5.

themselves are conceived by personalities with lofty ethical ideals and—if these ends are not stillborn, but vital and vigorous—are adopted and carried forward by those many human beings who, half unconsciously, determine the slow evolution of society. For these reasons, we should be on our guard *not to overestimate science and scientific methods* when it is a question of human problems; and we should not assume that experts are the only ones who have a right to express themselves on questions affecting the organization of society.[15]

The question is how to put this approach to work. How can we embrace scientific practice and knowledge as a distinctive and powerful way of producing truths without falling prey to its mystifications—chiefly, the modern myth of the "expert" capacity to objectively resolve problems? How do we affirm science without expecting too much of it politically? And where do Einstein's insights leave those environmental scientists who wish to "express [our]selves" on the social dimensions of climate change?

III

At the end of "Climate Change: The Evidence and Our Options," Thompson defines our three options—mitigate, adapt, or suffer—in these terms:

> Mitigation is proactive . . . it involves doing things to reduce the pace and magnitude of the changes by altering the underlying causes . . . Adaptation is reactive. It involves reducing the potential adverse impacts resulting from the by-products of climate change . . . Our third option, suffering, means enduring the adverse impacts that cannot be staved off by mitigation or adaptation.[16]

John Holdren (whose earlier proposal for a "Planetary Regime" was discussed in Chapter 2) introduced the mitigate-adapt-suffer formula to a wide audience in 2007. Thompson's paper was published in 2010. That same year, Holdren, in his capacity as the newly appointed Assistant to the US President for Science and Technology, repeated the argument before the US National Climate Adaptation Summit:[17]

> [W]e only have three options. One is mitigation, the steps we take to reduce the pace and magnitude of the changes in climate that our activities cause. The second

---

15   Ibid., 5, emphasis added.
16   Thompson, "Climate Change," 167.
17   John Holdren (see Chapter 2) became a major figure in environmental science in the 1970s after publishing several works concerning human population coauthored with the neo-Malthusian Paul Erlich. See, for example, Paul Erlich and John Holdren, "Impact of Population Growth," *Science 171*, March 26, 1971, 1212–17; this paper is the source of the well-known I = PAT formula (human impact on the environment (I) is a function of population (P), affluence or consumption levels (A) and technology (T)).

is adaptation, the measures we take to reduce the harm that results from climate change that we do not avoid, and the third option is suffering. It's really that simple: mitigation, adaptation, and suffering.[18]

To reiterate, this is a not a standard framing of "our options." International climate policy is premised upon the notion that we need to mitigate carbon emissions and adapt to the changing climate.

Moreover, while it is true that adaptation is by definition "reactive," certain adaptations are seen as proactive. The entire world is already adapting to climate change—but this is not necessarily good news. For example, air conditioning, a common mechanism through which to mitigate the effects of warmer environments, is certainly "proactive," in the sense that this adaptation to climate change required some degree of forethought and planning. The problem with air conditioning—a problem that makes it an excellent metaphor for many technical approaches to adaptation—is that air conditioning units operate by exchanging, not eliminating, heat. They do not change the laws of thermodynamics; they work with them to remove heat, blowing it out of a building or automobile. The result is a net increase in heat. Air conditioning is one cause of the well-known "urban heat island" effect, which precipitates augmented air conditioning use, which in turn further heats the urban island in a positive feedback loop. Air conditioning presents itself to each of its users as a simple form of adaptation, but at the scale of the *city*, more air conditioning only makes the problem we are trying to escape worse—not to mention the fact that the vast majority of air conditioning units, which require a lot of energy, are powered by electricity generated from burning fossil fuels. By one measure, air conditioning is already the third largest source of demand for fossil fuel-derived electricity in the world (with demand rising fast, particularly in fast-growing and fast-warming cities of developing countries).[19] Air conditioning is a quotidian, urban maladaptation to climate change: an adaptation that begets greater future suffering.

More important, while we appreciate the emphasis on suffering, the separation of suffering from mitigation and adaptation, occludes the fact that mitigation and adaptation are often forms of suffering, especially for the relatively poor and marginalized, for whom climate adaptation is almost always

18   Remarks by the Honorable John P. Holdren, Assistant to the President for Science and Technology and Director, Office of Science and Technology Policy, Executive Office of the President, to the National Climate Adaptation Summit conference, Washington, DC, May 27, 2010, accessed at climatesciencewatch.org. Judging from the pattern of references we find by searching the words "mitigate adapt suffer," it appears that Holdren began using this rhetorically attractive triadic formula around 2006; it is widely attributed to him in texts from 2007 (see, for example, the unattributed slide 60/69 at <belfercenter.hks.harvard.edu/files/jph_scienceupdate_2_07.pdf>). By 2010 it was used generally, without reference to Holdren.

19   On the political ecology of air conditioning, see Stan Cox, *Losing Our Cool*, New York: New Press, 2010.

something to be endured. In fairness to Thompson, his paper acknowledges the importance of inequalities:

> Everyone will be affected by global warming, but those with the fewest resources for adapting will suffer most . . . Clearly mitigation is our best option, but so far most societies . . . have done little more than talk about the importance of mitigation . . . There are currently no technological quick fixes for global warming. Our only hope is to change our behavior in ways that significantly slow the rate of global warming, thereby giving the engineers time to devise, develop, and deploy technological solutions where possible. Unless large numbers of people take appropriate steps, including supporting governmental regulations aimed at reducing greenhouse gas emissions, our only options will be adaptation and suffering. And the longer we delay, the more unpleasant the adaptations and the greater the suffering will be.[20]

The emphasis on suffering as a distinct "option" emphasizes the fact that someone—probably someone yet to be born—will suffer due to our failure to mitigate and adapt. As critique of the mainstream mitigation-adaptation formulation, Holdren and Thompson's approach, despite its analytical limitations, invokes an essential (if only implicit) political argument by insisting on what is typically excluded in debates on adaptation. Yet if Holdren and Thompson have tried make the fact of "suffering" visible in mainstream climate discourse, their framing also mischaracterizes it as an "option." What is at stake is our apparent inability or refusal to understand suffering—now or in the future—in a political or ethical register not beholden to the implicit utilitarian calculus of mitigation *versus* adaptation—a "choice" that is virtually always discussed in terms of comparative costs. That is why we should feel unnerved when scientists speak of mitigation as our "best option." On the contrary, especially for the relatively affluent and secure, it is our ethical and planetary imperative. Not because we need to buy time for one particular social group to find a "technological solution" ("the engineers" in Thompson's text, messianic "technology" in every fantasy of Climate Leviathan), but because all greenhouse gas emissions increase the suffering of others, both present generations and those to come.

IV

One way to understand the central place of "adaptation" in the age of accelerating climate change is via what is arguably the most important texts in the enormous climate adaptation literature: the IPCC Report, Technical Summary, and Summary for Policymakers, Fifth Assessment Review (AR5)

20 Thompson, "Climate Change," 167.

Working Group II.[21] They are essentially syntheses of current research, produced by an international group of scientists from different disciplines, selected with input from the member states.[22] For AR5 Working Group II, a large number of specialists—242 lead authors and 66 review editors from 70 countries—surveyed the entire field of relevant, published material (12,000+ references), then synthesized their findings in a Technical Summary of manageable scope.[23] A further round of diplomatic filtering was applied to the Technical Summary to create the Summary for Policymakers. The final AR5 Working Group II documents were released to the public on March 25–29, 2014, at the Approval Session in Yokohama, Japan, where the Working Group II Summary for Policymakers was "approved line-by-line and accepted by the Panel, which has 195 member Governments."[24] It represents something almost unique in the history of scientific literature: a text that at once synthesizes (again, in a relatively open and democratic fashion) the known scientific literature in a way that enables a kind of scientific *and* political consensus. The very nature of the text—its conditions of production, circulation, and characteristics—reflects the political imperative brought to bear upon contemporary environmental science, and its inseparability from the capitalist state.

The AR5 Working Group II texts have many valuable qualities. Above all, in dry yet dramatic language, they lay out many of the widely-anticipated consequences of climate change. For example, the Summary for Policymakers includes the following list:

- Many terrestrial, freshwater, and marine species have shifted their geographic ranges, seasonal activities, migration patterns, abundances, and species interactions in response to ongoing climate change (high confidence).
- Based on many studies covering a wide range of regions and crops, negative impacts of climate change on crop yields have been more common than positive impacts (high confidence).
- Differences in vulnerability and exposure arise from non-climatic factors and from multidimensional inequalities often produced by uneven development processes (very high confidence).

---

21   Like the other products of the IPCC assessment report process, the Report, Technical Summary and Summary for Policymakers are three expressions of one process. For the AR5 documents and explanations on their condition of production, go to www.ipcc.ch.

22   "The 'intergovernmental' nature of the IPCC is one of the key reasons why it has been lauded by so many as being successful and influential. Its reports are listened to by governments when engaged in geopolitical negotiations in ways that national science academies or independent assessments might not be"; Mike Hulme, "1.5°C and Climate Research after the Paris Agreement," *Nature Climate Change* 6, 2016, 223.

23   Data from Intergovernmental Panel on Climate Change, Working Group II Fact Sheet: Climate Change 2014: Impacts, Adaptation, and Vulnerability. For the AR5 Working Group II documents, see the Working Group II Home page, www.ipcc-wg2.awi.de

24   Intergovernmental Panel on Climate Change, Working Group II Fact Sheet.

- Impacts from recent climate-related extremes, such as heat waves, droughts, floods, cyclones, and wildfires, reveal significant vulnerability and exposure of some ecosystems and many human systems to current climate variability (very high confidence).
- Climate-related hazards exacerbate other stressors, often with negative outcomes for livelihoods, especially for people living in poverty (high confidence).
- Violent conflict increases vulnerability to climate change (medium evidence, high agreement).[25]

The parenthetical remarks at the end of each sentence indicate another valuable aspect of the IPCC documents: the assessment of the relative confidence and agreement in the literature regarding each point. This reflects the inherently social strengths of science: the AR5 Working Group II reports crystallize the collective findings of the community and openly acknowledge sources and the degree of consensus. The valve of the IPCC reports, including AR5 Working Group II, is not that they are beyond critique, but that they invite critique.

With these merits in mind, it is worth considering two criticisms of the work of AR5 Working Group II, which together suggest a critique of what Michel Foucault called the *episteme* (roughly, the horizon of thought possible in a given time and place), not the particular interests or specific actors involved.[26] First, the AR5 Working Group II Technical Summary and Report present a vision of the future in which fundamental and systemic risks to the world's political and economic system are essentially absent. Threats are enumerated and assessed, but not the political-economic stage upon which they will play out. The result is a model of a future defined by dramatic changes, yet without radically unexpected events—no "black swans" or system failures.

The top half of Figure 3.1 presents two possible warming pathways (RCP 2.6 and 8.5).[27] It describes the range of possible temperature increases expected by 2100 (relative to 1850–1900). In the low-mitigation scenario (RCP 2.6) average global temperatures would only increase by 1.5°C. As noted earlier, however, the planet has already reached a mean increase of approximately 1°C, without reducing global carbon emissions. Absent radical political change, RCP 8.5 ("business as usual"—no change from the current trajectory) is the most likely scenario. On that pathway, we might expect a global mean increase of 4.5°C by 2100, and rising.

---

25   IPCC, Top-Level Findings from the AR5 Working Group II Summary for Policymakers, available at www.ipcc.ch.

26   Michel Foucault, *Archaeology of Knowledge*, New York: Routledge, 2002 [1969].

27   IPCC, AR5 Working Group II, Box TS-5 Fig. 1. RCPs are Representative Concentration Pathways: scenarios of future global carbon emissions (relative concentrations of carbon in the atmosphere); effectively, predictions of the future.

Figure 3.1A. Rising temperatures and risks: Global mean temperature increase 1986 – 2005 relative to 1850 – 1900

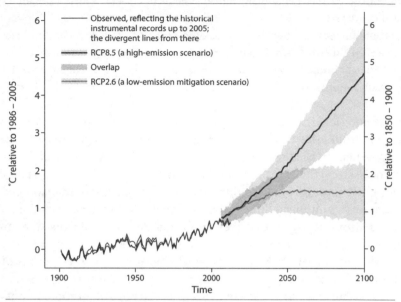

Source: Intergovernmental Panel on Climate Change, Fifth Assessment Report, Working Group III, 2014.

Figure 3.1B. Relative additional risk from five types of threats at differing levels of additional warming

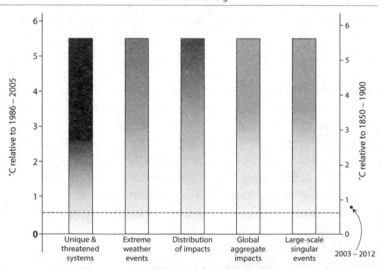

Source: Intergovernmental Panel on Climate Change, Fifth Assessment Report, Working Group III, 2014.

The bottom half of Figure 3.1 is AR5 Working Group II's novel contribution. It attempts to display the relative severity or level of additional climate change-induced risk we should expect in five key areas. (Although these five dynamics are interconnected, they are analytically distinguished in the diagram.) The simple message is that these risks increase in severity as mean temperature increases. But the difficult questions are how much, and to what degree? In the face of the inherent trickiness of these questions, the figure tempts us with a misplaced concreteness. Take, for example, the assessment of additional risks associated with a mean temperature increase of 2.5°C.[28] At that level, additional risk to unique and threatened systems is between "high" and "very high"; additional risk from extreme weather events is "high." Yet somehow, global aggregate impacts and the threat of large-scale singular events would only increase "moderately."

In other words, the figure seems to tell us that a temperature increase that would cause significant additional stresses on earth systems and trigger a significant increase in extreme weather would nonetheless have only modest implications for global political economy. The implicit claim—somewhere between assumption and assertion—is that the prevailing liberal, capitalist order is more robust than the global environment, and will adapt to the coming threat better than the ecosystems upon which it depends. But AR5 Working Group II provides no account of the political conditions for this moderation, nor any justification for its remarkably optimistic and ahistorical presumption of the stability of our political economic order.

It bears emphasis that the underestimation of systematic threats is not due to misrepresentation or the authors' bias, but to the literatures upon which the report is based, which for the most part take for granted both (a) the stability or even timelessness of our political economic order, and (b) that "adaptation" describes the technical means by which humans will figure out how to live on a hotter planet in a manner as much as possible like we do now. This is built into the scientific and methodological division of labour in the IPCC working groups. AR5 Working Group I reports, incorporated into the work of Working Group II, describe an analytically precise, natural sciences view of climate change grounded in widely accepted theories and models of physical processes. The major sources of uncertainty (the complex spatiality of clouds and ocean heat or long-term feedback dynamics in the Earth's climate system, for instance) are well-studied, and the degree of uncertainty is circumscribed. In other words, while we cannot possibly know how the Earth's climatic system will respond a century from now, at least we have a robust literature examining the climate models that support our predictions. The situation changes dramatically when we shift to

---

28   To reiterate, our political-economic analysis points to temperature increases consistent with RCP 8.5; but for the sake of discussion, a more conservative estimate is useful.

Working Group III, on mitigation. The future of mitigation is fundamentally a question of political economy, but the IPCC does not, or perhaps cannot, draw upon work that presents a critical model of capitalism. This causes a fundamental analytical problem. It would be like trying to model hurricanes without a theory of thermodynamics or an understanding of the effects of changing ocean temperatures on cyclone dynamics.

These difficulties are further compounded when we turn to Working Group II, on adaptation. Every analysis of adaptation to global climate change presupposes not only an estimate of future atmospheric carbon concentrations (which determine the rapidity and extent of climate change) but also a theory of how complex societies are likely to adapt in the face of complex changes. But the review process employed through the IPCC cannot produce a coherent political analysis of adaptation because the underlying literature, such as it is, does not have one. The strengths of the IPCC process meet their limit where we arrive at the challenge of predicting or analyzing potential systematic changes to our predominantly liberal, capitalist geopolitical economy.

When it comes to global aggregate impacts, these imprecisions are graphically finessed in Figure 3.1 by the use of shaded bars that portray a smoothly graded risk profile. In the shift from the rigorously quantitative upper part of the figure to the vague, qualitative lower part, aesthetics compensate for the inadequacy of the underlying model: it may not make much sense, but it definitely looks nice. Even when we reach the top of the Y axis the lower part of the figure, with a mean 5.5°C global temperature increase by 2100, the AR5 Working Group II figure says that the world faces no more than "high" risk of global aggregate impacts. This presumes more than we should about the stability of our world system. Note, too, the conservatism of the IPCC's temporal framing, which treats the year 2100 as a meaningful end point. Humans have lived on Earth for ~200,000 years; what we typically call "civilization" is thousands of years old. However unintentionally, setting the temporal horizon of our analysis at 2100 tends to suggest that the end of this century will mark a plateau, at which point we will have reached some sort of equilibrium, good or bad. But that is of course not true.

If we compare the different texts produced by AR5 Working Group II, we find varying degrees of precision and conservatism concerning systemic risks. In general, from the distillation of findings in the discrete sections to the final, diplomatically approved Summary, systemic risks are downplayed. They are more openly avowed in the full text chapters, acknowledged in the Technical Summary, and almost absent from the Summary for Policymakers. For example, the Technical Summary states that "human security"—in the broad sense of physical, social, and livelihood security—will be "*progressively threatened* as the climate changes," a claim not to be found in the Summary for Policymakers.[29]

---

29   IPCC, Fifth Assessment Report, Working Group II, Technical Summary, 25.

Similarly, the Technical Summary points out that one of the factors inhibiting strategies for successful mitigation and adaptation is that "privileged members of society can benefit" from current approaches to climate change. Indeed they can and do—a crucial fact for examining the political fault-lines surrounding climate adaptation.[30] This point is not in the Summary for Policymakers either.

As a final and important example, the Technical Summary includes a serious indictment of the standard economic conceptions of the costs of adaptation:

> Poor planning, overemphasizing short-term outcomes . . . or failing to consider all options can result in maladaptation (*medium evidence, high agreement*). Narrow focus on quantifiable costs and benefits can bias decisions against the poor, against ecosystems, and against those in the future whose values can be excluded or are understated.[31]

Here is how it appears in the Summary for Policymakers:

> Poor planning, overemphasizing short-term outcomes, or failing to sufficiently anticipate consequences can result in maladaptation (*medium evidence, high agreement*). Maladaptation can increase the vulnerability or exposure of the target group in the future, or the vulnerability of other people, places, or sectors.[32]

As mentioned earlier, the translation from the Technical Summary to the Summary for Policymakers entails the removal of unnecessary technical language. But that is not what is going on here. The Technical Summary's argument that we must "consider all options" is perfectly clear and nontechnical, but missing from the Summary for Policymakers. Similarly, there is nothing complex about the statement that a "[n]arrow focus on quantifiable costs and benefits can bias decisions against the poor," but it too is removed in favour of "target group" (if anything, a *more* technical term).

More examples are readily available, but the pattern is clear. The movement from the scientific literature to the Report to the Technical Summary to the Summary for Policymakers involves a cascade of translations. Scientific *and* political decisions are at work at each stage. The limitations of the present order, and the systemic risks it faces, are consistently de-emphasized. So too are the costs of the forms of adaptation imagined for the world—costs that will be borne by the poor, the nonhuman, and generations to come. It is hard not to suspect an anxious intent to suppress it.

The second critique to which the IPCC's AR5 Working Group II is subject— and with it, the current analysis of climate adaptation of which it is

---

30 Ibid., 7.
31 Ibid., 32.
32 Summary for Policymakers, 28

constitutive—concerns the concept of adaptation itself.[33] When the world is offered a limited set of options, it is worth paying close attention to the fine print, for this is where we find the metaphors we will live by.[34] "Suffering" is a moral and political concept at least as old as the story of Job. "Mitigation" is from physical sciences, physics and engineering. "Adaptation" is biological. Though much older than Darwin's theory of evolution, it has come to prominence because of its centrality to evolutionary theory. This biological provenance is worth consideration.

The words "adaptation" and "adapt" have a relatively simple etymology but a complex ensemble of meanings and resonances. The noun (an "adaptation" or "adaptive trait") refers to a quality or state a being has or expresses. The verb ("to adapt") refers to the process that brings about those particular things (traits, qualities). Synonyms include "to adjust, make fit"; "to conform to conditions"; "to adopt an appropriate form." To express an adaptation is to be adapted to a particular context. Since Darwin, "adaptation" has come to refer specifically to a species' modification through evolutionary change in ways that render it better adjusted to its environment. In evolutionary theory, the population is the unit of adaptation. The individuals in any given population will exhibit heterogeneous traits or qualities (phenotypic diversity—the outward expression of genetic variants of the members of that population), and environmental conditions will grant certain traits an advantage. Consequently, the population of the species will, over time, express a higher proportion of favored traits.[35]

Adaptation refers, then, to the process and the result of evolution by means of natural selection. Because the process is ongoing, the result is never fixed or permanent. Species and ecosystems are dynamic and mutable, integrating new genetic variants through immigration and mutation just as selection is acting on them. The genetic profile of a given species in a time and place will evolve across generations. While the relative frequency of deleterious genes will usually decline over time, they do not typically disappear entirely; a relatively small proportion of a population may carry genes for "unfit" qualities.

---

33   This subsection has benefitted from excellent critical studies of adaptation: Roman Felli, *La grande adaptation: Climat, capitalisme, catastrophe*, Paris: Seuil, 2015; Marcus Taylor, *The Political Ecology of Climate Change Adaptation*, London: Routledge, 2014; Michael Watts, "Now and Then: The Origins of Political Ecology and the Rebirth of Adaptation as a Form of Thought," in Tom Perreault, Gavin Bridge, and James McCarthy (eds), *The Routledge Handbook of Political Ecology*, Abingdon, Oxon, UK: Routledge, 2015, 19–50; and Jeremy Walker and Melinda Cooper, "Geneaologies of Resilience," *Security Dialogue* 42, no. 2, 2011, 413–60.

34   A reference to George Lakoff and Mark Johnson, *Metaphors We Live By*, Chicago, IL: University of Chicago Press, 1980.

35   While the unit of analysis for studying these processes in biology is the *species-population*, ultimately the changes occurs at the level of the genetic makeup of that population. For this reason, some evolutionary theorists speak of the gene as the unit of analysis. On this debate, compare Richard Levins and Richard Lewontin, *The Dialectical Biologist*, Cambridge, MA: Harvard University Press, 1985, and Richard Dawkins, *The Selfish Gene*, New York: Oxford University Press, 2016.

To see how this unfolds in actually existing socio-natural conditions, take the case of an agricultural plant species responding to climate change. The diet of most of the world's people (and the animals people eat) is dependent upon the production of a small number of major crop species, particularly wheat, maize, rice, potato, and soy. In centers of crop origin, where these species are often fundamental to local diets, farmers typically plant crop landraces (traditional varieties), whose seeds are saved by farmers year to year. Through natural and human mediated selection, these plant crops have evolved to suit particular environments.[36] Like all plants, they also experience stress as local environments change. For instance, the majority of the world's landraces are grown in the tropics, under natural precipitation (rain-fed, not irrigated). With climate change, tropical precipitation patterns have become more variable: some places are on average wetter, others drier, but the timing and level of precipitation are less predictable almost everywhere. Coupled with rising temperatures, this unpredictability poses significant challenges for crop production and the farmers who rely upon it.

Theoretically, we can expect crop populations to respond to climate change in multiple ways, including by adaptation to novel conditions. (Landraces of pearl millet in Africa, for example, have evolved shorter flowering time during decades of drought.[37]) In addition, adaptation may be facilitated by gene flow, or the introduction of new genetic variants through immigration. Changes in phenotype or traits can also occur through the expression of phenotypic plasticity, which does not require genetic change. Although these responses may in some cases allow crops to maintain productivity despite climate change, they may also be constrained, retarding optimization and lowering yield, sometimes significantly. All these evolutionary dynamics in crops are mediated and complicated by human management of the agroecosystem. If production declines enough, farmers may discard their landraces in search of better adapted seed lots or species.[38] They may also give up on farming altogether.

What about human societies? In contemporary discussions of climate change, "adaptation" refers to the social and biological at once, and the evolutionary roots of the metaphor are obscured. But what is the unit of analysis? When we say that "society adapts," what plays the role of natural selection?

---

36   On plant local adaptation, see Kristin Mercer and Hugo Perales, "Evolutionary Response of Landraces to Climate Change in Centers of Crop Diversity." *Evolutionary Applications* 3, no. 5-6, 2010, 480–93. We thank Kristin Mercer for her help with this paragraph.

37   Yves Vigouroux, et al., "Selection for Earlier Flowering Crop Associated with Climatic Variations in the Sahel," *PLoS One* 6, no. 5, 2011, e19563.

38   This conception of adaptation is rarely introduced in discussions of how to maintain the agronomic and economic viability of agricultural systems. In international fora, transgenics are often (problematically) upheld as critical technology for agricultural adaptation: see Kristin Mercer, Hugo Perales and Joel Wainwright, "Climate Change and the Transgenic Adaptation Strategy: Smallholder Livelihoods, Climate Justice, and Maize Landraces in Mexico," *Global Environmental Change* 22, 2012, 495–504.

What are the genes, what are the populations? This is where the political valences of the evolutionary metaphor have their chief effects. When we are told that "society must adapt to climate change" or that "we should adapt rather than suffer," the evolutionary metaphor guarantees we conceptualize human life in "biological" terms. This may not seem problematic (we are indeed biological beings) but the primacy of thinking about adaptation on biological terms has two crucial effects on social and political analysis.

First, it invites functionalism.[39] Functionalism is always a claim that explains the genesis of some aspect of the world as a product of a situation in which it was "called for" or even necessary. In evolutionary terms we may say that traits are "functional" when they increase the fitness of certain members of a given population. They develop because the environment solicits them by setting conditions in which they are encouraged: the long, thin beaks of nectar-eating hummingbirds, for example. But what does it mean to be "functional" in a *social* system? What does it mean to be fit, to be well-adapted?

In the social setting of human communities, all notions of what we might call "social fitness" are fundamentally and inescapably ideological. In every society, the conception of the world held by the ruling elite reflects their ideas about themselves and their rule that identify certain features they associate with themselves as particularly well-suited to "success" or status. These include, among other things, abstract notions of social fitness (or right) that justify their way of being. However ugly or distorted, these ideas ramify to some extent throughout society and thereby acquire social force—they can even become common sense, one of the key ways in which hegemony operates. A familiar result of this broader adoption of elite ideas of what is socially "functional" is (for example) the way in which "entrepreneurialism" has become an almost universally celebrated quality in capitalist societies, the ultimate individual "adaptation" to the contemporary moment. This ideological foundation of any conception of "fitness" has no correlation in the evolutionary process from which the metaphor derives. Ideology cannot be explained by evolution.

Second, praising humans abstractly for their capacity to adapt—a logical corollary of a functional view of social life, in which the way we live follows naturally from "sensible" adaptations to conditions that make them functional—not only obscures the ideological and hence political content of "adaptation," it is also a historical gesture of the reactionary right.[40] Whenever

---

39   Structural functionalism is a *bête noire* in the humanities, widely criticized but rarely seen. Watts's review of the meanings of adaptation for human geography makes the crucial point: "In the human sciences, the term 'adaptation' has . . . always been saddled by the baggage of structural functionalism on the one hand and biological reductionism on the other" (Michael Watts, "Adaptation," in Derek Gregory, Ron Johnston, Geraldine Pratt, Michael Watts, and Sarah Whatmore (eds), *The Dictionary of Human Geography*, 5th Edition, Hoboken, NJ: Wiley-Blackwell, 2009, 8; see also Watts, "Now and Then.") Our target here is the pedestrian variety that celebrates the human capacity to adapt as a basis for downplaying the planetary emergency.

40   "The aspect of the problem of adaptation that is probably the most disturbing is

political questions are rendered biological, their answers are attributed to nature (human or otherwise), and de-politicized in a way that legitimates the prevailing order as the outcome of dynamics that are beyond human influence by definition.

In other words, simply to claim that "society must adapt" is to represent social responses to climate change—from the mundane (air conditioning) to the exceptional (a state of emergency after a "natural disaster")—in a way that makes these adaptations seem natural and functional. This dynamic is firmly rooted in the dominant philosophical and metaphysical traditions of the liberal capitalist global North. In Chapter 1, we discussed the centrality for Hobbes of the notion of natural right, or the inherent naturalness of the sovereign: Leviathan's sovereignty is posited as nothing less than *the functional social adaptation to the state of nature*. This thread ties the entire Western European tradition of political theory together. Historically, appeals to nature and biology are always used to justify and secure the position of the prevailing elite. Nature sides with the powerful.[41]

None of this is to deny the value of scientific study of nature, the legitimacy of evolutionary theory, or valid uses of the concept "adaptation" in social and political analysis. We are all subjects of ideology. No one can wholly reject one's conceptual inheritance any more than one can wholly refuse the knowledge it affirms. But grave problems arise when we forget the irrevocably metaphorical quality of all natural and biological concepts that circulate in political life. With respect to climate change, the apparent naturalness of evolutionary metaphors like "adaptation" is fundamental to its politics. While it would be simplistic (and potentially functionalist) to blame this state of affairs on the capitalist class, the metaphysics of liberal capitalism undeniably rely on evolutionary language.[47]

Fortunately, there are strategies for dealing with mischievous metaphors. A radical historicism is essential. Only when we grasp the social life of science can we begin to appreciate its politics. There is no need for climate scientists to apologize for making political statements. On the contrary, it is the silence and passivity of most environmental scientists that requires justification. Those who increase our knowledge of the Earth's changes and also stick their necks out with politically responsible engagement make a dual intervention into natural history. This does

paradoxically the very fact that human beings are so adaptable. This very adaptability enables them to become adjusted to conditions and habits that will eventually destroy the values most characteristic of human life." René Dubos, *Man Adapting*, New Haven, CT: Yale University Press, 1965, 278.

41   "Not a single line has been written—at least within the Western tradition—in which the terms 'nature', 'natural order', 'natural law', 'natural right' . . . have not been followed . . . by an affirmation concerning the way to reform public life . . . When one appeals to the notion of nature, *the assemblage that it authorizes counts for infinitely more than the ontological quality of 'naturalness', whose origin it would guarantee.*" Bruno Latour, *Politics of Nature*, Cambridge, MA: Harvard University Press, 2004, 28–29 (emphasis in original).

42   Darwin's texts invited such appropriations; see Valentino Gerratana, "Marx and Darwin," *New Left Review* I:82, 1973, 60–82.

not mean they deserve acclamation as lone rebels, however. The heroism of science's occasional radical political involvement is always already social. James Hansen's 1988 Congressional testimony on climate change—when he told the US Senate that climate change had already begun, and was not a "natural variation," but anthropogenic—was the result of social labor and political struggle as much as scientific evidence.[43] Although we should celebrate those instances of scientific leadership, we must also heed Einstein's warning not to expect too much from science, because the transformation we need is essentially political. This truth is hidden by the language of adaptation. Consequently, we have to complement the work of IPCC Working Group II with a critique of adaptation as a technical rendering of a limit problem for the liberal imagination.

V

One may wonder if we have overemphasized adaptation, since international climate negotiations have focused almost exclusively on mitigation. The Kyoto Protocol was essentially a greenhouse gas abatement treaty. The signatories professed to recognize its importance, but adaptation was effectively left out of the protocol. While this could be interpreted positively— since the priority should be to reduce emissions as much as possible—the exclusion of adaptation is actually evidence of an inability to confront the politics of adaptation and thereby to produce international political agreement on adaptation.

The main obstacle to that agreement is obvious to anyone familiar with the UNFCCC process, namely, the world's massive inequalities: unequal wealth and power in the world system; unequal responsibility for climate change; and unequal distribution of its negative consequences. The oft-noted scandal of climate change is that those who caused it will not live to see its full consequences, and those who are suffering or will suffer worst did not cause the problem. This dynamic has a distinct spatial and temporal distribution, through which the living rich enjoy extraordinary privilege relative to the poor and yet to be born. For example, most low-lying, flood-prone, and island nations (like Bangladesh or the Maldives) are responsible for only the tiniest fraction of atmospheric carbon but face potential eradication, but Canada, where per capita emissions are among the highest in the world, is likely to be among the least affected by warmer global temperatures (which is not to say it will not be affected severely). The affluent parts of the world have emitted the most greenhouse gases, and the vast majority of those who benefited from the economic activity that generated those emissions have died or will be dead before the most severe consequences

---

43   Philip Shabecoff, "Global Warming Has Begun, Expert Tells Senate," *New York Times*, June 24, 1988. On the nature and effectiveness of Hansen's 1988 testimony, see Richard Besel, "Accommodating Climate Change Science: James Hansen and the Rhetorical/Political Emergence of Global Warming," *Science in Context* 26, no.1, 2013, 137–52.

have arrived. In rough numbers, approximately 7 percent of the world is responsible for half of all carbon emissions today, and half of the world is responsible for only approximately 7 percent.[44]

In discussions of climate politics this scandalous disproportionality is, understandably, typically framed by the nation-state: it is certainly legitimate for India to reproach the United States for failing to address its historical responsibility for the climate change that is now wreaking havoc across the subcontinent. But this critique should not be limited to the nation-state, which obscures as much as it reveals, since within every nation-state, the wealthiest social groups (the richest and most powerful people, in essence the capitalist class) are responsible for most of the consumption and carbon emissions that are causing climate change. Yet, while the global political-economic status quo puts the poor (including subaltern social groups of enormous heterogeneity) in the position most vulnerable to socionatural catastrophe, discussions of "adaptation" are almost always about how the poor must adapt.

There is something terribly wrong here. Surely if "adaptation" means "correction" or "adjustment," then the most important adaptation that the world could make to address climate change would be to redistribute wealth and power to end fossil fuel use and force those responsible for climate change to reallocate the wealth its drivers have helped them accumulate at the cost of billions of people's suffering. It is the world's wealthy and national elites who must "adapt" so the poor and future generations will not "suffer," and so we might prepare the bases of democracy necessary to deal justly with those already-irreversible impacts the future surely holds.

Any meaningful international agreement on adaptation would require ascertaining who should pay who to adjust to a warmer world—this is why it could not be resolved at Kyoto, or any subsequent climate summit. The liberal approach to this question (prevailing in international law) assumes the equivalence and mutual substitutability of justice and money. In other words, adaptation is reduced to the question of financial stocks and flows between nation-states. For what specific damages or adaptations should the United States pay India? What will "justice" cost, and for how long must one pay for it?

After the Paris Agreement the UNFCCC adaptation debate has stalled on precisely this issue—the construction of an acceptable framework for international law on "loss and damage," that is, who will pay who for damages caused by climate change. Cast in geopolitical terms, the impasse is evidence of the success of the core capitalist states' diplomatic strategy:

Adaptation was excluded from the agenda in the early years of climate policy

---

44 Shoibal Chakravarty, Ananth Chikkatur, Heleen de Coninck, Stephen Pacala, Robert Socolow, and Massimo Tavoni, "Sharing Global CO_2 Emission Reductions among One Billion High Emitters," *Proceedings of the National Academy of Sciences* 106, 2009, 11884–88; cited in Jamieson, *Reason in a Dark Time*, 131.

because it was seen as a defeatist approach that would reduce the incentive for greenhouse gas emissions. The "adaptation taboo" was akin to the distaste possessed by the religious right for sex education in schools: treated as an ethical compromise that will only encourage undesirable behavior. Politically, adaptation was an equally tough sell. Adaptation discussions in the UNFCCC are intrinsically linked with discussions on financing, which has always been a contentious issue in climate negotiations. Developed countries, which are responsible for the bulk of the historical emissions of greenhouse gases, have sought to restrict adaptation discussions because it then inevitably leads to the question of historic responsibility and who should pay for adaptation.[45]

In Paris, this issue moved to the top of the agenda but was defeated, once again, by the unwillingness of the United States to enter into any meaningful discussion of "loss and damage."

But let us imagine that the climate justice movement was larger, more organized, and powerful. Suppose we had seats at the table and could advocate, in a relatively unified fashion, for greater equality in the world system: fairness in the redistribution of carbon emissions, equality in levels of material comfort, and so on. Could the current arrangement of power in the world accommodate this change? How much room exists for a substantial consideration of adaptation to climate change in the existing world system of capitalist nation-states? Any approach to these questions must reflect deeply upon the manifest inequalities of power in a mode of global political-economic regulation currently constituted to a significant extent by liberal capitalism, including the UN system, the Bretton Woods institutions, free trade agreements, the European Union, and so on. This matrix has continually failed to produce a coordinated response to climate change, which is instead framed as a technical problem to be addressed by adaptation through financial investment (capital formation, not reparations) and governance (planetary management).[46]

These limits to the prevailing conception of adaptation plague the Paris Agreement. Although the concept is fundamental to it, the agreement does not present a coherent, tractable plan for planetary adaptation. It aspires to

45   Vikrom Mathur and Aniruddh Mohan, "From Response to Resilience: Adaptation in a Global Climate Agreement," ORF Occasional Paper 76, 2015, 2.

46   For example:

Existing and emerging economic instruments can foster adaptation by providing incentives for anticipating and reducing impacts (medium confidence). Instruments include public-private finance partnerships, loans, payments for environmental services, improved resource pricing, charges and subsidies, norms and regulations, and risk sharing and transfer mechanisms.

IPCC, "Climate Change 2014: Synthesis Report. Contribution of Working Groups I, II and III to the Fifth Assessment Report of the Intergovernmental Panel on Climate Change," Geneva, Switzerland, 2014, 107.

"enhancing adaptive capacity, strengthening resilience and reducing vulnerability to climate change" (Article 7.1), but the funds and political commitment necessary are not secured by the agreement. It also states that adaptation efforts will be "recognized" in accordance with "modalities to be adopted" (Article 7.3), and "support for and international cooperation on adaptation efforts" is "recognized" as important (Article 7.8). Legally speaking, this "recognition" requires little to no action. Moreover, the agreement contains no mandatory provisions to report adaptation strategies or commitments, although it encourages Parties to submit and update an "adaptation communication" (Article 7.10) in some form yet to be determined.

None of this changes the fact that the Paris Agreement is significant for the adaptation of the political. But the adaptation at work is not expressed directly in the text, because the underlying problems with adaptation in the UNFCCC negotiations go deeper. Political change has been slowed by both affluent sabotage (led especially by the United States) in addition to developing world resistance (as demonstrated by India, for example). As justifiable as the latter might be, it shares with the former a futile fidelity to the conventional economic thinking by which the nation-state-centered liberal-capitalist matrix operates, insofar as it relies just as heavily on the essentially technical determination of the distribution of costs and benefits. Negotiators seek to solve an optimization problem whose terms must include coefficients for colonialism, underdevelopment, massive historical displacement, and impoverishment. And this is to say nothing of inequalities internal to developing nation-states.[47] The impossible mathematics of this approach frustrates all market-based efforts to allocate a global pool of emittable greenhouse gases (and the powers-that-be know it cannot be anything less than global). The constant and necessary intrusion of the pesky politics of the unpriceable history of the present—inequality, colonialism, and underdevelopment—simultaneously legitimates Southern resistance and explains affluent nations' shirking of historical and moral accountability. For the South, it justifies the rejection of petty payments to forget the crimes of history. For elites of the North, for whom the ways and means of liberal capitalism are presumed, the way forward is through the erasure of the record of past wealth-producing emissions and the declaration of an atmospheric blank slate. "Save our global village," "we're all in this together": this is the political adaptation proclaimed by the global North. Furthermore, no mention is made of assisted migration—almost certainly a key aspect of any "adaptation".

This program suppresses—as it must—the fact that adaptation to climate change will not be cheap and many will suffer. In the liberal nation-state framework, it is impossible to broach the question in a manner that recognizes this truth. The underlying problem is that climate change cannot be addressed by

---

47 On inequality in global carbon emissions, see J. Timmons Roberts and Bradley C. Parks, *A Climate of Injustice: Global Inequality, North-South Politics, and Climate Policy*, Cambridge, MA: MIT Press, 2007.

liberal economic reason, which, denying itself a conscious politics—indeed, denouncing all "politics" as a distortion of economic rationality—cannot deal with history and hysteresis (that is, the irrepressible ways that history continues to matter). On orthodox economic terms, a global solution is not merely politically unlikely; it is logically impossible. No market-based "solution" can be devised for a massive problem whose "causes" took place before it was possible to price their repercussions. In short, there is no Coasian solution to climate change, no way for self-interested actors to address the "problem of social cost" when the very ground on which the problem must be addressed—the political—is disavowed.[48] This is emphatically not to deny the global environmental debt. That the luxurious life of the capitalist global North is dessicating West Africa and scorching South Asia is impossible to deny—but it is just as impossible to *price*. If, as we are often told, the market is by definition apolitical, then it is ridiculous to suggest it as a solution to what is in many ways today's defining political question: whose lives will pay the cost of adaptation to a warming planet?

We can be sure of at least one answer to this question: we know whose lands will be flooded or turned to dust. By some estimates, the world will have 500 million climate refugees by 2050, mainly from Asia (and mainly remaining in Asia). Granted, such estimates are highly uncertain, since it is impossible to predict diverse people's responses to climate change, and practically and legally impossible to define a "climate refugee." Since no one can escape the weather, everyone's movement is always already climatic in some abstract sense. Even in exceptional circumstances, it may be impossible to distinguish climate refugees from others who might have left otherwise. Migrating tends not to be an option for all; the poorest often cannot afford to leave. But even if they do not neatly fit into our analytical categories or models, in a rapidly warming world there is no moral alternative to giving much greater attention to climate refugees. We need a robust political language defending the right of people to migrate in anticipation of climate change. This requires a critical elaboration of these terms and especially a critique of the apocalyptic narrative of a world overrun by masses of unrooted peoples—which can only contribute to the "securitization" promised by a Climate Leviathan.[49]

---

48 Robert Coase, "The Problem of Social Cost," *Journal of Law and Economics* 3, 1960, 1–44; cf. Tamra Gilbertson and Oscar Reyes, "Carbon Trading: How it Works and Why it Fails," Dag Hammerskjöld Foundation, Occasional Paper no. 7, 2009, available at tni.org.

49 For two defenses of the concept, see François Gemenne, "One Good Reason to Speak of 'Climate Refugees,'" *Forced Migration Review* 49, 2015, 70–71; Matthew Lister, "Climate Change Refugees," *Critical Review of International Social and Political Philosophy* 17, 2014, 618–34. Climate migration is addressed in IPCC, AR5 Working Group II, 2014, Chapter 12, section 4, "Migration and Mobility Dimensions of Human Security." It summarizes major findings of the relevant literature as follows:

Climate change will have significant impacts on forms of migration that compromise human security ... Major extreme weather events have in the past led to significant population

Merely cataloging the many ways that people are adapting to and suffering from climate change (one tendency of "progressive" social science in our time) is analytically, ethically, and politically insufficient. We already know enough to ask the difficult questions; documenting the variations in a thousand ways adds nothing essential. Global warming is complex, uneven, and stochastic, but it is here, and intensifying. All political strategies concerning climate, however minimal, will therefore involve adaptation. Most of these changes are so micro-scale, spontaneous, or locally defined that they are unnoticeable at the planetary scale. For some, this is a source of hope, since it suggests that the challenge of adapting to climate change may be met by billions of local acts of adaptation that, taken together, transform our world without coordination by a Climate Leviathan.

But simply because climate change induces myriad geographically uneven, small-scale or granular reactions in no way precludes the emergence of Leviathan (or Mao or a reactionary Behemoth). Part of our argument is that it is precisely the variety and disarticulation of the many reactions to climate change—the lived particularity of adaptation as a process that must involve change in both "material" practices and politics—that invite these regimes. Thousands went to Copenhagen to endorse a Leviathan to whom they all would willingly submit, and they did so not despite but because of the disparate effects of climate change and probable lack of a coordinated response at the planetary scale; the American liberal, for example, wants global coordination to ensure that climate refugees from Bangladesh do not interfere with his or her adapta-tions. All social formations, at all scales, are shot through with specific *in situ* dynamics, forms of resistance, and so on. But the fact that history and geogra-phy happen "on the ground" does not end a conversation about their political life, the irreducibly multi-scalar social forces that shape them.

---

displacement, and changes in the incidence of extreme events will amplify the challenges and risks of such displacement. Many vulnerable groups do not have the resources to be able to migrate to avoid the impacts of floods, storms, and droughts . . . Migration and mobility are adaptation strategies in all regions of the world that experience climate variability. Specific populations that lack the ability to move also face higher exposure to weather-related extremes, particularly in rural and urban areas in low- and middle-income countries. Expanding opportunities for mobility can reduce vulnerability to climate change and enhance human security.

For critical perspectives on the story of a world overrun with climate refugees, see Sanjay Chaturvedi and Timothy Doyle, *Climate Terror: A Critical Geopolitics of Climate Change,* London: Palgrave Macmillan, 2015, Chapter 5; Giovanni Bettini, "Climate Migration as an Adaption Strategy: De-securitizing Climate-induced Migration or Making the Unruly Governable?" *Critical Studies on Security* 2, 2014, 180–95; Carol Farbotko and Heather Lazrus, "The First Climate Refugees? Contesting Global Narratives of Climate Change in Tuvalu," *Global Environmental Change* 22, 2012, 382–90; Roman Felli, "Managing Climate Insecurity by Ensuring Continuous Capital Accumulation: 'Climate Refugees' and 'Climate Migrants'," *New Political Economy* 18, no. 3, 2013, 337–63; Etienne Piguet, "From 'Primitive Migration' to 'Climate Refugees': The Curious Fate of the Natural Environment in Migration Studies," *Annals of the Association of American Geographers* 103, 2013, 148–62.

The failure of global efforts to mitigate carbon make it clear that any emergent Leviathan will be principally a beast of adaptation. That is why our argument about Leviathan emphasizes the *emergent* character of planetary sovereignty. With the tacit acceptance of runaway climate change, we should expect Leviathan to enable efforts to profit from it (through newly accessible resources in the Arctic, for example) while also stimulating and organizing intergovernmental and cross-territorial forms of governance—an adaptation to augment elite social groups' power and security.[50] Neither of these tendencies are new: climate change only intensifies existing dynamics. To come to grips with them, we must see through our ostensibly "post-political" moment, because the problem we face is not the disintegration of the political, but its distinctive adaptation.[51] If Timothy Mitchell is right that "the political machinery that emerged to govern the age of fossil fuels may be incapable of addressing the events that will end it," what will follow?[52] This is a question—the question of the political—to which the prevailing conception of adaptation is wholly inadequate. We must, therefore, look elsewhere.

---

50   McKenzie Funk, *Windfall: The Booming Business of Global Warming*, New York: Penguin, 2014. On the effort to "secure" and profit from the melting Arctic, see Leigh Johnson, "The Fearful Symmetry of Arctic Climate Change: Accumulation by Degradation," *Environment and Planning D: Society and Space* 28, no. 5, 2010, 828–47; Eric Bonds, "Losing the Arctic: The US Corporate Community, the National-Security State, and Climate Change," *Environmental Sociology* 2, no. 1, 2016, 5–17.

51   See Eric Swyngedouw, "Apocalypse Forever: Post-Political Populism and the Specter of Climate Change," *Theory, Culture & Society* 27 nos. 2–3, 2010, 213–32. James McCarthy's critique of Swyngedouw is apposite: "there are . . . very substantial, significant, and ongoing struggles around the politics and politicization of climate change that are directly at odds with some of the 'post-political' dynamics that Swyngedouw sees." James McCarthy, "We Have Never Been Post-Political," *Capitalism, Nature, Socialism* 24, no. 1, 2013, 23.

52   Timothy Mitchell, "Carbon Democracy," *Economy and Society* 38, no. 3, 2009, 401. We have learned much from Mitchell's analysis of the natural history of democracy, but unfortunately, as Mazen Labban remarks, "Mitchell eliminates capitalism altogether from the natural history of carbon democracy and replaces social relations between persons with the relations of things to persons such that, to borrow from Marx (1864), the 'definite social connections appear as social characteristics belonging naturally to things' " (Labban, "On Timothy Mitchell's *Carbon Democracy: Political Power in the Age of Oil*," *Antipode*, 2013, accessed at antipodefoundation.org).

4

The Adaptation of the Political

The basic innovation introduced by the philosophy of praxis into the science of politics and of history is the demonstration that there is no abstract "human nature," fixed and immutable . . . but that human nature is the totality of historically determined social relations, hence an historical fact.

Antonio Gramsci[1]

I

Climate change demands a fundamental shift in our understanding of the political, the terrain upon which all other calls for adaptation must inevitably rely. Everyone has an implicit theory of the political: an idea of what counts as political, and what kinds of things politics can or cannot change. These theories are not fixed: they change over time; they adapt in light of the world around us. The radical shifts involved in confronting climate change can be legitimated and realized only if our conception of the political changes. But what does it mean to say the political "adapts"? First, it suggests that the political has both a history—a natural history, perhaps—and a specificity in every time and place, because adaptation takes place over time and in response to particular conditions. Second, it also suggests that the political constitutes a distinct realm of the social world, some part of our lives we can isolate, at least analytically.

Today, many radical European philosophers and social scientists contend that the political as a realm of the social world is shrinking or disintegrating. They lament the "demise" of the political itself and the onset of a "post-political" condition.[2] As Žižek puts it, we are witness to the emergence of "a new bipolarity between politics and post-politics."[3] As will be clear in what follows, we do not find this position convincing. The lingo of post-politics is itself a result of the irreducibly political processes through which the realm of what counts as "true" politics is defined. Nothing could be more political than a shift, an adaptation, of what we consider politicized or politicizable.

Consequently, in our account, the category of the political is a defining quality of human life, a part of the social world that can only shrink or disappear

---

1 Antonio Gramsci, [Q13§20] *Selections from the Prison Notebook*, translated and edited by Quintin Hoare and Geoffrey Nowell Smith, New York: International Publishers, 1971, 133.

2 See, for example, Chantal Mouffe, Jacques Rancière, Alain Badiou, Slavoj Žižek, and others.

3 Slavoj Žižek, *Living in the End Times*, New York, Verso, 2011, ix.

as a result of politics itself. We define the political, therefore, as a realm characterized neither by particular political conditions or institutions (like individual freedom or the parliamentary system) nor by the existential fact of social struggle (so-called "agonism"). It is not merely the field of competing interests or agonistic confrontation or individual self-actualization in an inescapably social world. Instead, it is the very grounds on which such conditions, institutions, or struggles arise and are formulated. In this sense the political is not, strictly speaking, a relational concept. "The political" defines a relation *tout court*: the relationship between the dominant and the dominated. The political is not an arena in which dominant groups impose their interests and subaltern groups resist; it is, rather, the ground upon which the relation between the dominant and dominated is worked out.[4] In other words, there is no nonpolitical or apolitical domination. Thus the fundamental adaptation that climate change demands of humanity is political in this sense. It is the only way in which the dominant can continue to dominate—and the only way in which that domination can be undone.

Any politics assumes and asserts a historical and geographical terrain to which it lays claim. Insofar as the specifically political character of the capitalist nation-state is constituted in the separation of political and civil society (the standard binary of state and market or politics and the economy), these are the grounds upon which the nation-state's legitimacy stands or falls. Its hegemony in the contemporary political imagination underwrites our assertion that if Climate Leviathan is to emerge, it will do so through the adaptation of the political, a more or less radical shift in the existing form of sovereignty that will enable the world's most powerful states to engage in planetary management. This way of defining the political, however, clearly needs further elaboration, at least partly because it contrasts with many other definitions, implicit or explicit, and in particular with the common sense of most if not all liberal democratic traditions. How our way of defining the political differs from that common sense is crucial to our analysis of the current conjuncture and the ways in which the political is being shaped by climate change.

II

One of the more difficult challenges involved in thinking this through is that we keep running into concepts that we use almost every day, but terribly loosely. We cannot get at the political, and the force through which it adapts, without confronting the unspoken "common sense" conception of the political, a product of more than two centuries of liberal hegemony. Indeed, what is this liberalism that so shapes our lives? Almost nobody wants to define it—not even the

---

4   "Grounds" is thus an apposite term because implicit in any form of "the political" is a spatio-temporal context in which it unfolds and helps shape.

liberals—and for good reason: it is slippery, contingent, blurry, dynamic, and place- and time-specific. The range seems sufficiently vast to include definitions that are almost polar opposites. In the "classical" sense in which the term is often evoked by Europeans, liberalism refers to a more or less strict commitment to *laissez-faire*: individual liberty, formal political equality, tightly constrained state power, and "free" markets. In contrast, as the term gets used in North America, a liberal endorses big government and regulated markets, social safety nets, and protection of minority rights. Indeed, in the United States and Canada, liberals of the first variety are often considered conservatives but are also called neoliberals.

John Gray, a well-known liberal critic of social democracy, says liberalism entails a commitment to four main principles: individualism, egalitarianism, universalism, and "meliorism" (a belief in human "progress").[5] This is a liberal self-description, and an acritical one at that, insofar as it posits the fundamentals of liberalism to be a set of normative ideals. It makes reference neither to liberalism as a set of political practices nor to histories of actually existing liberalisms or liberals in action. It is a purely formal definition that asks as little of itself as it does of its audience.

Taking up a task Harold Laski initiated in the 1930s, the philosopher Domenico Losurdo has recently obliterated the idea that liberalism in action looks anything like the result of a commitment to Gray's abstract ideals.[6] To take only the most glaring evidence, racialized chattel slavery emerged with the very same times, places, and people that produced and championed liberalism. The history of liberalism, as Losurdo demonstrates, is as much a story of *unfreedom* as freedom, of the bourgeois consecration of a select "community of the free" which exposes liberalism's association with "universal" freedom as the mythology it is. As Laski put it, "to the demand for justice", the liberal community of the free "replied by the offer of charity."[7]

This chasm between liberal norms and liberal practice, between normative ideals and historical realities, disgraces any attempt to call up the former in defense of the latter. Consider classical liberalism's writings about slavery and colonialism: the paradigm is the work of John Locke, but that of Benjamin Franklin or de Tocqueville would do just as well. That work is usually dismissed by liberals as unfortunate products of the times, as if Locke, Franklin, or de Tocqueville were only ardent supporters of colonialism and racial slavery by historical chance. It cannot have had anything to do with liberalism *per se*, which, as an unqualified commitment to universal freedom, cannot be responsible for the unfortunate backwardness of the historical communities in which it was born. This liberal account of liberalism is simultaneously idealist and

---

5   John Gray, *Liberalism*, Second Edition, Minneapolis, MN: University of Minnesota Press, 1986: x.

6   Domenico Losurdo, *Liberalism: A Counter-History*, New York: Verso, 2011, 322.

7   Harold Laski, *The Rise of European Liberalism*, London: Routledge, 1996, 168.

idealized, and it completely dehistoricizes the ideas and the people who expressed them. Erasing liberal colonialism, slavery, racism, and gender oppression, it instead tells a fable of the emergence, in the thought of a privileged cadre of European and Euro-American white men, of a set of principles that become realized in the practice of the modern capitalist state and its bourgeois civil society. It portrays liberalism as a product of its own Idea, the universal dream of freedom realized in freedom itself.

Our criticism is not that liberalism contains a spirit of freedom that has been suppressed or betrayed, nor that its history is unfortunately marked by contradiction, irony, or paradox. Rather, it is that liberalism can never be anything other than the complex freedom-unfreedom dynamic it has always been.[8] To understand liberalism's hegemonic conception of the realm of the political, we need to grasp the dynamics of liberalism that enable this entanglement of freedom and unfreedom.

The contemporary liberal literature is of little use here, for it consists almost completely in intellectual histories, polemic, or endless normative debate between liberals. Foundational texts like John Rawls's *A Theory of Justice* or Jürgen Habermas's *Between Facts and Norms* provide competing how-to manuals for proper liberal thought,[9] in which the conversation largely revolves around questions like "What is tolerance?" "What is just?" "What should we prioritize, the right or the good?" and "How should we balance competing conceptions of the right or the good?" (The last, in liberal terminology, is Rawls's "problem of political liberalism."[10]) Other than the Olympian status of "the principle of liberty," there is rarely even an explanation of what makes the competing answers to these questions distinctively liberal, let alone what earthly social or political economic conditions might be adequate to their normative standards. Instead, we are stuck with "veils of ignorance" or "intersubjective discourse ethics," theoretical instruments that are somehow supposed to allow us to forget who we are and give us insight into what it is like to be simply anyone—not far from orthodox economics' "representative agent." This is depoliticization—the removal of the very possibility of even raising domination at the heart of the so-called public sphere. It makes the political in our sense impossible—first by radically narrowing the political realm and separating it cleanly from the messiness of material concerns like distribution and reproduction, and then by formulating a discourse or language in which domination is unspeakable and therefore erased.

Critics of liberalism have reacted to these developments in two ways, both of which have much to teach us about the contradictions inherent in the consolidation of a planetary climate regime committed to liberal capitalism. On the

---

8   This is the main argument of Losurdo's *Liberalism: A Counter-History*.

9   John Rawls, *A Theory of Justice*, Cambridge, MA: Harvard University Press, 1971; Jürgen Habermas, *Between Facts and Norms*, Cambridge, MA: MIT Press, 2004.

10   John Rawls, *Political Liberalism*, New York: Columbia University Press, 1993.

one hand, Left critics like Losurdo have exposed liberals' erasure of domination by highlighting the ways in which liberalism is, and always has been, as much about the production of unfreedom for some as it has been about freedom for the privileged "community of the free." On the other hand, antiliberals from the Right like Carl Schmitt have attacked liberalism for obscuring the political necessity and truth of domination. Schmitt—one of liberalism's more devastating critics—denounces "liberal normativism," the "assumption that the state can ultimately rest on a set of mutually agreed-to procedures and rules that trump particular claims and necessities."[11]

We can return to the question of domination at the heart of the political with these criticisms of liberalism in mind. In a 1965 discussion of hegemony, Nicos Poulantzas describes the liberal separation of the political ("regionalization," in his terms), and the effect it has had on modern state formation:

> [T]he state crystallizes the *relations* of production and *class relations*. The modern political state does not translate the "interests" of the dominant classes at the political level, but the relationship between those interests and the interests of the dominated classes—which means that it precisely constitutes the "political" expression of the interests of the dominant classes.[12]

For Poulantzas, the "specifically political character of the capitalist state" is not a result of the state's domination by capital, but is in fact constituted in the very "separation between state and civil society," that is, the separation of political society from the atomized realm of production and reproduction. The legitimacy of this separation is thus both founded upon and represents a seemingly "natural" result of "the characteristic of universality assumed by a particular set of values." What are these values? They are liberal capitalist values: "the 'universal' values of formal abstract liberty and equality," and their ostensible naturalness is a proof of hegemony:

> In societies based on expanded reproduction and generalized commodity exchange, we observe a process of privatization and autonomization of men as producers. Natural human relations, founded on a hierarchy involving the socioeconomic subordination of producers (witness slave and feudal states), are replaced by "social" relations between "autonomized" individuals, located in the exchange process . . . This appearance of social relations in the capitalist system of production in fact presupposes, as a necessary precondition, the characteristic

---

11 Tracy Strong, "Foreword: The Sovereign and the Exception: Carl Schmitt, Politics and Theology," in Carl Schmitt, *Political Theology*, Chicago: University of Chicago Press, 2005, xvi. For Schmitt, "nothing is more modern than the onslaught against the political" (*Political Theology*, 65).

12 Nicos Poulantzas, "Preliminaries to the Study of Hegemony in the State," in James Martin (ed.) *The Poulantzas Reader: Marxism, Law, and the State*, London: Verso, 2008 [1965], 80, 83, emphasis in original.

atomization of civil society and goes hand in hand with the advent of specifically political relations.[13]

Liberalism is founded upon the production of a separation in the social world between the political and the rest and a consequent neutralizing onslaught on the political that attempts to proceduralize and depoliticize domination, that is, the continual production of freedom for some and unfreedom for others. As we will see, this has crucial implications for the trajectory of Climate Leviathan. To elaborate, we turn to Antonio Gramsci, one of Poulantzas's sources of inspiration.

Before doing so, it is worth briefly discussing Michel Foucault's critique of liberalism, given its enormous influence on the Left today. Foucault's key insight was to approach liberalism neither as an abstract theory nor as an ideology, but rather as an ensemble of *practices*. He treats liberalism essentially as a method of governing, one mobilized for the "production of freedom" with "maximum economy": "the maximum limitation of the forms and domains of government action."[14] The principle of maximizing freedom with maximum economy—government that produces liberty at the lowest possible unit cost—is not only quasi-utopian, but has become a very useful "tool for the criticism of reality." Liberal governmentality is thus premised on political economy as both a knowledge and a way of knowing (*savoir et connaissance*, as Foucault said); the idealized free market becomes the mythic standard against which governmental practices are measured. Approaching liberalism in this way, Foucault is capable of fleshing out the principle of liberty, and showing how it really operates, in ways that liberal philosophers fail to do.

There are ways in which Foucault's account overlaps with that of other critics of liberalism like Losurdo and Schmitt. Foucault highlights the fact that liberalism "entails at its heart a productive/destructive relationship with freedom. Liberalism must produce freedom, but this very act entails the establishment of limitations, controls, forms of coercion, and obligations relying on threats, etcetera." He calls the latter "strategies of security"—"liberalism's other face."[15] There is also a way in which Foucault's emphasis on "maximum economy" echoes Schmitt's account of the liberal "onslaught against the political."[16] But, there are also important differences, and these ultimately render Losurdo's and Schmitt's arguments more powerful than Foucault's. First, the

---

13   Ibid., 83. By our reading, Poulantzas places the word "social" in ""social" relations" in scare quotes to emphasize that they are also natural relations. This passage, with its emphasis on the natural history of the formation of the political in capitalist society, lends support to Bob Jessop's assertion that "were he alive today, Poulantzas would be a political ecologist" (personal communication, May 2013).

14   Michel Foucault, *Birth of Biopolitics: Lectures at the Collège de France, 1978–1979*, New York: Picador, 2008, 317, n.21.

15   Ibid.; see also 64–65.

16   Schmitt, *Political Theology*, 65.

freedom–unfreedom relation at the core of Losurdo's account identifies the dominator and the dominated in the liberal order. This is radically different than Foucault's description of a "productive/destructive relationship with freedom"—a generalized dynamic through which "strategies of security" produce all subjects by definition. For Losurdo, liberalism produces a social group that is unfree and separated by the political from the community of the free who are liberalism's "winners." Foucault never really politicizes the problem of "economy" and ignores this dynamic. We might say that while Foucault brilliantly analyses the question of *how* liberalism works, he falls short of answering *why* it does.

Consider, for example, the quasi-neutrality with which Foucault describes liberal government's efficiency-maximizing "production of freedom": it is as if Foucault rejects liberalism's normative tail-chasing but accepts its account of itself. Indeed, since it is unclear what (if any) privileges Foucault thinks power in the conventional sense affords (accumulation, authority, and so forth being denied the driving force they are granted by other theories), it is hard to know why else power would operate other than because of a disinterested structure of "economy." Schmitt, in contrast, has a very clear idea of the privileges afforded by power—rule, domination, the authority to decide—and is therefore concerned that the liberal onslaught on politics is always a political matter. This is the reason he describes liberalism as a series of "neutralizations and depoliticizations" that "makes of the state a compromise and of its institutions a ventilating system."[17] One might even say that political economy (which Foucault designated liberal governmentality's knowledge and way of knowing) is *the* science of neutralization. But Foucault specifically steers us away from such a conclusion. Rather, his emphasis on economy as liberalism's organizing principle tends to obscure both the politics of that principle and the way in which it constrains the political as a category to the sphere of government.[18] Thus, although we can learn much from Foucault's critique of liberalism, in the end he cannot provide us with the theory we need.

The very features of liberal rationality that enrage Schmitt—its naive faith in individualism, its unwillingness to acknowledge a friend "we" and an enemy "they," its quietist substitution of procedure for authority, its passive "normativism"—are generally left undiscussed by Foucault, even though these features continually pose the most striking challenges to liberal rationality. As the history of liberalism suggests, when the moment of decision arrives—the

---

17   Carl Schmitt, *The Concept of the Political*, Chicago, IL: University of Chicago Press, 2007, 70.

18   That Foucault does not equate "government" with the state does not overcome the limits of his analysis of liberal politics. Indeed, to the extent that the state is rendered one among many modes of government, the specificity of its problems is obscured. This has its merits, because it highlights the ways in which the nonstate realm also governs, but it also makes it difficult to understand what it is about the state that makes it special (if less so than liberal political theory suggests) or at least distinct.

point at which we must either embrace these contradictions on principle or reject them in the interests of pragmatism—liberals almost always choose to reject them. Why, for example, are all liberal "freedoms" ultimately subject to state abrogation? There is no "right" in any actually existing liberal democracy that is unconditional. (The capitalist state may even declare an exception and suspend the right to private property.)

The reasons for this are not to be found in the principle of economy. It is not merely that it is complicated or costly to constantly expand the bureaucracy or make room for unconstrained individual autonomy. It is, rather, that such efforts impinge upon what cannot be restricted: sovereignty. Liberalism is a politics of categorical containment in a set of categories of social life that accurately allocate social phenomena to their appropriate domain, in the interests of containing problems to their "proper" sphere. As far as possible, the economy and politics are cleanly separated, just as are the public and private, the healthy and ill, and so forth.[19] This separation is critical to liberalism and cardinal to its legitimacy. Despite the vast inequalities between dominators and dominated that character-ize "the economy" of every liberal nation-state, all are posited as equal in "formal freedom," the political abstraction of individual meritocratic citizenship.

And yet the sanctity of the politics-economy separation is also a liability because, however justified or legitimate the naturalness of the separation appears, the practice of sovereignty makes its artificiality obvious to the liberal sovereign. Liberalism may depend existentially on encoding and monitoring the separation of economy (including social reproduction) from the political, but constructing the separation itself requires as "pure" an act of political will as one can imagine, a true Schmittian sovereign decision. This act of producing and maintaining the supposedly natural limits of the political is the key sover-eign responsibility in liberalism. We might even say that *the economy* is a de facto residual, the set of social relations defined precisely so as to stand outside politics.

Consequently, in modern liberal capitalism, the political is not founded in any idea or organizing principle, but always exists as the *product* of the exercise of sovereign power. The *form* the political takes in any given liberal conjuncture may work the way Foucault describes, but it will not always be so. He is guilty of a variation on the error of which Marx accused Hegel: he confuses the particu-lar conditions of his own time as the truth of a historical category; the content of the liberalism of his time becomes the form all liberalism takes. Liberalism is not defined by the familiar liberal procedures and institutions to achieve govern-ment of maximum economy; rather, liberalism is defined by the *sovereign natu-ralization* of a narrowly defined conception of what counts as politics, of what is legitimately politicizable. The phenomena that must be proscribed include the most fundamental questions for human communities: poverty, difference,

---

19   Schmitt, *Concept of the Political*, 71.

inequality, and nature. That the effort to keep these problems nonpolitical ultimately fails in no way renders that effort less essential to liberalism.[20]

Many in the environmental movement reject the liberal conception of the
political on precisely these grounds, that is, because nature is proscribed.
Ecological critiques of liberalism vary in their emphases and conclusions, but
in general they are based on the argument that liberalism simultaneously fixes
and obscures a fundamental distinction at the heart of the political between
humans and nature (or, more precisely, "non-human nature"). This critique
has been developed at length by many, like ecophilosopher Arne Naess, social
ecologist Murray Bookchin, feminist Val Plumwood, and actor-network theorist Bruno Latour (among others). While there are many important differences among these and other ecological thinkers, together they provide a
stimulating and provocative set of arguments against the exclusion of nonhuman nature at the heart of the liberal theory of the political. This is an essential
point, one to which we return below; but our account of the political in the
following sections does not draw explicitly upon these ecological critiques of
liberalism. It derives instead from Gramsci's work. Gramsci's and Schmitt's
approaches, presuppositions, and conclusions are radically different.[21] Schmitt
refuses the prospect of historicizing the political; Gramsci once called his
approach "absolute historicism." Schmitt advocated fascism, Gramsci communism. These differences notwithstanding, our reading of Gramsci draws upon
Schmitt's insights so that we may grasp the adaptation of the political in light
of planetary emergency.

III

Our turn to Gramsci does not mean setting aside the relation between
humanity and nature. On the contrary, we are searching for a means to
expose and overcome the liberal exclusion clause separating the human
from the nonhuman. Gramsci is quick to remind us (unusual for someone
writing in the Marxist tradition, not to mention in political philosophy
generally) that every confrontation with the question of the political raises
the problem of what he calls "the unity of history and nature."[22] We are
confronted with the realization—climate change epitomizes this predicament—that to ask "what makes history happen?" is also to ask "what makes
nature happen?" These are perhaps the biggest questions we can ask, and
one might at first glance assume they are unanswerable. Yet many people the

20   Geoff Mann, *In the Long Run We Are All Dead: Keynesianism, Political Economy and
Revolution*, London: Verso, 2017, 182–214, 366–96.
21   These differences are elaborated (and Schmitt is criticized) in Peter Thomas, "Gramsci and
the Political: From the State as 'Metaphysical Event' to Hegemony as 'Philosophical Fact'." *Radical
Philosophy* 153, 2009, 27–36.
22   Gramsci, [Q4§45] *Selections from the Prison Notebooks*, Vol. II, 194–5.

world over consider it more than possible to answer these questions, even to give the same answer to both: "God," for example. And, certainly, we would expect those who take these answers as Truth to act *as if* they were true; their ideas, therefore, take on "material force":

> Every philosopher is, and cannot but be, convinced that he expresses the unity of the human spirit, that is, the unity of history and nature. Otherwise, men would not act, they would not create new history; in other words, philosophies would not become "ideologies," they could not, in practice, acquire the fanatical granite solidity of "popular beliefs," which have the equivalence of "material forces."[23]

Just consider climate change denial. However crazy its content, denialism is neither "mere ideology" nor meaningless chatter, but a material force in the Earth's natural history.

The nature of our relation with nature, then, is partly a product of the "material forces" generated by our very understanding of it, an understanding that is shaped fundamentally by ideology and the hegemonic forces that determine it. To put it this way is to open a dialectical approach to the question of natural history in place of an orthodox materialism. Gramsci rejected the dogmatic materialism that contaminated much Marxist theory of his time— including some of Lenin's influential work.[24] Although he never directly attacked the materialism Lenin famously laid out in 1908 in *Materialism and Emperio-Criticism*, it is certain he read it, and equally certain he saw things otherwise:[25]

> In historical materialism, "matter" should be understood neither in the meaning it has derived from the natural sciences (physics, chemistry, mechanics, etc. . . . .) nor in the meaning it has derived from the various materialist metaphysics. Historical materialism takes the physical (chemical, mechanical, etc.) properties of matter into account, of course, but only insofar as they become an "economic factor" of production. The issue, then, is not matter as such but how it is socially and historically organized for production, as a *human relation*. Historical materialism does not study a machine in order to establish the physical-chemical-mechanical structure of its natural components; it studies it as an object of production and property, as the crystallization of a social relation that itself coincides with a particular historical period.[26]

To some orthodox readers, this kind of thinking is tantamount to resurrecting,

---

23   Ibid.

24   Lucio Colletti, "Introduction," in Karl Marx, *Early Writings*, London: Penguin, London, 1975, 8–15.

25   Lenin later seemed occasionally to distance himself from this rigid variety of materialism; see for example V. I. Lenin, *Collected Works*, Vol. 38, Moscow: Progress Publishers, 1972, 114.

26   Gramsci, [Q4§25] *Prison Notebooks*, Vol. II, 164–65.

within Marxism, something Marx and Engels had worked so hard to crush: the idea that the world as we know it is a product of our thoughts about it, as opposed to the other way around—the political implication being that the revolution could be in our heads. But these critics have no adequate account of the mode through which the organic relationships that constitute the political might be realized. If matter is all that matters, then politics is just a waiting game.

Gramsci's reconstruction of Lenin's theory of hegemony addresses this shortcoming. Lenin directed his materialist wrath at what he called "spiritualism" and "fideism," at the "Kantians" who denied a real, knowable world.[27] But Gramsci's historical materialism holds Marxism in tension with the influential idealist legacy in Italy—something Gramsci would have considered essential, precisely because of the influence of that idealism, and its consequent "material force" in the Italian context.[28] His historical materialism is therefore more historicist than materialist. This theoretical marriage leads Gramsci to redirect political praxis (the struggle for hegemony) away from an obsession with Marxism as a science and toward a philosophical critique of realism. He attacks the fundamentals of positivist materialist orthodoxy. Without naming names, he shows how Leninists cannot get beyond a commitment to a "scientific" one-sidedness. In the idealist-versus-materialist battle, Lenin said, only the "shame-faced" deny that "one or the other must be taken as primary".[29] Gramsci totally opposed this. The point, he said, was "to go beyond the traditional conceptions of 'idealism' and 'materialism.' . . . As for the expression 'historical materialism,' greater stress is placed on the second word, whereas it should be placed on the first: Marx is fundamentally a 'historicist.'"[30]

Thus, the distinctiveness of Gramsci's theory of hegemony is tied to his rejection of a radical materialism. Lenin conceived the problem of hegemony as concerning the proletariat's leadership of nonrevolutionary classes at determinate historical moments—even in a bourgeois revolution. This demanded a political strategy through which the peasantry and fractions of the bourgeoisie

---

27   "Kantian" is also the slur thrown at György Lukács after he wrote *History and Class Consciousness* (translated by Rodney Livingstone, London: Merlin Press, 1971). This was clearly a bad time to be a Kantian—something worth considering in light of Lucio Colletti and Kojin Karatani's compelling arguments that Marx was more Kantian than Hegelian. See Lucio Colletti, *Marxism and Hegel*, London: New Left Books, 1973; Kojin Karatani, *Transcritique: On Kant and Marx*, Cambridge, MA: MIT Press, 2003.

28   That of Antonio Labriola and Benedetto Croce in particular. Labriola, a Hegelian-Marxist philosopher much admired by Gramsci, coined what is usually taken to be the favorite code-phrase for Marxism in the *Notebooks*, "philosophy of praxis"; Walter Adamson, *Hegemony and Revolution: A Study of Antonio Gramsci's Political and Cultural Theory*, Berkeley, CA: University of California Press, 1980, 114. For an argument that "philosophy of praxis" is not just another word for Marxism, see Peter Thomas, *The Gramscian Moment: Philosophy, Hegemony, and Marxism*. Amsterdam: Brill, 2009, 105–108.

29   Lenin, *Collected Works*, Vol. 14, 292, 146.

30   Gramsci, *Prison Notebooks*, Vol. II, 153. In 1844, Marx wrote: "Here we see how consistent naturalism or humanism differs both from idealism and materialism and is at the same time their unifying truth. We also see that only naturalism is capable of comprehending the process of world history." Karl Marx, "Economic and Philosophic Manuscripts of 1844," *Early Writings*, London: Penguin, 389.

could come to see their material interests realized in that movement. In other words, for Lenin, hegemony described the need for alliance against the ruling class—a politics internal to one side of the class war, as it were.[31]

Gramsci starts with this seed and cultivates a powerful idea from it. For him, as we know, hegemony describes the mode of leadership of a historic bloc over society as a whole. The operation of hegemony involves more than an appeal to material or economic interest, and it saturates both productive and ideological relations across the social formation. It is not merely a Leninist strategy, but a Marxian historical-critical category and general social relation: the outcome of a process through which the masses consent—for reasons both economic and ethico-political—to a historic bloc's assertion of its particular interest as the universal interest.[32] Gramsci's hegemony transcends the materialist-idealist divide that Lenin claimed was theoretically insurmountable and politically decisive:

> [T]he most important philosophical combination that has taken place has been between the philosophy of praxis and various idealistic tendencies, a fact which, to the so-called orthodoxy, essentially bound to a particular cultural current of the last quarter century (positivism, scientism), has seemed an absurdity if not actually a piece of chicanery . . . What happened is this: the philosophy of praxis has undergone in reality a double revision, that is to say it has been subsumed into a double philosophical combination. On the one hand, its elements, explicitly or implicitly, have been absorbed and incorporated by a number of idealist currents . . . On the other hand, the so-called orthodoxy, concerned to find a philosophy which, according to their extremely limited viewpoint, was more comprehensive than just a "simple" interpretation of history, have believed themselves orthodox in identifying this philosophy fundamentally with traditional materialism.[33]

However much he credited Lenin with the conceptual breakthrough the concept of hegemony made possible, Gramsci's treatment at the hands of post-World War II Leninists leaves no doubt they were not fooled by his genuflection. In France, Althusser tried to rehabilitate him with an idiosyncratic, arguably disingenuous, anti-historicism in *Reading Capital*. In Italy, while the Communist Party under Togliatti opportunistically manipulated Gramsci's legacy, communist theorists like Della Volpe, Colletti, and Timpanaro wrote him off as an idealist. In England, Perry Anderson named him one of the

---

31   Perry Anderson, "The Antinomies of Antonio Gramsci," *New Left Review* I/100, 1976/77, 5–78.

32   This theory is also important to Marx: see Karl Marx and Friedrich Engels, *The German Ideology*, in: Robert Tucker (ed.), *The Marx-Engels Reader*, 2nd Edition, New York: Norton, 1978, 172–74.

33   Gramsci, [Q16§9] *Selections from the Prison Notebook*, 388–89.

founders of so-called "western Marxism" (along with Korsch and Lukács)—the increasing tendency to distance theory from real political struggle—a critique he chooses to mitigate by suggesting a rigorous "hidden order" in Gramsci's theoretical work.[34]

For our purposes, these attacks only underscore the extent to which a Gramscian approach to the politics of climate cannot be merely Leninist. The Leninist tradition has much to offer, certainly, but there is a reason that so few Marxists prioritized the question of nature during the twentieth century. Indeed, it was hardly even mentioned, which is unsurprising if politics is driven by the material conditions of production and nature is assumed to be a fixed external object of human domination. On this account, human labor works on a passive object to produce itself; nature is little more than ahistorical background to history.

Gramsci's engagement with nature is radically different, and a crucial factor in the production of ideology and its material force in the world. Not that "nature" and "world" are the same thing for him. Rather, as Benedetto Fontana puts it, "to acquire meaning and content nature can only be—or must become—history." History "is, for Gramsci, politics," because participation in history is always bound up in ideology: it involves "the formation and proliferation of a way of life and a way of thinking—that is, a conception of the world."[35]

What does this mean? How does nature become history, and what relation does it have to the role ideology plays in the political? The key question concerning nature and humanity in Gramsci's prison notebooks is posed (in rather grand terms) as "What is man?" (The unfortunate, gendered language is typical of the notebooks. Rather than fill the following paragraphs with square-bracketed corrections or "sic", we quote the original with apologies for not finding a reader-friendly way to remove this baggage.) This, he says, is "the primary and principal question philosophy asks."[36] He rejects any attempt to discover "humanity" in the common essence of individuals. The point is not some quality every human shares or embodies, but rather what it means to be human. In other words, with "the question 'What is man?' what we mean is: what can man

---

34   Althusser and Balibar, *Reading Capital*, London: New Left Books, London, 119–44; Martin Jay, *Marxism and Totality: The Adventures of a Concept from Lukács to Habermas*, Berkeley, CA: University of California Press, 1984, 424, 427; Colletti, *Marxism and Hegel*, 38, n.28 (a judgment Colletti later renounced; see "A Political and Philosophical Interview," *New Left Review* I/86,1974, 24-25); Sebastiano Timpanaro, *On Materialism*, London: New Left Books, 1975, 236; Perry Anderson, *Considerations on Western Marxism*, London: Verso, London; Anderson, "The Antinomies of Antonio Gramsci," 6; Joseph Buttigieg, "Philology and Politics: Returning to the Text of Antonio Gramsci's Prison Notebooks," *Boundary 2* 21, no. 2, 1994, 130–1.

35   Benedetto Fontana, "The Concept of Nature in Gramsci," *The Philosophical Forum*, XXVII, 1996, 223, 221. Fontana shows that Gramsci uses "nature" in five distinct ways in the *Prison Notebooks*: 1. nature as undifferentiated matter; 2. nature as "second nature"; 3. nature as the irrational, instinct; 4. nature as chaos and disorder; 5. nature as "(potential) overcoming of the domination and conquest of nature" (221).

36   Gramsci, [Q10II§54] *Selections from the Prison Notebooks*, 351.

become? That is, can man dominate his own destiny, can he 'make himself,' can he create his own life?"[37]

The very fact that Gramsci considers it axiomatic that the question of what it means to be human is the question of what we can become helps us understand some aspects of his conception of the political, which is a historicist, nondogmatic admixture of radical possibility and worldly constraints. He defines "man" as "the process of his actions," not in the sense of the work of humanity on an external nonhuman world, but rather in how we make ourselves and so become ourselves:

> we want to know what we are and what we can become; whether we really are, and if so to what extent, "makers of our own selves," of our life and of our destiny. And we want to know this "today," in the given conditions of today, the conditions of our daily life . . .[38]

Gramsci says the ideological orientation that results from this effort to "know what we are and what we can become" is a "conception of the world."[39] Every conception of the world originates in actual human beings' questioning of our lives and world. Gramsci affirms the universality of this questioning as a potential source of transcendence, but laments that it is typically short-circuited by religion—in Italy by Catholicism, which provided the dominant answers to these questions in the 1930s. (This is the reason Catholicism was fundamental to fascist hegemony.) Consequently, in the Italy of his day, "when we ask ourselves 'what is man?', what importance do his will and his concrete activity have in creating himself and the life he lives? what we mean is: is Catholicism a correct conception of the world?" For Gramsci, the answer is (unsurprisingly) no.

But it is not so simple to "prove" Catholicism, or any other conception of the world, is "incorrect." First of all, conceptions of the world are not simply right or wrong; they are differentially coherent, historicized, and self-sufficient. Second, Gramsci knows Catholics would respond to any demonstration that Catholicism is "incorrect" by pointing out that "no other conception is followed punctiliously either," and, of course, "they would be right. But all this shows is that there does not exist, historically, a way of seeing things and of acting which is equal for all."[40] This is why we cannot answer the question "what is man?" by discovering it in any given "individual." There is no key ingredient.

Gramsci defines humanity as a "process of actions" and also relationally. It is impossible to understand humanity solely on an individual basis: it is in fact "a series of active relationships (a process)" in which individuality is not "the only element to be taken into account." The humanity in each individual "is

---

37   Ibid.
38   Ibid.
39   Ibid.
40   Ibid., 351–52.

composed of: 1. the individual; 2. other men; 3. the natural world."[41] As Gramsci sees it, the greatest obstacle to new conceptions of the world is that "all hitherto existing philosophies" tend to "reproduce this position of Catholicism, that they conceive of man as an individual." They therefore fall victim to the fatal conceit that the transformation of humanity is a spiritual or "psychological" project—or even worse, an autonomous internal struggle—not the irreducibly social and political process of "active relationships" it must be. Moreover, at the risk of putting too fine a point on it, these active transformational relationships must reflect the fact that every individual is "composed of" other people *and* "the natural world"—not individually or collectively "connected to" or "dependent upon," but existentially *composed of*. In other words, any effort to transform humanity must take these socio-natural relations as fundamental to our consciousness of ourselves and our world. We do not "enter into relations with the natural world" just by being "part of the natural world, but actively, by means of work and technique": the "real philosopher [is] the politician, the active man who modifies the environment, understanding by environment the *ensemble* of relations which each of us enters to take part in."[42]

Thus, for Gramsci, "nature" and "society" are inseparable, active relations. And these relations are themselves inextricable from the processes through which we forge *critical* conceptions of the world. These are the result of earlier historical struggles that have laid down, "layer upon layer," the consciousness of "the right to live independently of the planning and the rights of minorities"— in other words, independently of the "rights" of elites to plunder subaltern social groups. This accumulating consciousness of rights has been won through "intelligent reflection, at first by a few and then by an entire social class," namely, the proletariat. Gramsci conceptualizes the transformation of our world as a historical process in which "intelligent reflection" is an integral element in fomenting struggle and reconstruction.[43]

---

41 Ibid., 352.

42 Ibid., emphasis in original.

43 Marx also wrestled with the interpenetration of humanity and nature. For Marx, labor, humanity's defining quality, is a metabolic relation between humans and nature, through which we transform the nature of which we are a part (Karl Marx, *Capital*, Vol. I, New York: Penguin, 1976 [1867], 283). But, of course, humanity is not the only force transforming nature. A good deal else is going on. If the nature of humanity consists in the always social and exclusively human work of transforming nature, there must be something that distinguishes the changes wrought by human labor from all the other changes constantly occurring through "natural" processes (ibid., 284). What, if anything, defines the *human* but no less natural contribution of this socio-natural process? Marx identifies the difference in what Gramsci calls "intelligent reflection"—"what distinguishes the worst architect from the best of bees is that the architect builds the cell in his mind before he constructs it in wax":

At the end of every labour process, a result emerges which had already been conceived by the worker at the beginning, and hence already existed ideally. Man not only effects a change of form in the materials of nature; he also realizes his own purposes in those materials. And this is a purpose he is conscious of, it determines the mode of his activity with the rigidity of a law,

Changing the world requires the labor of transforming our conception of the world. This labor, no less than any other, entails the metabolic transformation of socio-nature, but it does not just happen "naturally," like evaporation. Instead, it requires "intelligent reflection"—the critical construction of a conception of the world. This is not, as liberalism would have us believe, a struggle against a self-interested or acquisitive "human nature," because "*there is no abstract 'human nature'*, fixed and immutable (a concept which certainly derives from religious and transcendentalist thought)." What we call "human nature [is] the totality of historically determined social relations, hence an historical fact."[44] Once we recognize, Gramsci says, that "the relations between the social and natural orders" are always mediated by "theoretical and practical activity," "intelligent reflection" makes possible a stronger conception of the world "free from all magic and superstition" and provides

> a basis for the subsequent development of an historical, dialectical conception of the world, which understands movement and change, which appreciates the sum of effort and sacrifice which the present has cost the past and which the future is costing the present.[45]

IV

Let us pause for a moment at this formulation and use it is a way to think about what a Gramscian sensibility might suggest for our conjuncture. In what sense might critical thinking about the political help develop "an historical, dialectical conception of the world, which understands movement and change, which appreciates the sum of effort and sacrifice which the present has cost the past and which the future is costing the present"? There is a revolutionary conception of natural history built into this way of framing the problem. Struggle is the active force in history, history *is* politics, and the revolutionary ethico-political moment in natural history is the solidarity with the future that the present cannot shirk. The past sacrificed for the present—that is what defines it as "past"—and the present sacrifices for the future. This is what it means to conceive of the future as the result of natural history, the product of nature and humanity actively producing the world.

---

and he must subordinate his will to it. This subordination is no mere momentary act. Apart from the exertion of the working organs, a purposeful will is required for the entire duration of the work. This means close attention (ibid., 284).

Three elements align here that define Marx's conception of nature and social life: the practice of labor, the worker's conception of the object, and the realization of will in labor on the world. This unity of practice-consciousness-will distinguishes human labor as a socio-natural process.

44   Gramsci, [Q13§20] *Selections from the Prison Notebooks*, 133, emphasis added.
45   Ibid., [Q12§2] 34–35.

In the current conjuncture, with ecological and political-economic crises seemingly permanent features of life, this conception of natural history seems to us an enormously important resource. For, to state the obvious, the absolutely crucial outcome of the critical reconstruction of our conception of the world is an appreciation of the effort and sacrifice that the future *must* cost the present. The struggle for climate justice will proceed with the wisdom of that appreciation. A key question, then, is what the focus of a critical reconstruction of our conception of the world should be. What are the essential common senses we must undo to see the future for which we must struggle?

Some of Gramsci's most insightful responses to these questions were written around 1933, in a notebook focused on the ideas of Benedetto Croce.[46] One note on Croce, entitled "Progress and Becoming," questions the meaning of the "progress" so fundamental to liberal modernity. In his inimitable style, Gramsci asks a complex question, answers it directly, then unravels its historical and philosophical dimensions:

> *Progress and becoming.* Are these two different things or different aspects of one and the same concept? Progress is an ideology: becoming is a philosophical conception. "Progress" depends on a specific mentality, in the constitution of which are involved certain historically determined cultural elements: "becoming" is a philosophical concept from which "progress" can be absent. In the idea of progress is implied the possibility of quantitative and qualitative measuring, of "more" and "better." A "fixed," or fixable, yardstick must therefore be supposed, but this yardstick is given by the past, by a certain phase of the past or by certain measurable aspects, etc. (Not that one should think of a metric system of progress.)[47]

Progress and becoming are distinct but nested concepts. Becoming is a more generalized process, of which progress may or may not be part. Becoming is essential to any conception of history; progress is fundamentally ideological and must therefore be understood historically. The effort to do so, however, is complex, because the two concepts have intertwined in modern thought. In fact, progress seems to have absorbed becoming to such an extent that our conception of the perpetual change inherent to all being now presupposes the existence of some "fixable yardstick" with which to measure it.

---

46   Croce was an enormously influential Italian philosopher in the early twentieth century. A liberal idealist aristocrat, Croce took (for the most part) a brave stance against fascism, and thus for the years Gramsci spent in prison, his thought was actively suppressed. Prior to Mussolini's rise, however, and subsequent to his fall, Croce was among the most prominent figures in Italy. Gramsci developed both his radical historicism and his mistrust of strict materialism in part through his engagement with Croce.

47   Gramsci, [Q10II§48ii] "Progress and Becoming," *Selections from the Prison Notebooks*, 357–60. Q10II§48ii forms the second (longer) part of a note; the first part (Q10II§48i) concerns *senso comune* (on which see Thomas, *The Gramscian Moment*, chapter 8).

The challenge Gramsci identifies—of conceiving a form of being that is politically capable of becoming, but not already captured by the ideology of progress—is fundamental to our response to climate change. Can we construct a future without our current yardsticks as the measure? Can we become without merely progressing to an augmented version of what we already are? At this moment in history, can we, as critical agents in socio-natural transformation, become *other* than we are? Can humanity "adapt"? Gramsci contends that any radical approach to these questions must overcome the liberal ideology of progress. Only this will allow us to "appreciate the sum of effort and sacrifice which the present has cost the past and which the future is costing the present."

As always, for Gramsci this approach demands "absolute historicism." How was the idea of progress born? Is its birth a fundamental and epoch-making event? Gramsci's answer is yes. The birth of progress is epoch-making because it defines modernity. But how was it born? His answer is an account (like Foucault's) that emphasizes the emergence of a specifically modern rationality and mode of making life governable, but (unlike Foucault's) grounds modernity *qua* progress in socio-natural relations:

> The birth and the development of the idea of progress corresponds to a widespread consciousness that a certain relationship has been reached between society and nature (including in the concept of nature those of chance and "irrationality") such that as a result mankind as a whole is more sure of its future and can conceive "rationally" of plans through which to govern its entire life.[48]

Gramsci does not describe in any detail the specific relationship "reached between society and nature" captured in the "widespread consciousness" to which progress "corresponds." He is clear, however, that a critique of progress must be neither romantic nor nostalgic. "In order to combat the idea of progress," he says, both romanticism and nostalgia find recourse in "those natural phenomena which are still irresistible and irremediable," as if humanity's arrogant assumption that we control our fate is always undone by forces beyond our will. This is sophistry, because "in the past there were far more irresistible forces, famines, epidemics, etc., which, within certain limits, have now been overcome."[49]

Gramsci is no knee-jerk critic of modernity, as if the world would have been better without it. On key questions, he sides with the bourgeois-liberal tradition: "there can be no doubt that progress has been a democratic ideology. Nor is there any doubt that it has had a political function in the formation of modern

---

48 Gramsci, [Q10II§48ii] "Progress and Becoming," *Selections from the Prison Notebooks*, 357.
49 Ibid., [Q10II§48ii] 357–60. Gramsci comments parenthetically: "The past forces meanwhile have now been 'socially' forgotten, though not by all elements of society: the peasants continue not to understand 'progress'; they think of themselves as being, and still are all too much, in the hands of natural forces and of chance, and therefore retain a 'magical', mediaeval and religious mentality" (358).

constitutional states, etc."[50] These are surely developments to be celebrated, however uneven their implications, and as such, "attacks on the idea of progress are very tendentious and interest-motivated." Nevertheless, he says, progress in that form "is no longer at its zenith"—not "that the faith in the possibility of rationally dominating nature and chance has been lost, but in the sense that it is 'democratic.'" Progress has lost its democratic aspect because "the official 'standard bearers' of progress" (the bourgeoisie) have "brought into being in the present destructive forces like crises and unemployment, etc., every bit as dangerous and terrifying as those of the past," and it is clear that these forces are as much a result of "progress" as technology and scientific knowledge. Which is to say that the "crisis of the idea of progress is not therefore a crisis of the idea itself, but a crisis of the standard bearers of the idea, who have in turn become a part of 'nature' to be dominated."[51]

   Three points deserve emphasis here concerning climate change. First, in his time, a radical like Gramsci could still affirm a "faith in in the possibility of rationally dominating nature." On the Left, this faith holds no more, undone by everything from nuclear proliferation, growing awareness of mass extinction and other environmental crises, and by climate change. Second, despite this modernist "faith," Gramsci's political diagnosis still stands: what climate change forces us to acknowledge is that the human "domination of nature" is not and cannot be *democratic*. Modernity is at a crossroads: domination of nature *or* democracy. Third, our political condition results from an organic, as opposed to merely conjunctural, crisis of liberal hegemony. Liberal conceptions of democracy, freedom, politics, and so on remain hegemonic—these particular conceptions stand in for a presumably universal "common sense"—even though their glaring inadequacies to this moment in the planet's natural history are increasingly evident, even to liberals themselves. The ideology of progress was never about universal becoming. Still, we cannot simply disavow or refuse the concept of progress. Such "tendentious and interest-motivated" ahistoricism throws the baby out with the bathwater, ignoring the persistence and even origins of democracy in the concept of progress. A blanket rejection of progress confuses the idea and its standard bearers, who are now in fact part of the "natural order" in crisis.

   The problem is that we cannot somehow refuse the concepts we inherit to understand the world, remove ourselves from a critical or conceptual tradition, and start over with new ideas and meanings carefully crafted to suit our purposes, however noble they might seem. A clean separation of progress and becoming is impossible today because they "were born at the same time"—the combined product of political revolution, idealist philosophy, and liberal political economy—and bound together ideologically in the "widespread

50   Ibid.
51   Ibid.

consciousness" of what "civilization" means.[52] This is not without its bright side, Gramsci says, since with this twin birth a "measure of freedom enters into the concept of man."[53] So too, does the realization that "the objective possibilities exist for people not to die of hunger"—and yet "people do die of hunger," a fact that "has its importance, or so one would have thought."[54] This is where "progress" has failed us, in the production of unfreedom for billions, and now also in the catastrophic threat climate change poses to the very possibility of "civilization," which marks another step in this historical sequence. Progress and becoming remain intertwined, but climate change is reweaving them. The concept of progress as we knew it may be dead, but we do not know what we are becoming, and as yet we have no ideological bridge to overcome the resulting gap. With progress belied by planetary crises, we see no solution to the organic crisis of bourgeois hegemony—which has proven incapable of describing a future in which to become—other than more of the liberal progress that got us into this mess.

With the closure of the possibility that the effects of climate change might be subject to a meaningful degree of carbon mitigation, *adaptation is becoming the "progress" of our time.* Adaptation is to the ideology of Climate Leviathan what progress was to bourgeois liberalism in the nineteenth century. If it is true, as seems irrefutable, that we will have to adapt to the world that anthropogenic climate change is making (however different it is and will be), then the relevant question is not *whether* to adapt, as if a revolutionary social movement for climate justice can somehow decide against adaptation. The question, rather, is how—how to reshape a conception of the political in a very hot world.

---

52   Ibid., 357. Gramsci largely leaves political economy out of this account, but clearly classical economics had an important a hand in these developments. Our standard associations of increasing national wealth, productivity, and so on—in other words, growth—are in many ways what progress has meant for more than a century, and not only in capitalist societies.

53   Ibid., 360.

54   Ibid.

5

A Green Capitalism?

Those who, starry-eyed, put their confidence in the market, in its capacity to triumph over what they can no longer deny but that they call "challenges," have lost all credibility, but evidently that is not enough to give the future the chance not to be barbaric.

Isabelle Stengers[1]

I

The historical coincidence of the emergence of global capitalism and the transformation of our planet's atmosphere is no accident. The sharp rise in carbon emissions—the "blade" of the hockey stick in Figure 1.1—begins in the late eighteenth century, when capitalist social relations transformed much of the world. (This insight is behind the proposal to date the onset of the Anthropocene to 1775 with the invention of Watts's coal-powered steam engine.[2]) What is true for carbon is true to some extent for every major environmental issue: whether we consider an urban real estate project destroying wetlands, an oil spill in the Gulf of Mexico, or the destruction of tropical rain forest to produce soybeans and cattle, it is impossible to explain any environmental change today without a consideration of capitalism and its politics. This is not to deny capitalism's inherent dynamism, its capacity to produce enormous wealth (as long as "wealth" is defined by the volume of money and things). Rather, it is to emphasize that this social formation, so recent in natural-historical terms (humans have lived in capitalist societies for only approximately 0.01 percent of our natural history) has fundamentally changed our relationships with one another and with the Earth.[3]

Any substantial attempt to come to grips with climate change *must* contend with capitalism. Consider the drive to accumulate at the heart of all capitalist

---

1 Isabelle Stengers, *In Catastrophic Times: Resisting the Coming Barbarism,* London: Open Humanities, 2015, 28.

2 On the transition from steam to coal power and its implications for the history of capitalism, see Andreas Malm, *Fossil Capital,* New York: Verso, 2015. On the debate over when to date the beginning of the Anthropocene, see Simon Lewis and Mark Maslin, "Defining the Anthropocene," *Nature* 515, 12 March 2015, 171–80.

3 In round numbers, humans have been on Earth for 225,000 years, and the first capitalist society, England, only became fully capitalist in the last half of the eighteenth century; 225 years / 225,000 years = .01 percent.

economic organization. Capitalism is not a thing, but a social formation organized around commodity production and consumption, driven by the constant imperative to expand the accumulation of surplus by realizing positive returns on investment. Marx's general formula for capital, M-C-M′, tells the story as simply as possible. Money (M) is put into circulation by a capitalist to purchase labor power and means of production to produce commodities (C). This (M-C) is the process of production. The commodities produced must be sold, through which the capitalist obtains the return for his or her original expenditure in production. This second moment of the general formula for capital (C-M′) is consumption, allowing the value congealed in the commodity to be exchanged for money—more money, obviously, than originally invested (M′, where the prime symbol signals a quantitative increase in M).[4] Less some proportion the capitalist keeps as income, the money earned is reinvested in the production process, facilitating further accumulation. Capital's circulation and accumulation is the underlying source of the incessant expansion correctly associated with capitalist economies. There is a good reason that aggregate economic growth is a primary objective of all capitalist nation-states. A society organized on capitalist lines cannot operate otherwise for long. Accumulation begets accumulation for its own sake; this is the source of capitalism's undeniable dynamism.

The organization of social life to increase the production and sale of commodities and facilitate accumulation of money has important implications with respect to climate change. First, the expansion and accumulation of capital requires the constant conversion of the planet into means of production and commodities for sale and consumption. Although individual capitalists often embrace environmental commitments, as a *class*, capitalists must treat nature as a collection of resources. The problem is not only that the Earth's resources are finite, but that increasing concentration of atmospheric CO_2 (which has risen from approximately 250 parts per million before the emergence of capitalism to over 400 parts per million today) suggests far more immediate planetary limits to capitalism's growth imperative.[5] Social and technical responses that reduce or slow the effects of climate change may of course push these limits out into the future to some degree, but they cannot be eliminated. Responses that do not address the principle capitalist cause of climate change (that is, energy use to fuel the global capitalist economy) are in the end doomed to failure.[6]

---

4   It is possible, of course, that for any given investment, M > M′, and the capitalist loses money. But if capitalism produced that result at an aggregate scale for any length of time it would cease to operate; no one invests in production if they expect to lose money. Overall, capitalism only persists if surplus value is generated, i.e., M < M′.

5   There are also economic and social limits. Capital's drive cannot but produce periodic crises like the present one (Marx, *Capital* I, 1867; David Harvey, *The Enigma of Capital and the Crises of Capitalism*, London, Profile Books, 2011). Economic crises typically compel states to intervene to stimulate consumption (C-M′), a tendency that runs contrary to the response needed for climate change.

6   See also Stengers, *In Catastrophic Times*; Richard Smith, *Green Capitalism: The God That Failed*, Bristol, UK: World Economics Association, 2016.

Moreover, capitalism must be confronted in the struggle with climate change because of its crucial role in the production and exacerbation of inequality at various scales. It is no accident that the world has become dramatically more unequal with the emergence of global capitalism. Its very nature generates inequalities of wealth and power.[7] As Albert Einstein put it:

> Private capital tends to become concentrated in few hands, partly because of competition among the capitalists, and partly because technological development and the increasing division of labor encourage the formation of larger units of production at the expense of smaller ones. The result of these developments is an oligarchy of private capital the enormous power of which cannot be effectively checked even by a democratically organized political society.[8]

Recently, thanks to diverse processes—the global economic crisis that began in 2007, Occupy Wall Street, debates over Thomas Piketty's *Capital in the Twenty-first Century*, the spiraling wealth of the superrich—capital's inherent tendency to deepen inequalities of wealth and power has received a lot of overdue attention.[9] Too often these analyses leave open the idea that these inequalities can be brought to heel through measures such as modest redistribution through tax policy. The driver of inequality in capitalist society is the capital-labor relation itself, and its ramification through state power, so change is not so easy.[10]

For present purposes, the most significant missing piece in the conversation about inequality is nature. Climate change, which is sure to intensify and exacerbate disparity, has received far too little attention. Capital's tendency toward greater inequality is at the core of the challenge of confronting climate change, because meaningful response requires sacrifices, transnational alliances, and trans-class cooperation. Inequality is fatal to these efforts at two levels. First, within capitalist economies, inequalities in wealth and power make it difficult to build coalitions around shared sacrifice. Inequality also entrenches the capacity of the wealthy—who benefit disproportionately from economic growth—to prevent the conversion of our carbon-intensive economy into a more sustainable alternative. Consider the effectiveness of US energy companies in funding "climate skepticism" and lobbying politicians against a carbon tax.[11] Their power is rooted in private wealth. Second, between capitalist

---

7   Total socialized value ("wealth") and global median incomes have increased in the last two-plus centuries. But even with rising incomes, inequality undermines the capacity for collective action by reducing willingness to share sacrifices.

8   Albert Einstein, *Why Socialism?* New York: Monthly Review Press, 1951, 10.

9   See Thomas Piketty, *Capital in the Twenty-First Century*, translated by Arthur Goldhammer, Cambridge, MA: Belknapp Press, 2013; for a critique, see Geoff Mann, *In the Long Run We Are All Dead: Keynesianism, Political Economy and Revolution*, London: Verso, 2017, 335–65.

10   Nicos Poulantzas, *State, Power, Socialism*, London: Verso, 1979.

11   See Naomi Oreskes and Erik Conway, *Merchants of Doubt*, New York: Bloomsbury, 2011;

economies, the massively unequal dispensations of wealth and power in the world prevent the kind of global compromise that will be necessary to address climate change. In their trenchant analysis of international carbon production and climate change politics, Roberts and Parks show that the failure to achieve any global agreement to reduce carbon emissions is "rooted in the problem of global inequality: inequality in who is suffering the problem, who caused it . . ., who is expected to address [it], and who currently benefits disproportionately from the goods produced by the global economy."[12] As long as the world is capitalist, these inequalities will persist (see Figure 5.1), and so too will barriers to a cooperative global approach to climate change.

Figure 5.1. Cumulative CO_2 emissions by country, percent of world total 1990 – 2011

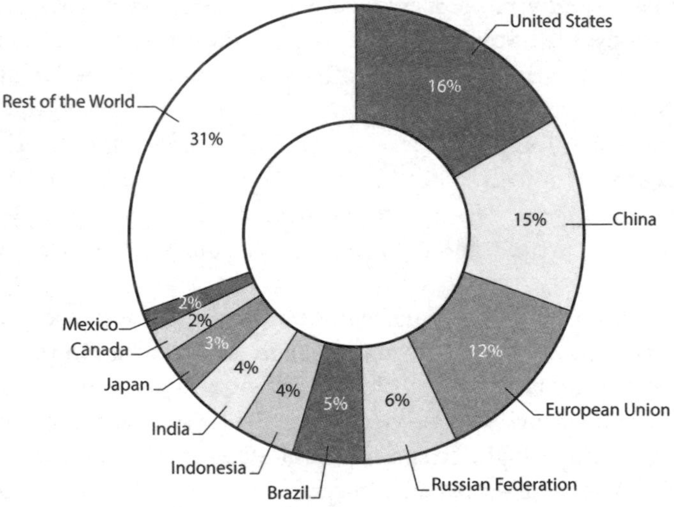

Source: World Resources Institute, 2013.

Liberals' faith in the adequacy of their values (freedom, the market, deliberation, "progress" and so on) on this problem to every problem we might ever confront—even those they cannot imagine—is proof of its status as ideology. The liberal capitalist "solution" to climate change thus proceeds by way of an "innovative" assembly of already existing political, economic, and technical resources, however inadequate they may be. The assembling of these resources is currently underway; Climate Leviathan is the end toward which it proceeds.

In this chapter, we examine this emerging assemblage, to understand it and

Hugh Compston and Ian Bailey (eds), *Turning Down the Heat: The Politics of Climate Policy in Affluent Democracies*, London: Palgrave Macmillan, 2008, 265.

12   J. Timmons Roberts and Bradley Parks, *A Climate of Injustice: Global Inequality, North-South Politics, and Climate Policy*, Boston, MA: MIT Press, 2007, 135

subject its logic to critique. We argue that Climate Leviathan is predicated upon the consolidation of existing forms of subjectivity, forms appropriate to the logic of rule in a liberal world—a logic patterned upon the liberal (or "bourgeois") conception of capital. However the problem in the relation between capitalism and climate change is not resolvable through state-coordinated "incentive alignment" and "credible commitment" on the part of firms. It lies, rather, at the foundations of capitalist society. While planetary warming accelerates ecological transformation and human suffering, liberal capitalism can only conceive of the buildup of anthropogenic greenhouse gases as a straightforward "market failure," for which various market-mending policies are proposed: cap-and-trade, carbon offsets, catastrophe bonds, mandatory risk disclosure, flood and hurricane insurance, and so on. Climate change is addressed by adjusting citizen-subjects' juridico-scientific status to include a role as emission source, so production and consumption can be properly regulated and governed. These changes—elements in the adaptation of the political—necessarily invoke the nation-state and are premised on the simultaneous adaptation of the political *qua* separation of state and civil society. For reasons explained below, we call this project "green Keynesianism."

II

The most symptomatic, and politically important, concept through which liberal capitalist reason domesticates climate change is that of the "collective action problem": a problem it is in everyone's best interest to fix, but about which no one agent has sufficient self-interested incentive to act without credible assurances that others will also. This framing rules out the possibility—as liberalism and capitalism virtually always do—that ethical commitments to shared social welfare and/or solidarity offer a viable response to such coordination problems (as they are also known). Orthodox analysis suggests that these challenges can be addressed in two basic ways, both of which rely on the exercise of state power. We can either displace private actors from the field of action (and make the state the coordinating mechanism), or we can construct institutions that lead agents to consent to act out of self-interest (use policy to organize optimal incentive structures).

In either case, many contemporary economists and policymakers conceive the collective action problem as a "market failure," a realm of human interaction in which, for any of a variety of reasons, markets do not mediate resource allocation optimally or do not exist at all. These situations are attributed to structural conditions imposed by nature—both "human nature" ("information asymmetry" means that self-interested private actors will not enter into some contracts because there is no way of overcoming counterparties' "natural" incentive to opportunism, for example) and nonhuman nature—like the fact that the atmosphere is impossible to privatize. In other words, market failures arise when, in the context of capitalist markets, either agents' rational self-interest or the materiality of the processes in question (or both) militate against the emergence well-functioning markets. These realms of interaction are deemed legitimate spaces for state intervention, either to provide the service itself, or (preferably) to create the institutions necessary for markets to function.

The classic market failure is a "public good" problem associated with a so-called "tragedy of the commons."[13] Public goods are resources characterized by non-excludability—in other words, they are difficult to commodify because those who do not pay for them can still access them or the services they provide: atmospheric oxygen, domestic security provided by national defense, or common grazing lands, for example.[14] The "tragedy of the commons" is the term ecologist Garrett Hardin used to describe the supposedly inevitable collapse of common-pool natural resources, due to what we now call market failure. The "tragedy" is a socio-ecological conjuncture involving agents motivated by an ineluctably "self-interested" human nature acting unchecked by effective institutions to manage resource use.

Some of the most oft-cited examples of a "tragedy of the commons" are fisheries.[15] Because of the dearth of information regarding supply (fish stocks are highly mobile and under water), the difficulty of monitoring fishing effort (the ocean is a difficult space to govern), the increasing effectiveness of harvesting technology, fisheries commons that lack an appropriately individualized incentive structure have a supposedly "natural" propensity to degradation. With climate change and the accelerating ocean acidification with which it is associated, declining abundance makes it increasingly imperative that existing stocks are managed sustainably, and fishing pressure must be constrained.[16] If one accepts the premise that cooperation or collective ownership of the resource is impossible because of human self-interest (this is *a priori* in all tragedy models), there is little incentive for any individual to practice stewardship, and users engage in a zero-sum harvesting competition with each other. Aware that they can neither exclude others from access to the resource nor ensure that others limit their use appropriately, all are motivated to take as much as they can as

---

13   Garrett Hardin, "Tragedy of the Commons," *Science* 162, no. 3859, December 13, 1968, 1243–48.

14   In economic theory, public goods are also characterized by so-called "nonrivalry," meaning that any one actor's use of the resource does not in any meaningful way diminish what remains for others. No matter how much oxygen we breathe, for example, it does not limit the available remainder. As we will see, however, many "public goods," like atmospheric greenhouse gas storage or oceanic carbon absorption are no longer so clearly "nonrival." This poses important challenges for market-oriented "solutions," because it introduces rivalry (scarcity) to a nonexcludable good.

15   See, for example, "The Tragedy of the Commons, cont'd," *The Economist*, May 4, 2005, economist.com.

16   J. T. Mathis, S. R. Cooley, N. Lucey, S. Colt, J. Ekstrom, T. Hurst, C. Hauri, W. Evans, J. N. Cross, and R. A. Feely, "Ocean Acidification Risk Assessment for Alaska's Fishery Sector," *Progress in Oceanography* 136, August 2015, 71–91.

quickly as they can. In so doing, together they destroy the fishery: "Freedom in a commons brings ruin to all."[17]

Since coordination or other solidaristic action is deemed impossible, this collective action "tragedy" is a "market failure," that is, the lack of the market-mediated cure-all orthodox economics says we should expect when agents are "free." The solution, it would seem, can only take one of two forms. We can impose complete state control of the productive apparatus, on the assumption that if the state is the only manager, it can organize its use with its subjects' (and, presumably, the ecosystem's) long-term interests in mind. This statist approach has a long history. Adam Smith himself highlighted the need for such proactive state initiative under conditions where "civil society"—a sphere where agents driven by their "natural" proclivity to "truck, barter and exchange" compete—failed to provide an adequate or accessible supply of socially necessary goods or services, and this logic underwrote state activity for much of the twentieth century.

Today, however, the preferred solution involves a combination of local coordination, state enforcement, and institutions of exclusive access—in other words, property rights. Liberal capitalism privileges market-mediated production and exchange relations whenever possible, on the proposition that they maximize efficiency, productivity, and "freedom," meaning merit-based returns to an imaginary subject-position, the rational, acquisitive individual with limited means: so-called *homo economicus*. Consequently, fixing market failures or mitigating the effects of "missing markets" has been identified as the primary function of the capitalist state since Adam Smith. This typically entails constructing an institutional matrix in which the price mechanism ensures actors are rendered responsible for their actions: a system that closes off access to all but those who pay the market-determined price, and privatizes the "right" of access so that it is exchangeable on the market. Theoretically, this should produce individual incentives that align with sustainability.

So, to take the case of fisheries, correcting market failure requires the assertion of national sovereignty over oceanic space and the creation of institutions like privately-held licenses and quotas, public investment in fisheries science (particularly monitoring), and so on. Together, this matrix should give each fishing agent an interest in careful fisheries management because the information, monitoring and incentive problems have been addressed: access itself is now a valuable commodity (in the form of exclusive and transferable rights to

---

17 Hardin "Tragedy of the Commons," 1244. Hardin's narrative is enormously influential, but false. There is a vast and robust literature on the management of commons that shows "tragedy" is by no means inevitable, and often much *less* likely under cooperative arrangements. The classic counterpoint is Elinor Ostrom's game-theoretical analysis of the management of common pool resources, reinforced by thousands of empirical studies of practical management (successful and unsuccessful) of diverse commons: see Elinor Ostrom, Roy Gardner and Jimmy Walker, *Rules, Games, and Common-Pool Resources,* Ann Arbor: University of Michigan Press, 1994.

fish), the state promises to monitor stock health, enforce harvest levels and ensure there are no free riders fishing "illegally," and thus it is in every agent's self-interest to steward their "property" in fish.

It bears emphasis that when market failures arise, liberals do not attribute them to a "failure" of the market model. On the contrary, a market failure is not taken as evidence of markets' "natural" limits, but rather as evidence of one of two types of state failure: regulating too much or regulating too little. In the first instance, the government does too much, limiting "freedom" by meddling in a realm of potentially profitable investment and discouraging private sector entry by (for example) restricting property rights and reducing the expected profitability of private investment. State-owned monopolies like energy utilities are frequent targets of this critique.[18] Alternatively, the state that regulates too little also abets market failure, most notably by failing to get producers to factor in the "social cost" of so-called "externalities." Externalities are "indirect," often nonmarket, effects of producing goods and services, born by more than the producer alone, usually by the community at large. Externalities can be positive or negative, but the positives are usually unintended. Indeed, with few exceptions, they are actively avoided because, by definition, they involve the provision of a good or service without a privately appropriable revenue stream, and hence enable so-called "free riders," market parasites who benefit from another agent's "initiative" but do not pay.

In environmental market failures, negative externalities are the main concern. The cry to "internalize the environmental externalities!" is the cornerstone of contemporary environmental economics. Typically, this entails imposing taxes or user fees for environmental damages on resource users and consumers to they pay something closer to the "full cost" of commodities. The blackboard theory for these taxes is simple and straightforward. By increasing the cost of environmental impact, the state would force the market to realize an ecologically "sustainable" equilibrium price. In other words, the new higher price is expected to reduce demand to a point at which degradation is deemed "acceptable," or, ideally, state revenues from the tax would enable it to "offset" the damages. Think of the tiny fee now paid for a plastic bag in many cities, essentially a plastic bag consumption tax: it works. Even a nominal fee sharply reduces plastic bag consumption.

One might wonder, then, why these taxes are absent in most markets in most societies in the world. To take the most glaring example, many

---

18   In British Columbia, Canada, for example, the repeal of laws against the construction of private "run-of-the-river" hydropower generating stations has been widely celebrated for "releasing" the power of markets to supply "green" energy. The program has been supported by a variety of voices rarely found on the same side of an environmental issue. See, for example, www.energybc.ca/runofriver.html; Amy Smart, "Ahousaht Run-of-River Project Could Power Tofino, Ucluelet," *Victoria Times-Colonist*, August 11, 2016; available at timescolonist.com.

economists, the World Bank, and some other important institutions of global capitalism presently support a carbon tax (a consumption tax on emissions-producing resources or activities, like gasoline or driving). A well-designed, suitably-priced carbon tax would help ensure that the socio-ecological impacts of greenhouse gas production are reflected in producers' consumption decisions. This would not only force consumers to pay a price that is closer to the "true" cost of their emissions, but spur innovation in low- and zero-emission technologies, given the increased incentive to minimize costly carbon emissions. As Nobel-winning economist Joseph Stiglitz puts it,

> Imposing a carbon price, reflecting the social cost of emissions, would significantly stimulate investment. To ensure a level playing field, we might have to impose cross-border adjustments. A carbon tax would simultaneously raise substantial revenues needed to finance [other] public investments.[19]

As Stiglitz makes clear, on the terms of its own reason, capitalism must be managed to keep the perpetual growth machine moving. Whether capitalism has the capacity to deliver on these promises is worth pondering. Despite the advice from economists (not to mention the demands of many concerned citizens), only a few capitalist states have any carbon tax, and the carbon taxes in place have proven too low to make a difference in global patterns of energy consumption.[20] In keeping with the diagnosis that a market failure is actually a state failure, most economists immediately attribute the ineffectiveness of these programs to "politics." This is not entirely wrong-headed, but since their conception of the political is so limited, it brings us no closer to an explanation of capitalism's failure to "do what it should" regarding climate change. It only feeds back into a fantasy of a society governed purely by the market.

Still, there is no shortage of economists writing technical, dry, policy-oriented reports with complex titles that boil down to "What Should Be Done About Climate Change," practically all of which are based in market-failure thinking. The following statement from one such report, a European Commission study on the forms of government regulation ("intervention") necessary to manage climate change, is exemplary:

> A certain degree of government intervention is initially needed [to address climate change] because of two market failures occurring simultaneously. First, there is little spontaneous demand for emission-reducing technologies, which chokes the supply of commercially viable non-polluting goods and services. Since a stable

19   Joseph Stiglitz, "How to Restore Equitable and Sustainable Economic Growth in the United States," *American Economic Review* 106, no. 5, 45.

20   For a map showing the extent of the world's carbon tax and trading schemes, see sightline. org/2014/11/17/all-the-worlds-carbon-pricing-systems-in-one-animated-map.

climate is a public good, the social benefits of climate action are not fully captured by those incurring the mitigation costs and autonomous climate change mitigation actions remain below the social optimum. Second, companies lack incentives to invest in clean technologies, because of the so-called appropriability effect associated with the expected post-innovation rents. Given society preferences, there could be pressure to widely disseminate outputs of green innovation. So, companies anticipate they will not be able to capture fully the market value of their investments in green R&D and therefore downplay their contribution to green innovation. By contrast, mutually supportive environmental and innovation policies could stimulate markets to deliver a wider portfolio of green technologies. These technologies would enable climate change mitigation at commercially reasonable costs and even provide opportunities for growth ... On that basis, our working hypothesis is twofold. First, an appropriate combination of environmental and innovation policies is desirable in order to address the combination of negative environmental and knowledge externalities. Second, an appropriate set of both policies will achieve [the] largest emission reductions at minimal fiscal burden.[21]

Recourse to the technical management of behaviour through the medium of the economy is a crucial strategy in green capitalist advocacy. Economics imputes to itself the capacity to correct behavior by "incentive alignment," thereby exposing it (and rendering it subject) to reason. In this frame, politics—whether in the narrow form of the state *qua* "political society" or in a broader conception—is not merely suppressed, it is made out as a purely negative field, which can do nothing but derail disinterested rationality. The economy must remain untainted by political "distortions." Only then can technical reason realize its potential to rescue us.

In sum, the market remains the ruling abstraction and institution of our time. It alone provides the pattern on which the fabric of all problems are cut. Economists and policymakers address climate change by slotting it into a "to do" file already labelled "market failure." Indeed, many economists now call climate change the greatest market failure in history—the problem being, again, that we do not pay the true cost of greenhouse gas emissions (a negative externality). In the words of the Stern Report (though an internet search confirms it could be the words of many others), "climate change ... must be regarded as market failure on the greatest scale the world has seen."[22] Toward what political strategy does this thinking lead?

---

21   Andrea Conte, Ariane Labat, Janos Varga and Žiga Žarni, "What is the Growth Potential of Green Innovation? An Assessment of EU Climate Policy Options," Directorate-General for Economic and Financial Affairs, European Commission, Economic Paper no. 413, June 2010: 1, 11.

22   Nicholas Stern, "Stern Review: The Economics of Climate Change," HM Treasury, 2006, 25. More recently Stern has written that "climate change represents the biggest market failure the world has seen because of the potential magnitude of the damage for so many people and the involvement of almost all in causing the externality." Nicholas Stern, *Why Are We Waiting? The Logic, Urgency and Promise of Tackling Climate Change*, Cambridge, MA: MIT Press, 2015, 195.

III

In a 2008 analysts' commentary published just weeks after the disintegration of Lehman Brothers helped take down the global financial system, Deutsche Bank economists attempted to spin the crisis (in which they were no minor players) as an opportunity for a global turnaround through investment in energy, technology, and infrastructure. They argued that the crisis had exposed an unprecedented "green sweet spot" for infrastructure stimulus that promised both social progress and environmental good sense.[23] Deutsche Bank was not the only organization that discovered the appeal of a green path out of the abyss. If we find it ironic to see a massive financial institution's cheery celebration of ecological opportunity, consider that the World Bank, the International Monetary Fund, and the International Energy Agency joined right in.[24]

The subject of Deutsche Bank's analysis was the state-funded stimulus package that the bank considered desperately necessary to save the financial system. Never mind neoliberalism; in 2008 the state was back, the only means to generate and coordinate the investment necessary to facilitate anything like a recovery, let alone an environmentally friendly one. Deutsche Bank CEO Josef Ackermann admitted he could "no longer believe in the market's self-healing power," and he was not alone.[25] In 2008, the usual complaints about public spending (it crowds out private investment, generates inflation, increases sovereign debt, and so on) went silent. Instead, the moment had arrived for a "Green New Deal" or "green Keynesianism."

Green Keynesianism has diverse advocates across what are usually less compatible camps, from influential Left critics like Susan George to orthodox policy insiders like Obama's former chief economic advisor, Lawrence Summers. There have always been, as it were, varieties of Keynesianism, not just because of the differences in national political economies but also for theoretical and political reasons.[26] Summers's and George's Keynesianisms are not identical. Nevertheless, at the most general level, their policy proposals are based on the same conceptual foundations. They seek a commitment to an economically "activist" state, coordinating and regulating the national economy through debt-financed state spending to promote employment, consumer demand, and

---

23 Deutsche Asset Management, "Economic Stimulus: The Case for 'Green' Infrastructure, Energy Security and 'Green' Jobs," November 2008, 4.

24 Others whom we might be a little less inclined to suspect of exculpatory distraction were no less enthusiastic, like the United Nations Environment Program, the UK's New Economics Foundation, and the Economic Policy Institute in the United States.

25 Quoted in Michael Skapinker, "The Market No Longer Has All the Answers," *Financial Times*, March 24, 2008.

26 Peter Hall (ed.), *The Political Power of Economic Ideas: Keynesianism Across Nations*, Princeton, NJ: Princeton University Press, 1989. This is an early volume edited by the political scientist who was later to establish the so-called "varieties of capitalism" literature: Peter Hall and David Soskice, *Varieties of Capitalism: The Institutional Foundations of Comparative Advantage*, Oxford: Oxford University Press, 2001.

political stability.[27] The environmental transition proposed by both George and Summers, though different in content, is based upon a shared recognition that the task of employment and demand "optimization" now requires attention to the environment. To be sure, the degree to which our environmental crisis looms is much less an issue for Summers than for George. But both trust the avoidance of political economic disaster and the possibility of progress or adaptation in the state's engagement in "stimulating" and "incentivizing" economic agents.

Green Keynesianism's advocates support a welfare-state model with an "environmental" reorientation.[28] They propose a variety of (mostly fiscal) policy tools for the environmentally conscious optimization of economic life. As Deutsche Bank suggested, infrastructure development and renewal is a priority; so too are research and development in clean energy, green building, and related sectors. Direct state investment in public transportation and wind power, for example, or mandated increases in energy efficient construction, are standard components of the green Keynesian programmes. Taxation plays an essential role, in the form of both negative or reduced taxes (subsidies and tax credits) to promote certain sectors and behaviors and positive emissions taxes to "internalize" the social costs (externalities) associated with greenhouse gas production. Examples include tax credits for research and development related to renewables and carbon taxes that penalize greenhouse gas generation.

Money is the lifeblood of these plans, of course, and various "green finance" mechanisms have been proposed: direct state funding and grant-making, targeted lending, loan guarantees, bond issuance and underwriting, and so on. Monetary policy has for the most part been isolated from these conversations. Although the lines between it and fiscal policy have gotten blurry at the edges (especially since 2008), when the green Keynesian state underwrites or even undertakes targeted lending to the solar industry, for instance, it is not a monetary policy operation. Neither is the form of bond issuance in question, even if

---

27   As Pierre Rosanvallon argues, Keynesianism understands the economy as a realm through which to optimize the operation of the state through bureaucracy; its goal is to simultaneously consolidate and modernize capitalism; Pierre Rosanvallon, "The Development of Keynesianism in France," in Peter Hall (ed.), *The Political Power of Economic Ideas: Keynesianism Across Nations*, Princeton: Princeton University Press, 1989, 171–93.

28   Why call this "green Keynesianism"? From the perspective of historical accuracy, it is indeed a bit of a stretch. John Maynard Keynes emphasized the priority of *monetary* policy as the means by which the state could prime the economic pump—lowering interest rates to make investment more attractive and saving less so—and advocated temporary fiscal measures only when monetary means could not do the job. However, post-World War II "Keynesianism" has nonetheless come to be associated almost entirely with fiscal policy (taxes and state spending) and a debt-financed, state-bureaucratic infrastructure, and we defer to this common definition in this conversation. See Geoff Tily, *Keynes Betrayed*, New York: Palgrave, 2010; Geoff Mann, "Poverty in the Midst of Plenty: Unemployment, Liquidity, and Keynes' Scarcity Theory of Capital," *Critical Historical Studies* 2, no. 1, 45–83.

issuing bonds is something monetary authorities do to manipulate interest rates and hence credit markets. Monetary policy is aimed at the control of the general price level (inflation) and the supply and cost of credit (the interest rate), but green Keynesian proposals for state bond issuance are not intended to influence the aggregate supply and price of credit, but rather to raise capital for specific "green" initiatives—energy efficient infrastructure upgrades, for example—in much the same way as cities issue municipal bonds to pay for public transit expansion.

All of these green initiatives are Keynesian in the conventional, fiscal-activist sense. They require repositioning the state and its sovereign power at the center of a supposedly market-determined civil society in the interests of sustainable economic prosperity. One might be forgiven for construing these ideas as an amalgam of climate panic and nostalgia for the post-World War II era. But it is not just the memory of capitalism's "Golden Age" that motivates arguments for a massive reinvigoration of the state's fiscal capacities. It is also a recognition that at the current conjuncture, monetary policies have reached the limits of their stimulative capacities, which the fallout of the financial crisis that began in 2007–2008 is forcing capitalist states to acknowledge, however reluctantly. When overall economic prospects look sufficiently grim and effective (anticipated) demand is low, employers are reluctant to invest even if credit is cheap and inflation is low (what Keynes called a "liquidity trap"). Under these conditions, central banks can drop interest rates to zero for years but it will not necessarily kick-start a capitalist economy, whether green, brown or any other color. This is exactly what central banks have been doing since 2008. Though it has lessened the severity of the crisis, the proof of its futility as an instrument to trigger economic recovery is readily apparent.

From a green Keynesian perspective, conventional monetary tools are extremely limited. Monetary policy is always a blunt and imprecise instrument, even under the conditions for which it is designed (that is, robust markets that have at least some effective demand for credit). For environmental aims, there is another wrinkle: at least as currently practiced, it cannot raise or lower interest rates in a particular sector, based on relative "greenness," and it cannot target prices in a one set of markets while leaving others unaffected. There is no monetary operating procedure presently available that can make borrowing or inputs more expensive for a coal-power plant than for a producer of electric cars. Only fiscal policy can do that. So, fiscal instruments are crucial to the green Keynesian program, and a legitimate, interventionist state is necessary. In many ways, the green Keynesian plan would resuscitate a state with a political economic footprint unseen since the 1930s and 1940s. Deutsche Bank envisions a National Infrastructure Bank to coordinate a green recovery in cooperation with local and regional governments and private partnerships (Figure 5.2). Nobel economist Joseph Stiglitz has called for something similar; so too has Thomas Piketty, arguably the best-known Keynesian of our time.[29] Remarkably, Deutsche Bank is proposing what looks remarkably like a New Deal program from the first Roosevelt administration—the interventionist institutions whose coordinating powers the U.S. Supreme Court ruled unconstitutional. That one of the largest and most influential financial firms on the planet could find itself endorsing a reincarnation of the National Recovery Administration is an indicator of how dire capital's outlook was at the close of the 2000s.

Figure 5.2. The National Infrastructure Bank can provide funding and coordination across the economy

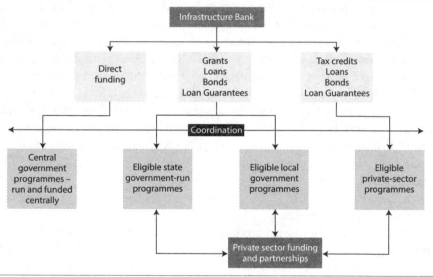

Source: Deutsche Bank's National Infrastructure Bank Model. From Deutsche Asset Management, "Economic Stimulus: The Case for 'Green' Infrastructure, Energy Security and 'Green' Jobs," November 2008, 9.

Following the financial chaos of 2007–08, green Keynesianism emerged as an important thread in the reaction to the crisis, particularly among centrists and progressives in liberal capitalist democracies. Its advocates included power insiders like Lord Nicholas Stern, economist and lead author of the British government's well-known 2006 review of the economics of climate change (the "Stern Report"). In a submission to the G20 for its 2009 London Summit, Stern and co-author Ottmar Edenhofer exhorted member states—who "account for roughly

---

29   Stiglitz, "How to Restore Equitable and Sustainable Economic Growth in the United States," 45.

two thirds of the world's population and three quarters of global gross national product, energy consumption and carbon emissions"—to acknowledge monetary policy's inadequacy in the face of the dual crisis of economy and climate.[30] The only option, they argued, is a massive green Keynesian project. Their proposal (Figure 5.3) is in many ways a multinational variation on the Deutsche Bank scheme:

> Governments should structure their approach towards a global green recovery in two phases. The first phase includes three measures that would boost aggregate demand and employment in the short term. Governments should focus on [1] improving energy efficiency, [2] upgrading the physical infrastructure of the economy to make it low-carbon, and [3] supporting clean-technology markets. The second phase focuses more on the medium term and comprises [4] initiating flagship projects, [5] enhancing international research and development and [6] incentivise investment for low carbon growth. Medium-term measures should provide the private sector with incentives to invest more resources in developing the markets that will underpin future growth. They can strengthen investor confidence now and provide the basis for sustained productivity growth in the future. Finally, [7] co-ordinating G20 efforts supports the effectiveness of all the other measures.

Reflecting upon these proposals almost a decade after the financial meltdown, we can make two observations. First, there is an intuitive logic to the proposals: they make practical sense. The state jumps back in with both feet; Keynesian stimulus reprimes the pump, but this time "ecologically." Financial innovation is reoriented from predatory or speculative debt-finance to the development of sophisticated markets for instruments to promote energy efficiency, biodiversity conservation, and financing for renewable energy and carbon abatement. The result is not your grandmother's Keynesianism, but one modified to spur employment and investment growth while reducing carbon emissions, improving productive efficiency, and stimulating demand. Variations on this thinking motivated disparate policy efforts like the Green European Foundation's "Green New Deal," the Obama administration's cash-for-clunkers program, and Lee Myun-Bak's "green growth" strategy for South Korea.[31]

---

30   Ottmar Edenhofer and Nicholas Stern, "Towards a Global Green Recovery: Recommendations for Immediate G20 Action," Report Submitted to the G20 London Summit, April 2, 2009, 6, 12–3, 16.

31   On Lee Myun-Bak's "green growth," see Sanghun Lee, "Assessing South Korea's Green Growth Strategy," in Raymond Bryant (ed.), *The International Handbook of Political Ecology*, London: Edward Elgar, 2017, 345–58. For a different, robust theory of different green capitalist projects, see Mario Candeias, *Green Transformation: Competing Strategic Projects*, Berlin: Rosa Luxemburg Stiftung, 2015. Candeias discerns differences between "authoritarian neoliberalism," "green capitalism," and "a green new deal," which we conflate.

Figure 5.3. A 'Green' Recovery for Global Capitalism

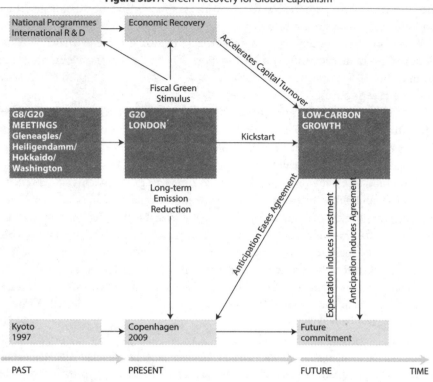

Source: Ottmar Edenhofer and Nicholas Stern, Towards a Global Green Recovery: Recommendations for Immediate G20 Action, report submitted to the G20 London summit, April 2, 2009, 17.

The second observation is possible only in retrospect: these intuitive and eminently reasonable arguments gained no purchase, and the proposals went nowhere. At least in terms of emissions reductions and environmental protection—let alone improvements in employment and investment levels—basically none of these plans have been realised thus far. Why? Certainly not for lack of incisive policy analysis or high-level endorsements. So is the answer really just a dearth of "political will," as we are so often told? Is the failure to realize green Keynesianism just a function of politicians' cowardice or corporate capture, of paralyzed electorates and the influence of climate denialism? No. These factors (especially the power of fossil fuel corporations) have helped squash the green Keynesian agenda, to be sure. But this cannot entirely explain why we have so little to show for all the talk, any more than they can explain why we are faced with likely-catastrophic anthropogenic global warming.

The apparent inability to realize policies that fix the problem of climate change *qua* market failure extends all the way up to the world scale. The challenge of building a green Keynesian political-economic strategy has been fundamental to both the promise and failure of the United Nations Conference of the

Parties (COP) process—the *promise* because only a would-be world state (like the UN) could deliver the green Keynesian goods; the *failure* because the United Nations COP basket remains empty.

The Paris Agreement epitomizes this binary. Its two key economic provisions are premised on the logic of correcting market failure. It recognizes the limited incentives for investors to finance projects that would, on one hand, mitigate greenhouse gases and, on the other, support adaptation measures. To address these shortcomings, the agreement takes us further toward a world where the market manages carbon everywhere. This may seem surprising, since the words "carbon market" do not appear in the final agreement, and carbon markets are not exactly buzzing right now. They remain modest in scale—covering less than half the world's carbon emissions in 2016—with less than modest volumes and prices. From the perspective of global financial flows, carbon markets are completely unimportant, and if they collapsed tomorrow most firms would not care a whit. The price to offset one ton of carbon in 2016 in the EU and California was around $13 per ton: far too low to trigger substantive shifts in investment or dramatic reductions in energy use.[32]

From a green-capitalist perspective, the solution is to create new mechanisms for trading carbon credits, including for those tons of carbon ostensibly abated by cross-border investments in energy efficiency or mitigation. Article 6 of the Paris Agreement, one of the few genuinely novel elements in the text, introduces a "Mechanism to Support Sustainable Development." This innocuously titled proposal describes a formula to enable the commodification of carbon in every ecosystem and economy:

> A mechanism to contribute to the mitigation of greenhouse gas emissions and support sustainable development is hereby established under the authority and guidance of the Conference of the Parties serving as the meeting of the Parties to the Paris Agreement for use by Parties on a voluntary basis. It shall be supervised by a body designated by the Conference of the Parties serving as the meeting of the Parties to the Paris Agreement, and shall aim:
>
> (a) To promote the mitigation of greenhouse gas emissions while fostering sustainable development;
>
> (b) To incentivize and facilitate participation in the mitigation of greenhouse gas emissions by public and private entities authorized by a Party;
>
> (c) To contribute to the reduction of emission levels in the host Party, which will benefit from mitigation activities resulting in emission reductions that can also

---

32   For a critical analysis of carbon markets, see Donald MacKenzie, "Making Things the Same: Gases, Emission Rights and the Politics of Carbon Markets," *Accounting, Organizations and Society* 34, no. 3-4, 440–55; Ian Bailey, Andy Gouldson and Peter Newell, "Ecological Modernisation and the Governance of Carbon: A Critical Analysis," *Antipode* 43, no. 3, 2011, 682–703. On the limits of markets for environmental conservation, see Jessica Dempsey, *Enterprising Nature: Economics, Markets, and Finance in Global Biodiversity Politics*, West Sussex, UK: Wiley Blackwell, 2016.

be used by another Party to fulfill its nationally determined contribution; and
(d) To deliver an overall mitigation in global emissions.

Simply put, the Paris Agreement creates a means for countries to invest in carbon mitigation by providing a global market-based framework for exchanging carbon credits: the REDD+ model gone global.[33] Pablo Solón, Bolivia's former ambassador to the UN climate negotiations, explains:

> [T]his Mechanism to Support Sustainable Development will be based on Article 12 and Article 6 of the Kyoto Protocol. Article 6 of the Kyoto Protocol has created carbon markets and offsets. And Article 12 of the Kyoto Protocol created the Clean Development Mechanism that handles those carbon credits. With [Article 6], the Clean Development Mechanism will most likely become the Sustainable Development Mechanism, and carbon markets will not be limited to developed countries (Annex I), but available to all countries at all different levels: global, regional, bilateral and national. In other words, all will be free to gamble on the future of the Earth system.[34]

Unsurprisingly, the liberal response to Solón's critique is to say, "we must do *something* (but cannot confront capitalism), so let's build an effective global institution that can monitor carbon emissions and regulate exchanges under Article 6 and the Clean Development Mechanism—a technical body that can correct existing market failures . . ." But how, exactly? Peek into the post-Paris COP negotiations and you find the details where the devil does his thing.

IV

The attraction of green Keynesianism to those on the progressive-liberal spectrum is easy to understand. At least in the contemporary global North, the vast majority of "us" (meaning, in this case, well-intentioned, progressive, environmentally conscious people) are beholden to the liberal capitalist order that is so entirely "normal" we cannot imagine otherwise. We seem stuck in capitalism, even those of us who perhaps wish it were not hegemonic, and from the inside, Keynesianism looks like the best or even only option. Since this is *not* true—it is not the best option, it is not the only option, and indeed it is quite likely that it is not an option at all—we must try to grasp what makes it *seem* like such a good idea to so many, including those who truly want to address the climate crisis (and not just so they might profit from it). Keynesianism and its green variety merit a critique in the proper sense of the term: not the polemical attack or

---

33   REDD+ is "reducing emissions from deforestation and forest degradation," a UNFCCC program established in 2005 to reduce emissions and carbon sequestration by providing incentives to maintain the viability of standing forests in developing countries.

34   Pablo Salón, "From Paris with Love for Lake Poopó," December 21, 2015.

out-of-hand dismissal that comes down to saying that Keynesianism is simply capitalism parading in social democratic disguise. There is an element of truth to this critique, but it does little to address the ideological problem, and the practical-political limits within which it constrains us. For this, we must specify the relations of our conjuncture, on which these ideas depend.[35]

Keynesians understand history to have demonstrated repeatedly that the "free market" or *laissez-faire* is a political economic disaster waiting to happen— but also to have shown that the disaster is not capitalism per se but only its "pure" liberal form.[36] The chaos of instability undoubtedly associated with "free" capitalist markets is neither natural nor productive. Keynesians begin from the premise that we do not need to endure the punishing economic volatility that Marx and Engels call the "freaks of fortune."[37] Keynesians are convinced that we are smarter than that, or at least some of us are, so if those people are in charge, our destructive tendencies to selfishness, herd behavior, and fear can be mitigated. Keynesianism is thus always structured by the dominance of technocratic and expert-based government, just as Keynes proposed. This does not mean that the

---

35   Our critique of Keynesianism differs fundamentally from that of the mainstream economists who have been sniping away at Keynesianism for decades. Though we recognize that the postwar "Keynesian" welfare state did indeed run up against some limits, most of Keynesianism's critics misunderstand these limits for two reasons. First, many of them substitute postwar Keynesianism for Keynes's economics, and thus they do not realize the degree to which they are often themselves Keynesians—if, that is, we associate that term with the ideas of John Maynard Keynes's *The General Theory of Employment, Interest and Money* (New York: Harcourt, Brace 1965 [1936]). Most critics know little of Keynes's economics, which is not primarily a fiscal scheme, but a monetary policy program—much like the one that governments have implemented since 2008 (and is widely credited with having prevented a second Great Depression). Second, the critics typically assume that Keynesianism is doomed for all time, as if the reasons it lost its disciplinary and policy dominance in the early 1970s are built into its DNA. But there was no inevitable force behind the fall of Keynesianism or the "Keynesian" welfare state. What brought it to an end was a specific constellation of political forces. For example, it is widely claimed that Keynesianism is inherently inflationary and that inflation destroyed it, and it is true that in Keynesianism's political crisis, conditions produced unacceptable levels of inflation. However, it was not Keynesianism, but rather the political conditions that were inflationary. The inflation of the 1970s was a product of social conflict. In the struggle over the distribution of income in the late 1960s, capital asserted a "right" to an enormous portion of national wealth, a right it took as natural and legitimate. Workers in the capitalist core, emboldened and empowered in the postwar years, demanded a greater share of the national wealth. They thereby threatened the "natural" status of capital's claims (in other words, what was considered an "acceptable" rate of profit). The state tried to contain this struggle by pleasing both parties—an option only made possible by inflation. But it need not have worked out this way. If workers had been able to claim a larger share of the pie (that is, if the idea that workers deserved a larger share of the national income had enjoyed widespread and entrenched political legitimacy), then there would have been no inflationary dynamic, but a redistributive one. Wages would have risen and profits would have fallen to a lower, but no less "acceptable" level. In short, Keynesianism is not more inflationary than other capitalist modes of economic theory and policy. Green Keynesianism does indeed face limits in our conjuncture, but the "neoliberal" critique from mainstream economics does not touch upon them. A critique of green Keynesianism from the Left must begin elsewhere. For a fuller discussion of these issues, see Mann, *In the Long Run We Are All Dead*.

36   Ibid.

37   Karl Marx. and Friedrich Engels, *The German Ideology* Amherst, MA: Prometheus Books, 1967 [1846], 89.

task ahead is merely a twenty-first century, green-tinted fine-tuning of what came before. Just because Keynesian political economy helped make sense of the 1930–1960s, that does not mean that it is ready for a reboot. The fact that Keynesian political economy is a set of political-theoretical-institutional commitments and practices constructed on the political-economic and policy foundations of a different era matters a great deal. Three key differences bear emphasis.

First, shifts in the international geopolitical order since the Keynesian "Golden Age" have radically altered the powers and discretion associated with the territorial, political-economic sovereignty that Keynesianism takes as given. This is critical because Keynesian policies are not readily scaled up beyond the national level. (Keynes himself understood this, which motivated his participation in the creation of the Bretton Woods institutions.) In contrast to the international economics common sense of our conjuncture, Keynesian economics and policy are premised upon nation-states' capacity to manipulate cross-border flows of goods, services, labor, and capital—to redirect, reduce, or restrict—and to make adjustments when it suits the national interest. Keynesianism also requires that states reallocate or coordinate internal investment flows, sectorally and spatially. These conditions are required because Keynesianism (and certainly any green variety) is structured on the basis of a theory of macroeconomic relationships that determine the level of investment.

According to that theory, investment, *not* consumption, is the driver of the capitalist system. Keynesian economics center, therefore, upon "investment demand," the forces that determine the decision to invest—especially the relationship between the interest rate and expected future rates of return on capital. Potential investors will not borrow to invest if the cost of borrowing seems likely to exceed anticipated profits. If uncertainty increases their "liquidity- preference" (meaning that expected returns are lower than the returns at which they are willing to risk lending), money-holders (also known as investors and capitalists) will sit on their money, keeping it out of circulation. Keynesian policy is thus concerned with the relationship between interest rates and the general level of "confidence" in the national economy; as mentioned earlier, and contrary to popular wisdom, it was designed first and foremost as a monetary policy program and not a fiscal regime (fiscal policy is posited as a backstop to monetary instruments).

Despite this theoretical and policy emphasis, the fixed-exchange rate system put in place by the Bretton Woods Agreement of 1944 abetted a shift in emphasis to the fiscal side by providing currency stability, which granted states significant discretionary freedom in the monetary realm, thus augmenting fiscal capacity.[38] In other words, if exchange rates are fixed, then monetary expansion

---

38   This is one key difference between the economics of Keynes and Green Keynesianism. The fiscal programs and policies at the core of proposals for Green Keynesianism play much less of a role in *The General Theory*, in which they are discussed largely as a means of shifting expectations, a second-choice security when monetary solutions prove inadequate. See Mann, *In the Long Run We Are All Dead.*

to support fiscal programs cannot be penalized (or speculated against) by international financial markets to anywhere near the same degree as is considered "normal" in the twenty-first century. The dismantling of Bretton Woods in the early 1970s brought the Keynesian house down, and the floating exchange rate system in place since then has helpfully greased the neoliberal wheels: sovereign debt has skyrocketed, alongside finance capital's power to "discipline" any polity, at any scale, that does not play by the fiscal rule of austerity.

In contrast to present global economic arrangements, which are organized around a reactionary state in virtually all policy realms but policing and the military, Keynesianism is fundamentally premised on a state that can have a meaningful effect on investment demand by influencing the expectations of local capitalists. Domestic expectations are the motor of this political economy. The global nature of modern trade and financial flows, not to mention of production and consumption, means it has become much more difficult, if not impossible, to manage these relationships. Domestic interest rates cannot necessarily influence expected return in a global market place, and in fact may have no relation to it. Moreover, uncertainty regarding future outcomes and the liquidity-preference that determines asset-holders' willingness to get the investment engine going are much harder to influence in a context of global flows and exchange-rate volatility. Investment demand is no longer determined at the domestic scale. Finance capital is transnational and policies that attempt to do anything other than bow and scrape before it are largely irrelevant.

The second significant difference between the present and prior Keynesian moments concerns finance. The financial structure of modern capitalism has changed radically since the 1970s. In the post-World War II era, but especially in the so-called post-Keynesian era since US President Richard Nixon, UK Prime Minister James Callaghan, and Prime Minister Pierre Trudeau of Canada, capitalism has become increasingly financialized. Financial motives, markets, actors, and institutions play increasingly powerful roles; the "pattern of accumulation in which profit-making occurs increasingly through financial channels rather than through trade and commodity production."[39]

There is nothing in the movement of financial flows per se that poses a problem for Keynesianism's viability as a political economic framework for policy and governance. Indeed, domestic flows between regions and sectors, intermediated by an integrated and stable modern financial network, are essential; coordinating such flows in the interests of employment and the efficiency of capital are fundamental to the Keynesian state's *raison d'être*. But international financial flows— especially of fast, unregulated, speculative capital—render Keynesianism extremely unstable, if not entirely unworkable. Not only are such flows myopic and volatile, but they also provide a space of investment opportunity that has no

---

39   Greta Krippner, "The Financialization of the American Economy," *Socio-economic Review* 3, 2005: 174.

real relation to employment—and even less to domestic employment anchored by secure and stable contracts (the sort that workers typically want). Profits are largely uncoupled from what used to be the best indicators of national economic well-being: income and employment levels. Almost unimaginable wealth is parked offshore, or circulates as virtually regulation-free hot money.

The third difference between Keynesianism then and what is necessary now is that, in both theory and practice, Keynesianism is driven by material through-put, whether that material is solar panels or organic avocadoes. The point of all the celebrated future green energy production is not just energy for energy's sake. All that clean energy is to be generated to power the industries that will supply all the employment, including the energy producers themselves. But factories and consulting services and restaurants all depend upon the endless production of stuff, and the circulation of commodities has ecological conse-quences even when it is powered by solar and grown next door.

Perhaps, though, as Fred Block suggests, while "a green mass consumption economy might sound like an oxymoron, it does not have to be." Maybe there is a way in which we *will* be able to consume or produce our way out of current ecological predicaments (although this is almost impossible if we expand the "we" to include those outside the already wealthy and secure liberal capitalist core). This hope, which characterizes virtually all proposals for Green New Deals and Green Keynesianism, is founded on the potential for an "accelerated shift in consumption from goods to services," which "could diminish the nega-tive environmental impacts of increased consumption since services tend to be less resource intensive than goods."[40] While this kind of thinking dominates organized labor's performative assessment of our climate futures, even the venerable *Financial Times* (which has become much more sympathetic to Keynesianism since 2008) has taken it up, arguing that "the investments needed to bring climate change under control are large but affordable and profitable."[41] Celebrating the "increasing profitability of an energy revolution" (falling renew-ables prices and rising generation capacity, negative abatement costs associated with green restructuring, and so on), columnist Martin Sandbu is convinced that "the positive effects of technology on the economics of climate change poli-cies are such as to take your breath away . . . 'cheap' does not quite capture it, 'profitable' is more like it."[42] (Believe it or not, this is to say nothing of the marvels he claims "techno-optimism" might let us imagine.)

All this sounds enormously attractive—enchanting, even. Imagine if it is true: we have in our political-economy toolbox means through which to

40   Fred Block, "Crisis and Renewal: The Outlines of a Twenty-First Century New Deal," *Socio-economic Review* 9, 2011: 44.

41   Romain Felli, "An Alternative Socio-Ecological Strategy? International Trade Unions' Engagement with Climate Change," *Review of International Political Economy*, 12, no. 2, 2014, 380; Martin Sandbu, "There Is Profit in Saving the Planet," *Financial Times*, June 16, 2015.

42   Ibid.

transform the potentially cataclysmic future into a non cataclysm (or better) of more stuff, more profits, and less First World guilt. Green Keynesian proposals are accompanied by the suite of institutions and policies associated in the ecological modernization literature with "just transition"—termination and reinvestment of fossil fuel subsidies (which amount to approximately $US 5.3 trillion annually, according to the International Monetary Fund), green investment initiatives, decentralized production and energy systems, green banks, and so on.[43] The whole package seems more than the only feasible option at this point, in addition to saving the planet from total ruin, it seems to promise a progressive solution to the problem of economic stagnation.

This is, in fact, just how Keynes intended it to appear. His goal in *The General Theory* was to provide a useful ("general") theory of capitalist modernity for the technocrats who manage a modern capitalist society. As the Marxian axiom goes, Keynes was certainly no radical. But he honestly believed that much more than capitalism was at stake: "Civilization," he wrote in 1938, is "a thin and precarious crust, erected by the personality and will of a very few, and only maintained by rules and conventions skillfully put across and guilefully preserved."[44] By the time his ideas were starting to circulate widely in the 1940s—at the end of more than thirty years of calamity in the heart of liberal capitalism—no small part of their attraction was attributable to the fact that the feeling that the whole of "civilization" was on a precipice was widely shared. This is *the* fundamental basis of Keynesianism, and today it is the existential precariousness of *civilization* (and not a general interest in Keynesian political economy) that makes the question of green Keynesianism so urgent. It promises a miracle: to organize a revolutionary transformation without revolution—we can just do what we already do, but "green", and we will be richer, more equal, *and* good stewards of Spaceship Earth. The desperate hopes placed in this regulatory response to capitalism's planetary challenges is likely to further concentrate power and resources in the hands of elites—the technocratic and economic groups with the knowledge and power to carry it out—thus rendering us even more beholden to the political status quo upon which those elites rely. This will only bolster Leviathan's pretensions to planetary sovereignty.

At this point, it is worth noting that one factor in the ongoing conflict between Leviathan and Behemoth is also one of the underlying causes of current geopolitical turbulence: the emergence of China as a global political-economic power. Unfortunately, in discussions of climate politics, China is usually considered only a problem, an amoral polluter. How often are we in North America or western Europe told our efforts to slow climate change are

43   Vitor Gaspar, Michael Keen and Ian Parry, "Climate Change: How to Price Paris," iMFdirect, International Monetary Fund, January 11, 2016, blog-imfdirect.imf.org.

44   John Maynard Keynes, "My Early Beliefs," in *Collected Writings*, Vol. X, Cambridge: Cambridge University Press, 1971–1989 [1938], 446–47.

meaningless because whatever "good" we do, "China" will ultimately render it futile? Sometimes this is a product of ignorance, sometimes of racist Eurocentrism, sometimes both.

China's capitalism clearly differs from that in Europe and North America. But this difference should be seen neither as a temporary peculiarity nor as a cultural "variety," but as the result of the specific historical and political path through which China has become fully capitalist—the consequences of which are increasingly definitive for the entire capitalist world.[45] Appreciating China's distinctiveness has important implications for climate politics and for Leviathan, and not only for the obvious reason that China's carbon emissions exceed that of all other nation-states (one quarter of the global total in 2013; per capita emissions are still relatively low, much less than half that of Canada and the United States, for example).[46] As Wang Hui explains, comprehending China's contribution to global climate change requires recentering our analysis on class politics and the international division of labor:

> In the West, many people understand China's energy consumption, environmental problems, issues with migrant workers and the exploitation of cheap labor in the context of human rights and other international protocols, but have never probed the relationship between these issues and the relocation of international industry. The relationship between China becoming the world's factory and the deindustrialization of the West should be obvious. Climate change, the energy issue, cheap labor and even the mechanisms of state oppression are all integral aspects of the new international division of labor.[47]

The dramatic rise in China's carbon emissions since 1990 is an effect of changes in the geography of the global political economy, in which China's industrial production and class relations play an increasingly central and contradictory role. China is the center of world commodity production, but most consumption occurs elsewhere. Who is responsible for the associated carbon emissions? The shift of

---

45   China is undoubtedly capitalist today, but the state controls the largest banks and owns more than 50 percent of industrial assets, which is hardly the historical norm. For divergent, compelling views of China's political economy, see G. Arrighi, *Adam Smith in Beijing: Lineages of the Twenty-first Century*, London: Verso, 2007; Joel Andreas, "Changing Colors in China," *New Left Review* II/54. 2008, 123–42; M. Blecher, *China Against the Tides: Restructuring through Revolution, Radicalism and Reform*, London: Continuum, 2010; Minqi Li, *The Rise of China and the Demise of the Capitalist World Economy*, New York: Monthly Review, 2008; Wang Hui, *China's Twentieth Century*, New York: Verso, 2016. On China's political economy and climate change, see Minqi Li, "Capitalism, Climate Change, and the Transition to Sustainability: Alternative Scenarios for the US, China and the World," *Development and Change* 40, 2009, 1039–62; Dale Wen, "Climate Change, Energy, and China," in Kolya Abramsky (ed.), *Sparking a Worldwide Energy Revolution*, Baltimore and Oakland: AK Press, 2010, 130–54. On the scale of state-owned enterprises, see World Bank, "State Owned Enterprises in China," 2010, blogs.worldbank.org.

46   Zhu Liu, *China's Carbon Emissions Report 2016*, Cambridge, MA: Harvard Belfer Center for Science and International Affairs, October 2016, belfercenter.hks.harvard.edu.

47   Wang Hui, *China's Twentieth Century*, 292.

industrial production from Europe and the United States to China has shifted the social and environmental consequences of production. The local impacts (ecosystem destruction, urban environmental degradation) have generated considerable resistance, but so far it has mostly been contained by the Communist Party.

At some point this century, the local, regional, and planetary effects of China-centered global commodity production will coalesce, accentuating the social and ecological contradictions of the current order. How will the Chinese state respond? This is undoubtedly one of the most significant questions in the world today, and notoriously difficult to assess. The absence of a formal parliamentary-democratic state apparatus with multiparty elections makes the capitalist state in China "exceptional," potentially more prone to crises in hegemonic transitions.[48] Moreover, it is difficult to measure the effectiveness of hegemonic processes in a society where signs of dissent are so effectively suppressed.[49] No doubt the waxing and waning politicization of the masses—a dynamic at the heart of modern Chinese history—will continue; but we cannot predict its direction, temporality, and effects.[50]

Although we cannot answer these complex questions, China's increasingly global leadership makes Climate Leviathan more likely than Behemoth. Simply put, elites in China are more likely to advocate capitalist planetary management than accept global disorder. Yet much depends on China's leadership and its class basis in decades to come. An abstract ideological commitment to scientifically harmonious society, like that currently advocated by the Communist Party of China, in no way guarantees its realization. The present form of hegemony in China is certain to crack and change in the face of fundamental challenges, including deepening social inequalities and environmental problems that climate change will only exacerbate. With the world's largest economy and population,

---

48   The simple existence of norms of liberal bourgeois political order do not guarantee stability, but they do facilitate nonrevolutionary transitions. As Poulantzas explains:

> one of the functions of the parliamentary-democratic state (universal suffrage, pluralism of political parties and organizations . . .) is to permit the balance of forces within the power bloc to change without a serious upheaval in the state apparatus; this is particularly the role of the constitution and of law. The parliamentary-democratic state, with an organic circulation of hegemony among different fractions of the power bloc by way of their political representatives, or even a certain regulated separation of powers between the dominant classes and fractions, only ever manages this goal in a partial way. But this proves totally impossible in the exceptional form of state.

Nicos Poulantzas, *Crisis of the Dictatorships*, London: NLB, 1976 [1975], 91. China today comprises an exceptional capitalist state not simply because it fails to meet some classical European or liberal norm, but because of its "authoritarian capitalist" quality and relative lack of civil institutions mediating between state power and the masses.

49   For instance, elites in China (the Communist Party of China) advocate an ideology of "scientific development" to build a "harmonious society:" should the apparent acceptance of this ideology by the masses be read as active consent, passive agreement, or repressed silence (or a varied combination of these)?

50   See especially Wang Hui, *China's Twentieth Century*.

the geopolitical power of the state will be enormous, but this cannot ensure its cities will be livable or its citizens satisfied with extant political arrangements. Moreover, the movements of potentially hundreds of millions of climate migrants in Asia will present important challenges to China's regional hegemony. Consequently, China will almost certainly be more powerful, but more unstable, in decades to come, even if a sudden collapse of the Communist Party of China, which has proven to be more durable and dynamic than any of the other such parties in the twentieth century, is not on the horizon.

Climate change may not, therefore, be the undoing of the hegemony of the Chinese state, but instead might trigger its reformation in the direction of planetary green Keynesianism. This is not as unlikely as it might seem at first glance. However limited or contradictory, China's climate leadership has proven much more substantive than that of almost all other capitalist societies, and if nothing else, the party's elites recognize that its self-interest requires global carbon mitigation and adaptation to rapid climate change. When President Xi warned Trump not to pull the United States out of the Paris Agreement at the 2017 Davos summit, his offered a neoliberal defense of capitalist globalization blended with Mao: "It is important to protect the environment while pursuing economic and social progress—to achieve harmony between man and nature, and harmony between man [and] society."[51] This is easier said than done, of course. Since China's capitalist political economy rests upon the transformation of commodities from around the world to produce commodities for the world over, any attempt to build a "harmonious" and/or "green" capitalist future will force the question of planetary sovereignty.

V

Like Keynesianism of any variety, green Keynesianism requires a vigorous state. Its political limits lie here, for the liberal-democratic state—at least as it currently exists—is entirely unlikely to create a green Keynesianism, at least one adequate to the problems we face. And were it capable, it would take too long. Green Keynesianism is thus a contradiction on political grounds; one with great consequences.

Perhaps Keynesianism's greatest flaw is its inability to even imagine that the

---

51   Recall that when the US and Chinese heads of state signed their climate agreement in 2014—the diplomatic event that opened the way from the post-Kyoto deadlock to the signing of the Paris Agreement—they announced it in front of the Great Wall of China. The symbolism was unmistakable: the G2's acceptance of planetary responsibility, staged on China's grounds. See The White House, Office of the Press Secretary, "US-China Joint Announcement on Climate Change," November 11, 2014. The United States and China adopted distinct positions in Paris but made a mutual commitment to it; Coral Davenport, "Obama and President Xi of China Vow to Sign Paris Climate Accord Promptly," New York Times, March 31, 2016. After the election of US President Trump, China's leadership made several strong statements reminding the United States of the importance of international leadership on climate; Chris D'Angelo "China Warns Donald Trump Against Pulling US Out of Paris Climate Pact," Huffington Post, January 17, 2017.

work required might be done without the state, because it assumes a priori that the market is the state's only "outside."[52] For Keynesians (and perhaps for all liberals), the state and market fill all the space of the social; they cannot conceive of a world in which there are multiple social fields, other spaces in which organizational or allocative work is possible. This conceptual limit is perfectly coextensive with elite common sense: all important action happens in the realm of the state *or* the market, and it is a zero-sum game (this is why liberals accuse state-backed investment of "crowding out" private capital—from their perspective, there is nothing else out there to be pushed aside). Consequently, since the market has already demonstrated its inadequacy to the task, the state is an existential *sine qua non*. For all the libertarian babble of "free markets," there is no elite social group in the world that wants the state to disappear. On the contrary, the capture of the state is almost always a defining characteristic of elite status. This helps explain why Keynesianism—green or otherwise—is so attractive in moments of crisis, and why other options seem so utopian, futile, or doomed.

Keynesianism in any one nation assumes and requires a sovereign state monopolizing both the legitimate use of violence and the legitimate allocation of resources within its territory. But planetary warming exposes the territorial nation-state as insufficient to address the crisis. With the surface of the globe covered in a chaotic and lumpy arrangement of adjacent but supposedly distinct and non-overlapping parcels, each of which has some capacity to contribute to everyone else's calamity, it is clear to global elites that no individual or subgroup of contemporary states are up to the task. What is obviously necessary is a means of governance that is not beholden to modern state sovereignty, at the same time that this necessity is denied by some of those very sovereign states. For a green Keynesian solution to the problem of catastrophic climate change, the problem of the state resolves itself only in its seemingly inescapable lack of resolution. The regulatory and decision-making role of the state, not to mention the form it takes, is completely and utterly indeterminate. The scale of the problems is so great, it seems impossible to confront them without the state, but it seems just as impossible that the state as currently constituted is going to get the job done. We face a situation in which there is, under current geopolitical and geoeconomic arrangements, no right answer.

To restate the political paradox more sharply: to address its contradictions—including the ecological contradiction that capital's growth is destroying

---

52 Keynesians' determined reinsertion of the state at the center of political economy is a product of Hegelian liberalism, that is, the legacy not of the free marketeers, but of those who understand the modern state as both the solution to the centrifugal forces of civil society and as the means to a practical quasi-utopia (the latter distinguishing Hegel from Hobbes). But just as someone like Miguel Abensour is set to convince us that politics and democracy do not need (or cannot abide by) the liberal-democratic state, so too must we recognize that the turn to the state might constrain what must be done because of what cannot be done with and by the state. See Miguel Abensour, *Democracy Against the State: Marx and the Machiavellian Moment*, Cambridge: Polity, 2011 [1997]; Mann, *In the Long Run We Are All Dead*.

the planet—capitalism needs a planetary manager, a Keynesian world state. But elites have proven reluctant to build it, and it appears unlikely to miraculously realize itself. So, the only apparent capitalist solution to climate change is presently impossible; the only even marginally possible green Keynesianism that could save us is still predicated upon the territorial nation-state. The necessary, logical corollary is to scale all the way up: in the face of planetary climate change, the success of green Keynesian programs in any one nation depends upon the commitment of all other nations. Hence the motivation to create a kind of global Green New Deal, a "Green Bretton Woods," which is clearly the idealized objective of liberal and progressive forces at every COP from Copenhagen to Paris (or wherever we next invest our hopes).[53]

This planetary Keynesianism is supposed to diminish the otherwise "inevitable" *realpolitik* that corrupts an aggregation of merely domestic arrangements by limiting the free rider or collective action problems associated with the market failure that plagues the "quintessential case of global commons." As Dani Rodrik puts it, "absent cosmopolitan considerations, each nation's optimal strategy would be to emit freely and to free-ride on the carbon controls of other countries"—the "tragedy of the commons" at a planetary scale.[54] Because Keynesianism is constructed on the assumption that self-interest and public interest can only be reconciled by the state, a pragmatic, liberal realism would look for an answer in a higher power, one that could suppress or at least contain the urge to free ride. But because of its irreducibly sovereign basis, no green Keynesian program can imagine anything other than a cosmopolitan basis for doing so, a basis which violates its own foundation in state-based sovereign autonomy. It cannot propose to construct a mechanism with a "self-interest" in planetary "ecological stimulus"[55] because that mechanism or institution would obviously require coercive power over the national component parts of the planet in which its power is "interested."

The logical conclusion of this line of thought is as clear as it is significant. A transnational Keynesianism can only be predicated on the consolidation of a transnational variation on the sovereign subject without which Keynesianism is inconceivable. A planetary green Keynesianism, the only kind that might have a hope of confronting the problem in its scale and magnitude, is thus forced down one of two planetary paths—both of which lead, ultimately, to the same destination.

The first path involves the construction of a consensual global agreement in which all parties find, if not something good, at least something better than

---

53   See, for example, Jamieson, *Reason in a Dark Time*.

54   Dani Rodrik, *The Globalization Paradox: Democracy and the World Economy*, New York: W. W. Norton, 2011, 247–49. Rodrik argues that, given the "beggar-thy-neighbor" terms in which geopolitics is currently structured, in "the case of global warming, self-interest pushed nations to ignore the risks of climate change" (249).

55   Piketty, *Capital in the Twenty-first Century*, 568.

the status quo. As Stiglitz says, "effective action has to be global; but given the deficiencies in the current system of global governance, action adequate to what needs to be done has yet to be taken."[56] Thus the contortions required by the climate treaty planners to make such an agreement imaginable, let alone workable; a plan that is essential is impossible—yet *something* must be done.[57] This is why the proposals always seem so formulaic and empty, and virtually never involve substantive targets or means and timelines for implementation.[58] The diagnosis of the problem continually takes us to the edge of the chasm between what we know is necessary and the common sense judgment that it is totally impossible.

So, to delay acknowledging that the impossible is necessary, "we" gather together at the precipice and list to each other all the qualities of a geopolitics that would make the chasm disappear. One recent assessment by influential US economists, for example, tells us that any effective global agreement will have to involve all of the following: global cooperation, adequate incentives for participation and compliance, equitability, cost-effectiveness, consistency with the international regime, verifiability, practicality, and realism.[59] The very conditions these thought experiments impose on the structure of agreements (a paradoxical response to a problem associated with *realpolitik*) make such proposals effectively unrealizable. It is like designing a bridge—a universalist, participatory, climate ethics that crosses the chasm of the "world's biggest collective action problem" to a global village on the other side—that we know will never be able to support our weight. From Kyoto to Paris, we are left stranded; hearts filled with hope, feet on crumbling soil.

We therefore come face to face with the cruel specter of the second possible path: the emergence of one nation-state, or a small set of nation-states, that arrogate to themselves the impossible institutional capacities that come with an interest in supranational "ecological stimulus." This is a Climate Leviathan that can bear the burdens required of a planetary Keynesian subject, capable of coordinating investment, distributing productive and destructive capacity, and managing free riders.

The differences between the results of these two sovereignties, if any, is unclear. Both could fill the role of Leviathan. And, to the extent that it is reasonable to expect war as the solution for a world in which isolated nation-states

---

56 Joseph Stiglitz, "Sharing the Burden of Saving the Planet: Global Social Justice for Sustainable Development Lessons from the Theory of Public Finance," in Mary Kaldor and Joseph Stiglitz (eds), *A New Global Covenant: Protection without Protectionism*, New York: Columbia University Press, 2013, 186.

57 See for example Daniel Perlmutter and Robert Rothstein, *The Challenge of Climate Change: Which Way Now?* Oxford: Wiley, 2011.

58 See for example Joseph Aldy and Robert Stavins, "Designing the Post-Kyoto Climate Regime," in Mary Kaldor and Joseph Stiglitz (eds), *A New Global Covenant: Protection without Protectionism*, New York: Columbia University Press, 2013, 205–30.

59 Ibid., 212–15.

pursue their struggles against an uneven wave of environmental disasters, even domestic green Keynesianisms lead here. We must not forget that Keynesianism was a product of world war and depended deeply upon it. One way or another, however reluctantly, the logic of capital in the Anthropocene points toward planetary sovereignty. We must therefore consider the conditions for its potential emergence.

6

Planetary Sovereignty

[Society] is gaining increasing control over its citizens but this control grows in tandem with the growth in its irrationality. And the combination of the two is constitutive . . . [T]he world is not just mad. It is mad and rational as well . . . The fact is that there is an authority that has the potential to prevent total catastrophe. This authority must be appealed to.

Theodor Adorno[1]

I

We believe the political is adapting to accommodate planetary sovereignty. The left half of our two-by-two heuristic (or "Punnett square") in Figure 2.2 represents two broad trajectories along which our world might proceed: planetary sovereigns of capitalist and noncapitalist form, technically and spatially adequate to catastrophe-as-norm, justified by the need to save life on Earth. But what could facilitate the emergence of planetary sovereignty? How could we get from our "Westphalian" world to planetary management? (And might we get there in a way that somehow preserves the territorial nation state?) In this chapter, we take up these questions. This will require us to proceed in conversation with students of international relations, where the prospect of a "world state" has been debated since the birth of the discipline. This will also involve some consideration of the philosophical sources of these debates, particularly Kant and Hegel. It may seem pedantic, but we hope to show that identifying the roots of contemporary thinking can provide a stronger basis for analyzing geopolitical changes to come.

The goal is not to predict the future. We cannot, of course, nor can anyone else. But, thanks to planetary climate change, most of us cannot help trying. Who hasn't tried to anticipate what the world's food and water will look like in thirty or a hundred years—and, more importantly, who hasn't imagined how people will react to those conditions? What parent, on a scorching summer day, has not conjured up (usually with dread) their children's or grandchildren's future? And who on the Left has not dwelled, at least briefly, on how to ensure those dreadful futures do not come to pass?

---

1 Theodor Adorno, in Adorno and Max Horkheimer, *Towards a New Manifesto*, New York; Verso, 2011[1956], 38–40.

On political and existential grounds, then, the Left needs a strategy—a political theory, one might say—for how to think about the future. It will no longer do to repeat Marx's insight that all predictions of the future are at best idealist, at worst reactionary (though there is still much wisdom in it). For all its limitations, thoughtful speculation is analytically and politically superior to all the other options currently available: pretending everything is "normal", embracing the false hopes peddled by techno-utopians, abandoning ourselves to nihilism ("we're fucked"), or, worse still, validating the visions of the apocalyptic books and films that transmute our fears into spectacular, dystopian commodities. If there is a low bar against which we can measure thoughtful speculation, it is Hollywood's aestheticization of anxiety and panic.

Careful speculation must be well-grounded, attentive and skeptical. Despite the best intentions, it is easy to succumb to simplistic and partial analyses. Even when thoughtful and well-informed scholars speculate regarding our climate-political futures, like Naomi Oreskes and Eric Conway do in their "cli-fi" novella *The Collapse of Western Civilization*, the results can be less than convincing. The book is an attempt to diagnose the present by projecting it into a dystopian future, a post-apocalyptic year 2393:

> [W]arnings of climate catastrophe went ignored for decades, leading to soaring temperatures, rising sea levels, widespread drought and . . . the Great Collapse of 2093, when the disintegration of the West Antarctica Ice Sheet led to mass migration and a complete reshuffling of the global order. Writing from the Second People's Republic of China on the 300th anniversary of the Great Collapse, a senior scholar presents a gripping and deeply disturbing account of how the children of the Enlightenment—the political and economic elites of the so-called advanced industrial societies—failed to act, and so brought about the collapse of Western civilization.[2]

The introduction explains how "a second Dark Age had fallen on Western civilization" thanks to "an ideological fixation on 'free' markets."[3] The adoption of the future-anterior allows the narrative to moralize about the ills of neoliberalism and the dystopian world we are told ("retrospeculatively") to which it will

---

2   Naomi Oreskes and Erik Conway, *The Collapse of Western Civilization*, New York: Columbia University Press, 2014, cover. *Collapse* is their second book together. The first, *Merchants of Doubt: How a Handful of Scientists Obscured the Truth on Issues from Tobacco Smoke to Global Warming*, New York: Bloomsbury Press, 2010, traces the rise of climate denialism in the United States. It focuses on the work of Cold War scientists, specialists in nuclear and rocketry research, who later collaborated with right-wing think tanks to lay the basis for climate denialism. *Merchants of Doubt* provides valuable, original research. Unfortunately, as in *The Collapse of Western Civilization*, climate change is ultimately blamed on neoliberal ideology—the explanation for scientists' willingness to collaborate with the fossil fuel industry—without an analysis of neoliberalism. The relation between the liberal framework implicit in *Merchants of Doubt* and the neoliberal object of its critique is left unexamined.

3   Oreskes and Conway, *The Collapse of Western Civilization*, ix.

lead: Chinese-led, state-governed, and "Neocommunist."[4] Orestes and Conway spell out the moral of the story in the penultimate paragraph: "China's ability to weather disastrous climate change vindicated the necessity of centralized government, leading to the establishment of . . . Neocommunist China . . . By blocking anticipatory action, neoliberals . . . fostered expansion of the forms of governance they most abhorred."[5]

What is most striking about this fantasy—which is, it bears emphasis, a liberal fantasy about the defeat of neoliberalism—is its explicitly geographical framing: planetary climate change causes the collapse of *Western* civilization and abets the consolidation of a Chinese (and therefore *non*-Western) civilization, upon which the future world-state is centered—*if* neoliberalism wins the day in today's "West." The novella thus maps the contemporary climate debate on Orientalist terms: inaction on climate change today means China wins and the "West" is lost.[6] The narrative is not only Eurocentric but deterministic, with shades of Malthus for full effect. The collapse of Western civilization is credited to the break-up of the West Antarctic Ice Sheet. Causal mechanisms are not specified, but ensuing mass migration and disease are implied.[7]

The future world map is stark. The only countries of what was once Western civilization are the United Kingdom (rechristened "Cambria"), Germany, the United States, and Canada. None of Africa's 54 countries is ever named. Indeed, the fate of Africa comes up only three times in the book, always as a metaphor for disaster: first, starvation; then when "governments were overthrown, particularly in Africa"; finally as African "populations" are wiped out, at which point the continent leaves the stage, its narrative function fulfilled.[8] The story lies elsewhere, with Western thinkers, who fail to

---

4 Ibid., 42–52. *The Collapse of Western Civilization* blames neoliberal ideology for "civilizational" collapse, and in that sense shares a problematic quality with Naomi Klein's *This Changes Everything* (and many other texts circulating in the climate justice movement): it attributes our problems to neoliberalism, which is to say the problem is not capitalism, but the current version of capitalism. We are unconvinced. Capitalism may not be the *only* problem, but it is surely one of the big ones.

5 Ibid.

6 The unwillingness of Oreskes and Conway to give the story's "Chinese" narrator any subjective qualities, narrative function, or even a name, exacerbates the text's Orientalism. Their anonymous China is solely a screen foisted by Western writers in front of themselves on which they project their anxieties about "civilization." This narrative loses all its force without the assumption that China's return to pre-eminence in the world system is necessarily a negative development. A useful counterpoint is Giovanni Arrighi's *Adam Smith in Beijing: Lineages of the 21st Century*, New York: Verso, 2007.

7 "The ultimate blow for Western civilization came . . . [with] the collapse of the West Antarctica Ice Sheet" (29). It might be a fantasy novel, but this is textbook environmental determinism. The place in the text where a causal hypothesis about the "collapse" belongs is, appropriately enough, marked by a blank (31). The unnamed narrator fills this void with the statement, "There is no need to rehearse the details of the human tragedy that occurred" (31).

8 Oreskes and Conway, *The Collapse of Western Civilization*: Africa's "starvation" (25), "governments . . . overthrown" (25); "wiped out" (33).

appreciate the disaster awaiting their civilization. "It was the rare man," we are told, who appreciated what was coming to the West. One "exception" was "Paul Ehrlich, whose book *The Population Bomb* was widely read . . . but *considered to have been discredited*."[9] The implication could not be clearer: Paul Erlich was right. We should have built the Planetary Regime he and Holdren proposed. Our failure to do so will precipitate the collapse of the West and the victory of the East.

This is a best-selling book.[10] It is a fantastic account by US "progressives" of their own worst nightmare, in which the ascendency of a planet-saving Climate Leviathan is blocked by reactionary Climate Behemoth (represented by the "neoliberal" denialism and market fundamentalism the book was written to attack), which forces the world on to the path of Climate Mao ("neocommunist" China). Donald Trump's election might tempt us to buy into this fantasy, but if the Left has any hope in the struggle for a better world, we must do speculation better than this. This means taking up the challenge of speculating on political futures to tell a better story—but all the while laying out our analytical assumptions, historicizing our concepts and claims, and addressing the capitalist social relations that define our political-economic order accurately and without despondency.

The problem of causality is of course a major challenge in these efforts. We cannot simply avoid causal claims, or our speculation will lose all coherence. But we must avoid the pitfalls of functionalism ("It must be this way for the system to function") or misplaced concreteness, which is a common problem from science ("By 2100 the sea level rise 2.2 meters; that means chaos"). But how can we speculate without falling back on mechanical causality (or wild guesses)? With respect to climate politics, most models are premised on a simple logical progression: rapid climate change → resource conflict → violence → social breakdown; or rapid climate change → resource conflict → social breakdown → violence, and so on. The order of the last three "stages" varies because climate change involves a vast array of physical changes. In any event, the narrative permutations are endless. Oreskes and Conway's story, for example, goes like this: West Antarctic Ice Sheet collapse → mass migration and disease → end of Western civilization.

Notwithstanding an impressive body of literature that draws correlations between discrete effects of climate change (such as more or less rain) and social conflict (more or less fighting), social scientists are a long way from being able to establish the "truth" of any of these simple causal models.[11] Certainly these

---

9   Ibid., 3–4, emphasis added.

10   As of June 21, 2016, it was the fourth bestseller in climatology and fifth in environmental policy at amazon.com (United States). At its peak, the book was the best seller in both categories.

11   There is at least one large, well-funded group of intellectuals at work on these models, because they are understood to be fundamental to the success of their organization: the US military. The literature on climate and US national security (or in more critical studies, "climate

models cannot be scaled up from empirical cases to support meaningful claims about the future of the entire planet. There are simply too many analytical problems involved.[12] Moreover, many so-called solutions to the changes these models predict (in other words, adaptations) are themselves expressions of the "problems" being modelled. For example, US military models suggest that water shortages in the Middle East will increase social conflict later this century. This is difficult to dispute, particularly given temperature trends for the region that are "projected to exceed a threshold for human adaptability:"

> A plausible analogy of future climate for many locations in Southwest Asia is the current climate of the desert of Northern Afar on the African side of the Red Sea, a region with no permanent human settlements owing to its extreme climate.[13]

The US military has already been charged with planning for these developments. Anyone with cursory knowledge of the results of the past century of US involvement in the Middle East would expect the US response to these changes to be "adaptations" that are themselves violent and destabilizing, even if their exact forms and consequences are impossible to predict.

Fortunately, we on the Left need not bang our heads against these walls, as there is another way to approach this. We do not need the "correct" causal model of climate change and civilization for our thinking and politics to be coherent and effective. The impossibility of accurate prediction does not mean we should throw up our hands and give up trying to anticipate a range of futures. Instead, the challenge of all climate futures centers on the question of the political. How the world will respond *politically* to climate change and its effects is the key question in every model or theory. Indeed, given the importance of anthropogenic impacts on climatic processes in the decades ahead, political responses will matter enormously to both human and nonhuman communities. In fact, it would be more accurate to speak of our object of analysis as the "climate/

---

change and securitization") has grown rapidly over the past decade. A good starting point is a pair of 2007 documents from the US foreign-policy and intelligence communities: Joshua W. Busby, *Climate Change and National Security: An Agenda for Action,* Council on Foreign Relations, CSR No. 32; and Kurt Campbell, Jay Gulledge, J. R. McNeill, John Podesta, et al., *The Age of Consequences: The Foreign Policy and National Security Implications of Global Climate Change,* Washington, DC: Center for a New American Security (available for download online; republished as a book by the Brookings Institution in 2008). See also Daniel Moran (ed.), *Climate Change and National Security: A Country-Level Analysis,* Washington, DC: Georgetown University Press, 2011 (a product of a workshop organized by the US National Intelligence Council). For more critical perspectives, see Michael Redclift and Marco Grasso (eds), *Handbook on Climate Change and Human Security,* Cheltenham, UK: Edward Elgar, 2013. Very little scholarly work has been published on the US military's programs for predicting future climate change (dis)order.

12   For example, specifying variables. What constitutes meaningful climate change for one place may not be meaningful elsewhere. Moreover, for complex planetary systems, it is impossible to draw boundaries between objects or processes inside and outside the model.

13   Jeremy S. Pal and Elfatih A. Eltahir, "Future Temperature in Southwest Asia Projected to Exceed a Threshold for Human Adaptability," *Nature Climate Change* 6, no. 2, 2016, 197–200.

political change complex." That complex could never be modelled on a simple causal basis.[14]

Where does this leave us? If we return to our focus on the adaptation of the political, our approach to causality has at least two requirements. First, we must aim to identify tendencies and contradictions in the prevailing political-economic order, and thereby to sketch out the possible pathways by which it could change. Second, we must historicize the very political and philosophical concepts through which we understand these tendencies and contradictions. The goal is not a mechanistic model of the future but a complex, theoretically informed lens through which to speculate coherently.

II

The idea that the political is adapting toward planetary sovereignty has many antecedents. A long history could be written on fantastic projections and rejections of "world government," extending at least as far back as Plato. These works—which include those of Kant, for example, or more contemporary thinkers like Hannah Arendt and Antonio Negri—raise an important line of questions. If earlier thinkers anticipated world government (or something like it) and yet it still does not exist, then how can we judge the merits of our claims about Climate Leviathan? And yet, to prevent tomorrow's catastrophe, to what forms of authority do we appeal today? Our aim in this chapter is to approach this question through a brief history of the idea of a world state. This is not a causal history but an attempt to ground our analysis in the ideas of some engaging thinkers who thought they knew where we were going.

Like Hobbes, Kant is a foundational "modern" thinker, but he is not always thought of as a political philosopher. His most important political writings were composed after the *Critique of Pure Reason* (1781), when Europe was in the midst of profound upheaval. Kant's life coincided with the consolidation of the capitalist nation-state in Western Europe, and his analysis of the ethical prospects for life was a response to its emergence. He is among the best-known advocates of the rights and dignity of the reasoning individual, a position typically interpreted as a way-station between Rousseau and modern liberalism. But this interpretation leaves ample room for debate and the politics of his writings are not easily fixed. Some read Kant's political works as justifying the emerging order, similar to Hobbes's *Leviathan*. Others, however, point to the fact that Kant criticizes Hobbes for his "authoritarian view of sovereignty . . . and his

---

14   In fairness, these insights can be gleaned from Intergovernmental Panel on Climate Change, Fifth Assessment Report, Working Group II, 2014, www.ipcc-wg2.awi.de. Chapter 12, "Human Security," open to multiple interpretations. For a critical survey of recent literature on the climate–violence nexus, see Eric Bonds, "Upending Climate Violence Research: Fossil Fuel Corporations and the Structural Violence of Climate Change," *Human Ecology Review* 22, no. 2, 2016, 3–23.

explanation of society based on a psychological assumption, that of the fear of sudden death."[15] More importantly, Kant's political analysis points toward a radically different world than the one in which he lived. We can read his political writings as both an analysis of change underway in Europe, but also as speculative critique.

His discussion of cosmopolitanism is central to this critique. Kant postulated a politics in which people act as if they were ethically responsible to all others, even those who are different. This position is often equated with the liberal multiculturalism of our times, a contradiction-riven ideology that has proven more than useful to US hegemony and imperialism. But if we return to his outline of cosmopolitanism in his famous essay, "On Perpetual Peace" it is not so straightforward. When Kant was writing, Europe was caught up in the upheaval initiated by the French Revolution. The standard interpretation is that Kant wrote "On Perpetual Peace" to outline a liberal vision of the outcome of these transformations, an argument for the creation of a federation of republican constitutional states that solidified some legacies of the Revolution (like bourgeois freedom), while subduing others (like popular resistance to the state). But Kant also specifies conditions to guarantee the stability of that kind of federation, conditions that would have been considered quite radical in his time (and in some respects still are):

> The Sugar Islands, that stronghold of the cruellest and most calculated slavery, do not yield any real profit; they serve only the indirect . . . purpose of training sailors for warships, thereby aiding the prosecution of wars in Europe. And all this is the work of powers who make endless ado about their piety, and who wish to be considered as chosen believers while they live on the fruits of iniquity.
>
> The peoples of the earth have thus entered in varying degrees into a universal community, and it has developed to the point where a violation of rights in *one* part of the world is felt everywhere. The idea of a cosmopolitan right is therefore not fantastic and overstrained; it is a necessary complement to the unwritten code of political and international right, transforming it into a universal right of humanity. Only under this condition can we flatter ourselves that we are continually advancing toward a perpetual peace.[16]

These lines were written in 1795, during the Haitian Revolution, and reflect Kant's critique of European colonialism, slavery, and war. He equates cosmopolitanism with the "right to the earth's surface which the human race shares in common" and criticizes those who would justify European colonization on the grounds of natural right.

---

15 Hans Reiss, "Preface," in Hans Reiss (ed.), *Kant's Political Writings*, Second Edition, Cambridge: Cambridge University Press, 1991, 10.

16 Kant, "On Perpetual Peace," in *Political Writings*, 107–8, emphasis in original; see also Proverbs 22:8, "He who sows iniquity will reap vanity"; and Job 4:8, "Even as I have seen, they that plow iniquity, and sow wickedness, reap the same."

[T]his natural right of hospitality, i.e. the right of strangers, does not extend beyond those conditions which make it possible for them to *attempt* to enter into relations with the native inhabitants. In this way, continents distant from each other can enter into peaceful mutual relations which may eventually be regulated by public laws, thus bringing the human race nearer and nearer to a cosmopolitan constitution.[17]

This "cosmopolitan constitution" is not exactly a "world government," but it is not so far from one either. Kant's federation of republican states respecting rights "the human race shares in common" presupposes a degree of collectivity. But he also presumes the federation's members will be republican governments, because he believed it would be impossible to bring every state (or territory) under a single power. This might sound like a proposal for something like the United Nations (UN), but the contemporary UN system falls far short of Kant's conditions for peace: he called for the elimination of standing armies and an end to all preparation for war, and he insisted the Republic should not be led by a subgroup with the capacity to dominate the others.[18] Virtually every member of the UN has a standing army, and the system is dominated by a Security Council, composed of a handful of capitalist nation-states with the most powerful militaries in history.

This is not to suggest that Kant was some naïve Pollyanna, crossing his fingers in the hope that everyone would be nice to each other and it would all work out in the end. On the contrary, he was highly skeptical of the capacities of either humans or states to realize their conscious wills or good intentions. He was far closer to Hobbes on this count than the idea of a "perpetual peace" might superficially suggest. As Kojin Karatani—who understands Kant as far more radical than he is usually taken to be—puts it, Kant "was fully aware of the deep-seated violence in human nature, which he called 'unsocial sociability.' At the same time, he believed that this violence could ultimately be contained . . . According to Kant, the federation of states, and subsequently a world republic, will be brought about not by human goodwill and intelligence but through 'unsocial sociability' and war."[19]

Other problems arise when equating Kant's vision with the existing liberal world order, both in the political-institutional and the political-economic realms. As much as he has been recruited in support of enormously influential liberal models of civil society (by John Rawls and Jürgen Habermas, for

---

17   Ibid., 106. For contrary views, compare Chad Kautzer, "Kant, Perpetual Peace, and the Colonial Origins of Modern Subjectivity," *Peace Studies Journal* 6, no. 2, 2013, 58–67; and Inés Valdez, "It's Not About Race: Good Wars, Bad Wars, and the Origins of Kant's Anti-Colonialism," *American Political Science Review* 111, no. 4, 819–34.

18   The UN "is far from the Kantian idea of the federation of nations." Kojin Karatani, "Beyond Capital-Nation-State," *Rethinking Marxism* 20, no. 4, 2008, 592.

19   Ibid., 591 2.

example), Kant was by no means uncritical of the economic mechanisms that (almost always implicitly) make every one of these models tick: capitalist markets mediated by money. In all liberal models, civil society is built upon— sometimes even constituted in—capitalist exchange. But in "On Perpetual Peace," Kant calls money the "most reliable instrument of war," and thus a major obstacle to cosmopolitanism.[20] He proposes a social life based on the recognition of the dignity of all, and dignity is "above any price."[21]

This "cosmopolitan constitution" founded in universal dignity sits in an uncomfortable but very common political position, a speculative proposal that is simultaneously radically progressive and romantic, even nostalgic. When Kant mourns the fact that in his day, it seemed increasingly true that "I need not think, *so long as I can pay*; others will soon enough take the tiresome job over for me," he is celebrating the possibility that enlightenment might overcome this vulgarity.[22] The "universal community" in which he says "the peoples of the earth" are now united is a speculative contribution that attempts to address both these concerns. It is a political step forward in history, away from war and hate, but also a step up, away from the gritty and crude concerns of self-interested production and exchange, and toward the idealized realm of "public reason," a "universal community—a world society of citizens."[23]

If the latter sounds a lot like Rawls's "original position" or Habermas's "intersubjective discourse ethics," that is because these ideas are indeed close relatives. This is the Kant that has become so central to liberal political theory, while remaining much less central—even a little annoying—to liberal political economy. Kant sneers at civic life organized around money and exchange, and his announcement of the "world society" of reasoning citizens is his performative sublation of the contradictions of modernity—enlightened reason alongside crass self-interest—in the hope that it will help make it so. This vision of a peaceful universal community has been continually set aside by the political economy that has dominated the ensuing centuries but always with the promise that at some point, capitalism will make us wealthy enough to realize it. In that sense, at least, all liberalism secretly anticipates a world government on the horizon of history.

III

Hegel could not see any worldly basis for Kant's cosmopolitan, demilitarized, perpetual peace. To him, the idea of something "above" the state that could resolve interstate conflict was wishful thinking. As he put it in the *Philosophy of*

---

20   Kant, "On Perpetual Peace," 95.
21   Immanuel Kant, *Groundwork of the Metaphysics of Morals*, Second Edition, Cambridge: Cambridge University Press, 2012, 46.
22   Kant, *Political Writings*, 54, emphasis added.
23   Kant, "An Answer to the Question, What is Enlightenment?" in *Political Writings*, 54–60.

Right, written in the wake of the seemingly endless wars initiated by Napoleon's liberal imperialism:

> There is no praetor to adjudicate between states; but at most arbitrators and mediators, and even the presence of these will be contingent, i.e. determined by particular wills. Kant's idea of a *perpetual peace* guaranteed by a federation of states which would settle all disputes and which, as a power recognized by each individual state, would resolve all disagreements so as to make it impossible for these to be settled by war presupposes an *agreement* between states. But this agreement, whether based on moral, religious, or other grounds and considerations, would always be dependent particular sovereign wills, and would therefore continue to be tainted with contingency.[24]

In short, specific conflicts between states must give rise to some kind of trans-state institution (like a UN envoy attempting to facilitate negotiation between states to resolve a boundary dispute), but there is no way for such contingent and limited instances to "grow" into Kant's "world society of citizens." In instances where different states are in conflict, Hegel leaves two paths open: they can come to some agreement, or, "if no agreement can be reached between particular wills, conflicts between states can only be settled by *war*."[25]

It is not impossible that Hegel's skepticism regarding the prospects for a "cosmopolitan constitution" was based in part on living through the reactionary ruins of what might be seen as Napoleon's failed and bloody attempt to realize it. In any event, his critique points toward two possible political conclusions.[26] On one hand, from what we might call the "realist" position, Kant's conception of cosmopolitanism is a fanciful dream. World government is simply impossible. This view, which may seem justifiable today, sees the existing state-based world order as the "natural" geopolitical equilibrium. It might occasionally be unsettled, but in the long-run it is a stable and permanent order.

On the other hand, it is possible to draw a dramatically different conclusion from Hegel's critique. If the "realist" position takes it as affirming the ultimate inevitability of the state-based logic of the existing order, and therefore of inter-state war, it does so essentially by countering the idea of "perpetual peace" with its "realist" opposite, perpetual (or at least inevitable) war. But one could also understand Hegel's argument not as asserting the impossibility of peace (because we will always have war), but rather the impossibility of perpetuity *per se*. If so, the problem is not Kant's speculative perpetual *peace*, but his uncritical assumption that we can have a perpetual condition, or historical equilibrium, of any

---

24   G. W. F. Hegel, *Philosophy of Right*, Cambridge: Cambridge University Press, 1991, §333, emphasis in original.

25   Ibid., §334, emphasis in original.

26   There is a large literature on Hegel's philosophical criticisms of Kant. For a helpful overview, see John McCumber, *Understanding Hegel's Mature Critique of Kant*, Stanford, CA: Stanford University Press, 2014.

kind at all. From this perspective, we should expect unceasing contradiction and political change, or what we would now call struggles for hegemony.

> Since the sovereignty of states is the principle governing their mutual relations, they exist to that extent in a state of nature in relation to each other, and their rights are *actualized* in a universal with constitutional powers over them, but in their own particular wills . . . [I]nternational law remains only an *obligation*, and the [normal] condition will be for relations governed by treaties to alternate with the suspension of such relations.[27]

These struggles within states (involving different social groups) and between states (for recognition, resources, territory and so on) drive an ensemble of interrelations from one order to another in a constantly shifting dynamic. This process has no necessary end, and could always result in any number of outcomes—in other words, it will "continue to be tainted with contingency."

IV

Political economy was essential to Hegel's political analysis. The earthly concerns of people going about their days in nothing if not contingent ways was for him not a quotidian distraction from modern politics, but its heart. Justice or "Right" might always be bound to reason, but it was also inseparable from lived necessity. If, as Hegel thought, Kant abandoned those concerns in anticipation of a supranational "world society" that could live forever on the nourishment of reason, he was of little help to those of us who remained tied to a tumultuous state-centered world. In that world, there is no perpetual stability, and philosophical concepts manifest in the cruder grammar of international relations and political economy: great powers, hegemony, empires and dynamic social conditions inside and between the dynamic collectivities we call states.

Nevertheless, this is the world in which Alex Wendt, a "constructivist" international relations theorist, identifies forces compelling us toward what he calls an "inevitable world state."[28] Both propositions (a world state and its inevitability) might seem ludicrous. Indeed, in his 2009 presidential address to the International Studies Association, Thomas Weiss quipped that "[t]he surest way to secure classification as a crackpot is to mention a world government as either a hypothetical or, worse yet, desirable outcome."[29] But the prospects for some

---

27 Hegel, *Philosophy of Right*, §333.
28 Alexander Wendt, "Why a World State is Inevitable," *European Journal of International Relations* 9, no. 4, 2003, 491–542. Constructivist international relations focuses on the construction of forms of recognition among and between states.
29 Thomas Weiss, "What Happened to the Idea of World Government?" *International Studies Quarterly* 53, 2009, 261. See also Weiss, *Thinking about Global Governance*, New York: Routledge, 2012.

form of world government are still very much alive in the form of planetary sovereignty. The simple reason for this is, as Adorno says in this chapter's epigraph, the demand for "an authority that has the potential to prevent total catastrophe" (he was thinking of nuclear annihilation). In the face of catastrophe, "[t]his authority must be appealed to."[30]

As mentioned earlier, many have wondered at the possibility of a world government or, more accurately, a world state. In the wake of the multiple catastrophes of the 1940s and after—World War II, the Holocaust, the annihilation of Hiroshima and Nagasaki, not to mention the Korean war, anticolonial wars the world over, and on and on—there was a vibrant philosophical debate on the merits of and prospects for a world state. Albert Einstein and Bertrand Russell, among others, were among its most passionate advocates. They argued that the existence of weapons capable of rendering the planet uninhabitable created a situation in which humanity faced a clear binary choice: to either overcome the interstate system's anarchic tendency toward conflict (thus realizing Kant's dream of a peaceful republic), or to destroy itself.[31] Renewing Kant's proposal in the context of looming catastrophe, Einstein argued:

> A world government must be created which is able to solve conflicts between nations by juridical decision. This government must be based on a clear-cut constitution which is approved by the governments and nations and which gives it the sole disposition of offensive weapons.[32]

Days after the United States bombed Hiroshima in August 1945, Bertrand Russell wrote:

> It is impossible to imagine a more dramatic and horrifying combination of scientific triumph with political and moral failure than has been shown to the world in the destruction of Hiroshima . . . The prospect for the human race is sombre beyond all precedent. Mankind are faced with a clear-cut alternative: either we shall all perish, or we shall have to acquire some slight degree of common sense . . . Either war or civilization must end, and if it is to be war that ends, there must be an international authority with the sole power to make the new bombs. All supplies of uranium must be placed under the control of the international authority, which shall have the right to safeguard the ore by armed forces. As soon as such an authority has been created, all existing atomic bombs, and all plants for their manufacture, must be handed over. And of course the international authority must have sufficient

---

30   Adorno and Horkheimer, *Towards a New Manifesto*, 40.

31   See Catherine Lu, "World Government," in Edward N. Zalta (ed.), *Stanford Encyclopedia of Philosophy* (Winter 2016 Edition), plato.stanford.edu.

32   Albert Einstein, "Towards a World Government," in *Out of My Later Years*, New York: Wings, 1956 [1946], 138, cited in Lu, "World Government."

armed forces to protect whatever has been handed over to it. If this system were once established, the international authority would be irresistible, and wars would cease.[33]

This "nuclear one-worldism," was attractive to many on the Left after World War II.[34] Whatever its philosophical merits, it was defeated by history—another victim of the Cold War. To his credit, Russell predicted this in 1945. "But I fear all this is Utopian. The United States will not consent to any pooling of armaments, and no more will Soviet Russia. Each will insist on retaining the means of exterminating the other."[35]

Most political philosophers did not follow the Einstein-Russell line of thought. In the shadow of the world-historical division between the United States and the Soviet Union, for many, the unity between sovereigns seemed not only impossible but terrifying. As Hannah Arendt put it, the purpose of the "World Government" that so many dreamed would save the planet from nuclear annihilation "is to overcome and eliminate authentic politics, that is, different peoples getting along with each other in the full force of their power."[36] Throughout her life, Arendt associated the aspiration to a world state with totalitarianism, for which all opposition, anywhere, is treason.[37] This connection could not even be severed by a well-intended "supernational authority," which would "either be ineffective or be monopolized by the nation that happens to be the strongest, and so would lead to world government, which could easily become the most frightful tyranny conceivable."[38]

It might seem from this assessment of our political prospects that Arendt is reprising the "realist" critique of Kant. Unlike individuals who have their own dignity and yet may unite through a collective will, multiple states never form a general will. With respect to one another, they always remain in a state of nature. Their fundamental bond is effectively negative—as she said, "a guaranteed peace on earth is as utopian as the squaring of the circle." However— and this is a crucial "however"—this is only true "so long as national independence, namely freedom from foreign rule, and the sovereignty of the state, namely, the claim to unchecked and unlimited power in foreign affairs, are identified."[39]

Arendt's argument is by no means a firm endorsement of Kant's perpetual

33   Bertrand Russell, "The Bomb and Civilization," *The Glasgow Forward* 39, no. 33, 18 August 1945, accessible at russell.mcmaster.ca.

34   Daniel Deudney, *Bounding Power: Republican Security Theory from the Polis to the Global Village*, Princeton, NJ: Princeton University Press, 2007.

35   Russell, "The Bomb and Civilization."

36   Arendt, *Origins of Totalitarianism*, 142, n. 38.

37   Ibid., 420.

38   Hannah Arendt, "Thoughts on Politics and Revolution," in *Crises of the Republic*, New York: Harcourt, Brace, 1972, 230.

39   Ibid., 229.

peace, but neither is it a resigned realism. The existential crisis of "mutually assured destruction" shaped her thinking no less than Russell's, but the conclusion she drew was more "conceptual" (if in the most "applied" manner possible). In a world in which war "among the great powers has become impossible owing to the monstrous development of the means of violence," we have outgrown "the state concept and its sovereignty," which together ensure "between sovereign states there can be no last resort except war."[40] Like Kant, she sees "federation" as the only institutional solution, but an explicitly "*inter*national authority."[41] That authority would be interstate, but founded on a "new state concept"—in other words, an adaptation of the political—in which "the federated units mutually check and control their powers."[42]

Is it possible to imagine transcending this proposal—toward a nontotalitarian world state of collective recognition? After many years on the sometimes cranky margins of political debate, the debate on world government is back on the agenda—partly because of the end of the Cold War, and partly because of a growing recognition of global ecological crisis. Alex Wendt has been central to this revival, and his "Why a World State is Inevitable" proposes a teleological argument that world government is not only coming, but is inevitable.

His claim is based in the logic of weapons development. States naturally compete with one another because they must defend themselves (their citizens). This leads them to seek "defense," that is, weaponry sufficient to compel other states to recognize them. Since the development of weapons technology is temporally and spatially uneven, different states will have different capacities for "defense," which generates a persistent anxiety regarding one's capacity to ensure recognition. For international relations realists, this leads to a cul-de-sac in world affairs, where the omega point of interstate relations is a perpetual anarchy of mutual suspicion, competitive preparations for "defense" (war) and, at best, stability through hegemony. But, in a manner that recalls earlier contributions to the debate, Wendt argues that the development of ever-more-dreadful weaponry fatally undermines this argument. Interstate defensive competition has led to a situation in which the destruction of states (perhaps all of them) is likely. There are just too many weapons of mass destruction. The end-state or *telos* to which the world state system tends must shift, "the struggle for recognition between states" leads to a new phase: "collective identity formation and eventually a [world] state."[43]

Wendt's theory builds explicitly on Kant's and Hegel's thoughts on the

40   Ibid., 229–30.
41   Ibid., 231, emphasis in original.
42   Ibid., 230.
43   Wendt, "Why a World State Is Inevitable," 493.

political order that emerged out of the French Revolution. He accepts both Kant's pessimistic assessment of humans' "unsocial sociability" and Hegel's diagnosis of the dynamic and ongoing struggle for recognition. For Wendt, "the struggle of individuals and groups for recognition of their subjectivity . . . is channeled toward a world state by the logic of anarchy, which generates a tendency for military technology and war to become increasingly destructive."[44] The difficult question—which many might legitimately believe unanswerable—is toward which ends is the interstate system driven by these dynamics?

> Three end-states suggest themselves—[1] a pacific federation of republican states, [2] a realist world of nation-states in which war remains legitimate, and [3] a world state. The first is associated with Kant and the second with Hegel, both of whom based their projections on explicitly teleological arguments. In rejecting the possibility of a world state, therefore, they agreed that, strictly speaking, anarchy would remain the organizing principle of the system, albeit different kinds of anarchy. As to the mechanism of progress, in different ways Kant and Hegel also both emphasized the role of conflict— Kant in man's "unsociable sociability," and Hegel in the "struggle for recognition" . . . While envisioning a tendency for conflict to create republican states, Kant did not expect them to develop a collective identity. His states remain egoists who retain their sovereignty. Hegel provides the basis for a different conclusion, since the effect of the struggle for recognition is precisely to transform egoistic identity into collective identity, and eventually a state. But Hegel expects this outcome only in the struggle between individuals. States too seek recognition, but in his view they remain self-sufficient totalities. Their struggle for recognition does not produce supranational solidarity, leaving us at the "end of history" with a world of multiple states . . .[45]

From this combination of Kantian and Hegelian premises (recast along teleological lines), Wendt finds a basis for the emergence of a world state. There are two crucial conditions for this pathway. First, states' struggles for recognition must to lead to a type of collective identity. There must be some emergent principle that unites the most powerful states (the rest will follow), undoing the conditions in which, as Hegel put it, "the relations of states to one another has sovereignty as its principle."[46] Second, there must be some means for the world state to be realized, not only in principle but concretely; in other words, the world state would need to meet the criteria of a state. If these two conditions hold, Wendt argues that "the struggle for recognition between states will have the same outcome as that between individuals, collective identity formation and eventually a state."

---

44   Ibid., 491.
45   Ibid.
46   What other principles these could be with respect to Climate Leviathan is a question to which we will return.

> One reason for this concerns . . . the role of technology. Kant rejected the possibility of a world state in part because the technology of his day precluded it, and in positing an end-state in which war remained legitimate Hegel did not think its costs would become intolerable. Neither anticipated the dramatic technological changes of the past century, which are in part caused by the security dilemma and thus endogenous to anarchy. As Daniel Deudney convincingly argues, these changes have greatly increased the costs of war and also the scale on which it is possible to organize a state.[47]

The basic logic of Wendt's "inevitable" world state is the same as Russell's and Einstein's in the 1940s, although the weapons have become much more powerful, accurate, and mobile (which only makes the Einstein-Russell arguments more sensible).[48] In effect, the Cold War suspended the world-state debate: its end, while sometimes celebrated as the "end of history," has also brought another conclusion: the return of the prospect of world government.

Wendt says the struggle for recognition among states, combined with changes in technology, will drive the system toward a world state. In other words, he shares Arendt's conclusion that war is no longer a viable "last resort". Arendt, however, seemed to have little faith in the power of looming obliteration to compel the adaptation of the political that might enable the world to attain peace. Moreover, she associated pretensions to world government with the "most frightful tyranny." Wendt is much more "optimistic," both insofar as he expects that reaching the threshold of assured destruction will force the world to adapt, and in his faith that nontotalitarian world government is not an oxymoron.

---

47   Ibid., 493, emphasis added. See Deudney, *Bounding Power*.

48   The logic of nuclear one-worldism has interesting historical intersections with climate politics. The development of the global climate change models at the heart of the IPCC reports emerged out of Cold War-era models of the world used for guiding intercontinental ballistic missiles and predicting the effects of nuclear war ("nuclear winter," for example). There is a growing literature in history and science studies on the climate–nuclear nexus. See, for example, John Cloud, "Crossing the Olentangy River: The Figure of the Earth and the Military-Industrial-Academic Complex, 1947–1972," *Studies in the History and Philosophy of Modern Physics* 31, no. 3, 2000, 371–404; R. Doel, "Constituting the Postwar Earth Sciences: The Military's Influence on the Environmental Sciences in the USA after 1945," *Social Studies of Science* 33, no. 5, 2003, 635–66; Kristine Harper, "Climate Control: United States Weather Modification in the Cold War and beyond," *Endeavour* 32, no. 1, 2008, 20–26; Jacob Hamblin, "A Global Contamination Zone: Early Cold War Planning for Environmental Warfare," in J. R. McNeill and Christine Unger (eds), *Environmental Histories of the Cold War*, New York: Cambridge University Press, 2010, 85–114; P. Edwards, "Entangled Histories: Climate Science and Nuclear Weapons Research," *Bulletin of the Atomic Scientists*, 68, no. 4, 2012, 28–40. In the introduction to this chapter we criticized the fiction of Oreskes and Conway; but they have also done excellent work on the Cold War origins of climate denialism. Naomi Oreskes and Erik Conway, "Challenging Knowledge: How Climate Science Became a Victim of the Cold War," in *Agnotology: The Making and Unmaking of Ignorance*, Stanford, CA: Stanford University Press, 2008, 55–89; see also Oreskes and Conway, *Merchants of Doubt*.

This "optimistic" analysis raises some difficult questions that Wendt leaves unanswered. First, if technological development drives this change, which technologies and why? Wendt only mentions weapons of mass destruction, but more than sixty years after Hiroshima and Nagasaki, we are not much closer to a world state than we were at the end of World War II.[49] Second, if the world state will come about through "collective identity formation", what will provide the ideological basis of the collective? (Clearly, nationalism will not do.) Third, how is the emergence of a world state affected by the specifically capitalist character of most of the world's actually existing nation-states (and almost all of the most powerful)? Wendt brackets the question of capitalism, except to say that the logic of capital will only further contribute to the emergence of a world state, without explaining how.

Here, we can only attempt to elaborate Wendt's ideas by tackling the first question. But for the sake of clarity, let us briefly consider the others (which merit much fuller discussion). The ideological basis of collective identity in a (nontotalitarian) world state might seem like a magic elixir. If we knew what that could be, we would be one big step closer to "universal citizenship." We noted earlier that one possible ideological form through which the struggle for recognition among states could be resolved is as "stewards" of life on Earth. Suppose that elites mainly from two leading capitalist states, the United States and China, are capable of reconfiguring the political so that sovereignty is organized and legitimated on a planetary basis. Those elites may well present their interests as if they were representative of the general interests of the whole planet. Even if, at the level of the state system, this represents a fundamentally elite program, they might be granted substantial legitimacy in a context of perceived planetary emergency.[50] This very feature of any likely movement toward a world state also provides some hint at the role of capital—which is almost certain to be fundamental to any elite project. Consequently, as far as the role of capital is concerned, we agree with Wendt that the logic of capital may drive a world state, since maintaining the basis for the circulation and accumulation of capital—not to mention the reproduction of labor power—will require solutions to "collective action problems" that capital can only achieve on a planetary basis (see Chapter 5). Giovanni Arrighi argues, in fact, that in the history of capitalism the movement of capital's contradictions has always driven toward larger political and geographical scales of resolution/governance, and arguably, after the United States' *belle époque*, there is

---

49   One key exception, the project of the European Union, is looking very weak at the time of writing.

50   Of course, the elite nature of the project is unlikely to matter at the scale of the state system along. The class, gender and other hierarchies that plague human communities would also mean it would, very likely, also be exercised via white masculine domination. The almost certain centrality of China to any such process of collective identity formation makes the Euro-American character of this process much less sure.

only one greater scale possible: the planetary.[51] Moreover, this is likely to put capital at the heart of any claim to Climate Leviathan's legitimacy, because barring revolutionary ideological transformations of which Wendt gives no hint, if the elite project to save the planet is to succeed it is going to require a legitimacy that, at least right now, only capitalism can give it. Still, all of this could change quite quickly.

Acknowledging how much more could be said, let us return to the question of technology as it intersects with sovereignty and collective identity formation. Wendt emphasizes the "logic of anarchy" that compels states to continually seek recognition from one another. All states thus contribute to a massive collective action problem, as each refines their military capability to destroy the others, perpetuating the need for ever greater investment in "defense." Others writing on the same problem affirm both the importance Wendt places on military technology and the "logic" of world government as a response to what Arendt called "the monstrous development of the means of violence." But "logical" does not mean "inevitable."[52] For Wendt's colleagues Bud Duvall and Jonathan Havercroft, for example, the emergence of world government hinges on details that Wendt overlooks, perhaps because he is so beholden to the long tradition of nuclear one-worldism. What if technology—in this case, military technology, specifically—influences both what sovereignty is understood to involve, and the collective identity in whose name it is exercised?

According to Duvall and Havercroft, one particular field of military technology—space weaponry—is crucial, and likely to have decisive effects. They tell us that "shifts in military technology (along with other processes) generate changes in the forms of political societies" and in "the nature of relationships among them." Their object of analysis is the "constitutive effects that emerging space-weapons technologies will likely have on the ontology . . . of the political societies that compose the international system, which . . . is to say on sovereignty."[53] These claims might seem to validate all those years world-state talk spent on the cranky margins of political theory. What kind of space weapons are we talking about?

On the near horizon lie three potential military uses of orbital space. The first, which has been a US pursuit since at least the 1980s [and which is already available, if imperfect] is intercepting missile attacks—a space-based missile-defense

---

51   See Giovanni Arrighi, *The Long Twentieth Century: Money, Power, and the Origins of Our Times*, New York: Verso, 1994. Though Arrighi's account explains a great deal, capital's drive toward larger scales is always cross-cut by the possibility of exploiting spatial difference to sustain specific "smaller capitals." As Poulantzas reminds us, "within capital as a whole" there is no general principle or "instance capable of laying down who should make sacrifices so that others may continue to prosper": (*State, Power, Socialism*, 182–83).

52   Raymond Duvall and Jonathan Havercroft, "Taking Sovereignty out of This World: Space Weapons and Empire of the Future," *Review of International Studies* 34, 2008, 755–75.

53   Ibid., 756.

shield. Second, there is serious discussion of developing "space control," which the US Department of Defense defines as "the exploitation of space and the denial of the use of space to adversaries [particularly China]. A third is force application from space: weapons of varying types . . . placed in orbit, with the ability to attack objects either flying in the Earth's atmosphere or on or near the Earth's surface.[54]

Duvall and Havercroft suggest that only the United States is in a position to "develop an effective space weapons project," but it is not clear why.[55] Bracketing this claim, however, their analysis is compelling:

> Space control represents the extension of US sovereignty into orbital space. Its implementation would . . . reinscribe the "hard shell" border of the US, now extended to include the "territory" of orbital space. US sovereignty is projected out of this world and into orbit. Under Article II of the 1967 *Outer Space Treaty*, "Outer Space, including the moon and other celestial bodies, is not subject to national appropriation by claim of sovereignty, by means of use or occupation, or by any other means." The US project of space control would entail a clear violation of this article. In addition to expanding the scope of US sovereignty.[56]

These processes will entail a very specific kind of development or adaptation in the "forms of political society," because this violation of international law would

> produce a distinctly capitalist sovereignty. In Volume One of *Capital*, Marx chided classical political economists for their inability to explain how workers became separated from the means of production. Whereas political economists such as Adam Smith argued that a previous accumulation of capital was necessary for a division of labour, Marx argued that this doctrine was absurd. Division of labour existed in pre-capitalist societies where workers were not alienated from their labour. Instead, Marx argued that the actual historical process of primitive accumulation of capital was carried out through colonial relations of appropriation by force. While not a perfect analogy, because of the lack of material labour, the value of which is to be forcibly appropriated in orbital space, space control is like such primitive accumulation in constituting a global capitalist order through the colonisation of space as previously common property [effectively remaking it into a new] form of "real estate." By controlling access to orbital space the US would be forcibly appropriating the orbits, in effect turning them into primitively accumulated private property. In this way, the US becomes even more than it is now the sovereign state for global capitalism, *the global capitalist state*.[57]

---

54 Ibid., 761.
55 Ibid., 756.
56 Ibid., 765.
57 Ibid., 765–66, emphasis in original.

In other words, Duvall and Havercroft anticipate that in the coming decades, the United States is likely to pursue and achieve a global monopoly on space weapons, which will trump Earth-bound military force. This could include a "missile shield" coupled with offensive space-based weapons, nuclear weapons, and air and sea dominance. For the first time, they suggest, one state would meet the Weberian criteria for statehood—"that institution which claims the *monopoly of the legitimate use of force* [*Gewalt*] within a given territory"—in a situation in which the "given territory" is the entire planet.[58] A new era of US-centered imperialism will arrive, with the United States at "the centre of a global extensive . . . empire, a sovereign of the globe."[59]

On what grounds could space weaponry contribute to Climate Leviathan? It sounds like conspiracy theory, but the fact is that something very like space weapons will be mobilized to defend life on Earth: atmospheric geoengineering. With the growing awareness that the mitigation window has closed, we hear more of plans to "geoengineer" our way to safety through massive techno-social mitigation-by-atmospheric-manipulation.[60] Consider, for example, sulfate aerosol injection, sometimes known as solar radiation management (SRM), to artificially increase atmospheric albedo.[61] One recent essay advocating SRM characterizes it as "albedo modification—a kind of geoengineering intended to cool the planet by increasing the reflectivity of the earth's atmosphere." The mechanism is straightforward. Injected synthetic aerosols will "reflect sunlight into the stratosphere;" like "wearing a white shirt in the summer."[62]

The big difference, of course, is that if you wear a white shirt in the summer, you are the one to decide what to wear. Who decides to inject synthetic aerosols into the stratosphere, and how much?[63] Geoengineering

---

58   Max Weber, "Politics as Vocation," in Hans Gerth and C. Wright Mills (eds), *From Max Weber: Essays in Sociology*, London: Routledge, 1991, 78, emphasis in original. *Gewalt* translates as both "force" and "violence."

59   Duvall and Havercroft, "Taking Sovereignty out of This World," 768.

60   David Keith, "Geoengineering the Climate: History and Prospect," *Annual Review of Energy and the Environment* 25, 2000, 245–84; Clive Hamilton, *Earthmasters: Playing God with the Climate*, New South Wales, Australia: Allen & Unwin, 2013; Alan Robock, "Albedo Enhancement by Stratospheric Sulfur Injection: More Research Needed," *Earth's Future*, 4, 2016, doi:10.1002/2016EF000407.

61   See Keith, "Geoengineering the Climate"; James Fleming, "The Pathological History of Weather and Climate Modification: Three Cycles of Promise and Hype," *Historical Studies in the Natural Sciences* 37, no. 1, 2006, 3–25; James Fleming, "The Climate Engineers," *The Wilson Quarterly* 31 no. 2, 2007, 46–60; Hamilton, *Earthmasters*; Dale Jamieson, *Reason in a Dark Time*, Chapter 7; Mike Hulme, *Can Science Fix Climate Change? A Case Against Climate Engineering*, London: Wiley & Sons, 2014.

62   David Keith and Gernot Wagner, "Toward a More Reflective Planet," Project Syndicate, June 16, 2016, project-syndicate.org.

63   Other commonly proposed strategies include artificially generating cold-water upwelling to lower surface temperatures or altering ocean chemistry to absorb more carbon. See David Keller, Ellias Feng and Andreas Oschlies, "Potential Climate Engineering Effectiveness and Side

projects like SRM are qualitatively different than projects to create resilient infrastructures or to produce drought-resistant seed stock. Large-scale carbon capture and storage belongs in the same discussion, since depositing gigatons of carbon in the Earth's crust for thousands of years will involve considerable geological engineering. But SRM is arguably the most plausible and significant form of geoengineering on the way, and it has enormous consequences for the adaptation of the political. Any attempt to modify the world's albedo will require decisions over the fate of the Earth's climate and energy, nothing less than life and death; every large-scale geoengineering project will involve a relatively small group of actors experimenting with global systems in the most improbable of missions: to materially reconfigure planet Earth so as to avoid having to rework human political economies. The greatest problem with SRM, so-called "governance," is really the problem of sovereignty, because the fundamental question is not "How shall we design appropriate institutions to govern geoengineering?" but rather "Who can declare the emergency?"[64]

> Sulfate aerosol injection . . . would involve injecting sulfate aerosols into the stratosphere where they would scatter sunlight back into space. Even if this approach were successful in reducing mean surface temperature, it would likely produce substantial regional variations in temperature, precipitation, and intensity of the hydrological cycle, even perhaps disrupting the Indian monsoon. The 1991 eruption of Mount Pinatubo, which many consider a "natural experiment" in sulfate aerosol engineering, produced a substantial decrease in precipitation over land and brought drought to some parts of the tropics.[65]

These changes would result from shifts in the distribution in the Earth's capacity to absorb solar radiation: relatively less in the tropics (where aerosols would be concentrated) and more at higher latitudes. Thus, SRM means taking responsibility for changing the weather everywhere in a radically uncertain and geographically uneven direction. There is also a temporal dimension to SRM's political implications. "If we were to embark on any SRM program while continuing to increase the atmospheric concentration of carbon dioxide," which is almost certain, "we would risk catastrophic climate change if we were to lose the capacity or will to manage solar radiation anytime during the next millennium

Effects During a High Carbon Dioxide-Emission Scenario 2014," *Nature Communications* 5, article 3304; doi:10.1038/ncomms4304. For a review of approaches to geoengineering, see Zhihua Zhang, John C. Moore, Donald Huisingh, and Yongxin Zhao, "Review of Geoengineering Approaches to Mitigating Climate Change," *Journal of Cleaner Production* 103, 2015, 898–907.

64   Daniel Bodansky, "The Who, What, and Wherefore of Geoengineering Governance," *Climatic Change* 121, no. 3, 2013, 539–51; Martin L. Weitzman, "A Voting Architecture for the Governance of Free-Driver Externalities, with Application to Geoengineering," *Scandinavian Journal of Economics* 117, no. 4, 2015, 1049–68.

65   Jamieson, *Reason in a Dark Time*, 220.

or beyond."[66] That is to say, the state or sovereign that initiates SRM would arrogate to itself its own perpetual necessity. Which raises the crucial political questions:

> Many people think that geoengineering technologies should be developed but only deployed (notice the military word) in case of a climate emergency . . . How do we know when we are experiencing a climate emergency? Who has the authority to declare such an emergency?[67]

Jamieson poses these questions rhetorically, but they are not rhetorical. They arise from the logic of planetary sovereignty, and we will have to answer them, actively suppress them, or formulate better questions.

To be sure, geoengineering alone will not bring Leviathan into being because Climate Leviathan is emerging at the intersection of several interlocking processes. Still, the recognition that any means of evaluating geoengineering projects will be intensely political explains the logical appeal for a legitimate planetary authority to adjudicate the merits of experimentation. That authority will come cloaked in the white coat of techno-scientific expertise: "Either we are smart enough to craft that feedback mechanism ourselves, or the Earth system will ultimately provide it."[68] It is Reason versus the state of nature. Between them stands the planetary sovereign: the one that declares the (experimental) exception in the name of life itself. Planetary sovereignty thus emerges in what might be called *Weltrecht*, the arrogation of the authority and duty to remake the world to save it.

VI

Whenever one discusses technologies that do not yet exist, there is always a threat of lapsing into technological determinism or a teleology of scientific "progress."[69] Our point is not that change will be causally driven simply by technology. Every field of science and technology is always already social, and the potential creation of these specific technologies would be an effect of (and contribute to) political change. Their geopolitical dimensions already rend the globe, contributing to deep tensions between the United States and China, for example. We agree with Duvall and Havercroft that these technological changes could bolster US hegemony, but we should not presume that they will do so. The technologies may develop slowly, after some consolidation of global power (in

---

66   Ibid., 220–21.

67   Ibid., 221.

68   Edward Parson and David Keith, "End the Deadlock on Governance of Geoengineering Research," *Science* 229, 15 March 2013, 1279.

69   For a technological determinist argument regarding space weapons, see David Baker, *The Shape of Wars to Come*, Cambridge, MA: Patrick Stephens, 1981. For an alternative account of space weapons, see Duvall and Havercroft, "Taking Sovereignty out of This World."

the form of a "G2," for instance—hegemonic rule by the combined states of China and the United States), or after a war or other event that dramatically weakens US hegemony and/or increases China's geopolitical power.

Indeed, these uncertain dynamics highlight one of the most worrisome conclusions of our analysis: if the principal change wrought by climate change is the adaptation of the political, the greatest source of uncertainty in its adaptation lies in the complex geopolitical-economic relations between the United States and China. We could see world war between two spheres of influence, leading to a collapse in the world system, or the consolidation of Climate Leviathan through collaboration between the United States and China, or a US-centric Leviathan. There are other prospects, too, of course. Ultimately, in all cases it is impossible to produce a strong predictive model of the climate change-political complex.

To close the chapter, lets take stock of its arguments. Like Wendt, we too anticipate a shift toward a world-scale authority and are persuaded by his argument that the logic of the interstate system points toward its creation. However, he sidesteps the question of capital and its technological dynamism (especially non-military technology), both factors that would seem to make world government not so much "inevitable" as "likely." What seems much more inevitable is the fundamental shift in sovereignty that both Wendt and Duvall and Havercroft try to outline.

We identify three distinct logics that all point toward planetary sovereignty. The first is the logic of weaponry, particularly weapons of mass destruction, elaborated in a tradition that runs from Einstein and Russell to Arendt to Wendt (even if their specific responses to this dynamic differ). The second is the central emphasis of the Marxist tradition: capitalism's tendency toward crisis. Its logic tends toward forms and scales of sovereignty deemed capable of resolving its increasingly global or planetary contradictions (see Chapter 5). The third, which underlines the essential novelty of the present conjuncture, is the "logic" of ecological catastrophe and the ensuing imperative to save life on Earth through geoengineering, which finds its most advanced expression in SRM. These logics cohere in an emergent Climate Leviathan for which the political is constituted, therefore, in the necessities crisis and catastrophe demand: hegemonic military-political capacity at a scale adequate to "save the planet," the production and protection of geoengineering or related socio-technological mechanisms to realize this goal, and finally, the sovereign power to name the emergency, initiate the institutional and technical responses deemed appropriate, and ensure (as far as possible) their legitimacy.

Though they are already underway and are sure to worsen, accelerated environmental changes like rising sea levels and intensifying droughts will not solicit on their own the coming political transformations climate change will demand. Rather, it is the ensemble of the spectres (and reality) of mass migration and conflict, coupled with the promises of geoengineering that make planetary sovereignty "necessary." Processes are more likely to drive the creation of Leviathan if [a] they present an existential threat; [b] they are large scale (global); and [c] they pose challenges for the existing political order. In this view, SRM and new planetary governance (particularly if it is introduced along with space-based weaponry), could be the decisive trigger for planetary sovereignty. This could, as we argued earlier, take one of two broad political-economic forms: capitalist or postcapitalist. But to this we can now add that it could emerge through one of two geopolitical paths—producing, in effect, one of two types of empire, geopolitically distinct "Climate Leviathans" (both much more likely to be capitalist than postcapitalist, so both scenarios reflect the upper-left quadrant of Figure 2.2).

The first is a US-centered Climate Leviathan. In this scenario, the United States maintains it's current military dominance, and exploits the "need to save life on Earth" as the ideological basis of a new imperial hegemony. The United States is not only the global leader in the technologies of destruction, but also of geoengineering, particularly SRM. Any such US-led planetary management would unfold on a massively unequal geopolitical terrain, in which planetary sovereignty effectively took the form of imperial rule. A US-centered Climate Leviathan like this could conceivably last a long time, since any attempt to defeat the United States militarily would also seem to unsettle the very management of life of Earth. Attempts to resist US hegemony would be treated as treasonous "terrorism" of an extreme type, confronted with overwhelming military technology.

The second scenario emerges if we begin by recognizing that the United States is not in fact globally hegemonic (for example, if we do not assume that the United States *alone* is likely to achieve rapid advances in military technology like space weaponry). On the contrary, the United States is already competing with several other capitalist nation-states for "great power" status—most notably China, but also Russia, India, and others—and this competition already involves a new cold war of cyber-warfare, diplomatic conflict, and the race to develop sophisticated weaponry (including space weapons).

In this scenario, which seems more likely, one or more of these competing powers will continue to compete with the United States. History would seem to suggest this will lead to war, and it may well. But, for our purposes, what is critical is that the United States would fail to establish political, military and technological dominance. The implication is that the management of the planet would unfold in the context of a world system that is neither democratic (since the vast majority of nation-states and peoples would have no real involvement in the important decisions about the Earth's management) nor clearly dominated by one hegemonic power. Planetary governance would unroll on a lumpy, conflictual geopolitical terrain upon which elites continue to seek "adaptations" that meet their needs—political stability, continued accumulation, and so on. For example, it does not seem entirely outrageous to imagine the United States and

China (or some other small cohort of globally influential powers) deciding to reorganize the world system in a sort of grand compromise that includes shared planetary management, a "G2" concentration of the existing order bilaterally constituted to save life on Earth.

From the perspective of anyone hoping for something like climate justice, none of these future paths (or variations upon them) are acceptable. Is there any alternative? What would realizing alternatives involve?

Part III

7

After Paris

We refuse this shadow of the future, we will not bend to the politics of fear that stifle liberties in the name of security. The biggest threat to security, to life in all its forms, is the system that drives the climate disaster.

Climate Games Response to Recent Paris Attacks, December 2015[1]

I

In October 2012, Hurricane Sandy hit New York City. By diameter, it was the largest Atlantic hurricane on record, and the destruction was massive.[2] More than 200 people died amidst $75 billion in direct damages.[3] Some of these costs were due to power outages that affected 2 million people.[4] Low-lying, low-income communities across northern New Jersey and Brooklyn were especially badly hit by a lack of electricity and water, flooded living spaces, broken transit, illness, and other hardships. But not everyone suffered. In the darkness of lower Manhattan, the global headquarters of Goldman Sachs was aglow, a beacon to the city, thanks to the building's emergency backup generators (see Figure 7.1).

This true story is a metaphor for Climate Leviathan. The world's wealthy and powerful are already adapting to rapid planetary changes. Through massive private investment and the exploitation of their ties to powerful state institutions, the elite are cementing structures to protect their wealth, status, and power. They recognize that the present world order is incapable of stemming accelerating climate change. Wall Street cannot prevent the next Superstorm Sandy, but with enough concrete and generators, it can buffer itself from the worst effects, and with catastrophe bonds it can more than cover the increased cost of doing business in the storm surge. If the need to rapidly reduce carbon emissions is the world's greatest collective action problem, then the prevailing patterns of adaptation—which entrench profound inequalities—reflect the

---

1 "Climate Games Response to Recent Attacks," December 1, 2015, creativeresistance.org/climate-games-response-to-paris-attacks.

2 United States Department of Energy, Office of Electricity Delivery & Energy Reliability, "Hurricane Sandy Situation Report #6," October 31, 2012, available at oe.netl.doe.gov.

3 Most measures of damage caused by Sandy focus on damage in the United States, where quantifiable costs were greatest. Yet immense harm was also caused to Haiti, Cuba, and other Caribbean countries. Measuring in monetary terms always diminishes the losses of the poor.

4 United States Department of Energy, Office of Electricity Delivery and Energy Reliability, "Hurricane Sandy Situation Report #6."

premeditated refusal of elites to solve it. The relatively poor and least powerful are left to fend for themselves.[5]

Figure 7.1. Goldman Sachs headquarters illuminated during Hurricane Sandy, 2012

Source: Eduardo Munoz/Reuters.

Two years after Sandy, on September 21, 2014, New York City hosted the People's Climate March, one of the largest political marches in US history and possibly the largest environmental march anywhere, ever. Held the day before a one-day United Nations Climate Summit, an estimated 311,000 people (including representatives of more than 1,000 organizations) gathered in central Manhattan to demand action on climate change.[6] (Smaller solidarity events were held in dozens of other cities.) More celebratory than confrontational, New York's People's Climate March was colorful and life-affirming; it was, in the words of the organizers, an "amazing display of the size and beauty of our movement." The legally permitted march clogged the main arteries on the west and south side of Central Park, but it was well-regulated by participants and marked by little friction. Images of the march look like postcards sent from a beautiful society where citizens demand change but everyone gets along. As the People's Climate March summary explained:

---

5   On the inequalities exposed and exacerbated by Sandy, see David Rohde, "The Hideous Inequality Exposed by Hurricane Sandy," *The Atlantic*, October 31, 2012; Maya Wiley, "After Sandy: New York's 'Perfect Storm' of Inequality in Wealth and Housing," *The Guardian*, October 28, 2013.

6   On the People's Climate March, see 2014.peoplesclimate.org. The *New York Times* cites the organizers' count at 311,000. Lisa Foderaro, "Taking a Call for Climate Change to the Streets," *New York Times*, September 21, 2014. Joel Wainwright participated in the New York and Paris demonstrations discussed here.

With world leaders coming to New York City for a landmark summit on climate change, people around the world took to the streets to demand action to end the climate crisis. Now, more than ever, we are a big, beautiful, unified movement. We are coming together around the world like never before to demand a brighter and more just future for everyone.

Like all demonstrations, the march was a type of spatial performance. The aim was to march on (or at least toward) the headquarters of the United Nations, site of the next day's Climate Summit. The New York Police Department refused to permit this, so the march made a right turn at 42nd Street, leading us west, away from the United Nations. The masses dissolved into the city a few blocks after leaving the staging ground. For such an enormous (and supposedly significant) political event, the march travelled a remarkably short distance. The protesters were well-ordered spatially: the hundreds of thousands of marchers were effectively sorted into social groups: Indigenous peoples and "front-line communities" leading, followed by students, scientists, and so on.[7] At the very head of the march was a special section of those who, by virtue of office or fame, signaled the participation of elite groups, people like Hollywood star Leonardo DiCaprio, former US Vice President Al Gore, New York City Mayor Bill de Blasio, and Secretary General of the United Nations Ban Ki-Moon.

The following morning—the day of the UN meeting—New York City awoke to more climate protest, but of a very different sort. Echoing Occupy Wall Street, a call to "flood Wall Street" brought hundreds of climate justice activists to the financial district in an effort to shut it down, however briefly, to draw attention to the crucial link between planetary emergency and global capital. Their slogan was "Stop Capitalism. End the Climate Crisis."[8] Unlike the People's Climate March, so enormous it brought central Manhattan to a standstill, the group of radicals who attempted to flood Wall Street was far too small to seriously disrupt business as usual in lower Manhattan. But this demonstration was immediately attacked by police; more than 100 protesters were arrested.[9] Why such rough

---

7   We intended to march with a group called "we know who is to blame" but never made it through the crowd to the proper position, landing instead with a group of scientists and university students (appropriately enough). In any event, our segment of the march never actually marched. The roads were so full, and we were so far from the front, that two hours after the start of the march we were still in the same place.

8   See the Flood Wall Street site: floodwallstreet.net.

9   On the state/police repression of Occupy Wall Street, see The Global Justice Clinic (NYU School of Law) and the Walter Leitner International Human Rights Clinic at the Leitner Center for International Law and Justice (Fordham Law School), "Suppressing Protest: Human Rights Violations in the US Response to Occupy Wall Street," 2012, available at leitnercenter.org. On the arrests at Flood Wall Street, see Amanda Holpuch, "Dozens Arrested as Police Face off with Flood Wall Street," *The Guardian*, September 22, 2014, and "Over 100 Arrested at "Flood Wall Street" Protest against Climate Change," Democracy Now! September 23, 2014. On the politics of the two 2015 New York protests, see Terran Giacomini and Terisa Turner, "The 2014 People's Climate March and Flood Wall Street Civil Disobedience: Making the Transition to a Post-fossil Capitalist, Commoning Civilization," *Capitalism Nature Socialism* 26, no. 2, 2015.

treatment from a state that only the day before watched so serenely as 300,000 people filled the streets? The question almost answers itself. It can hardly be attributed solely to the fact that the financial district protesters did not have a permit. The state cannot prevent the ocean from flooding New York City, but the police can protect Wall Street. Better flooding tomorrow than anticapitalists today.

These two New York scenes bring into relief some of the complexities and contradictions of the climate justice movement. In its relatively brief history, it has achieved some notable successes, particularly in Europe. And yet, most of us are aware of the enormous mismatch between our present capacities and our political aims. We face difficult challenges, questions that arise with every planning meeting, action, and campaign. What do we mean when we say "climate justice movement"? Who is in the movement and who is not?[10] In whose name does anyone who says "our movement" speak? Is there a specific geographical, class, or other basis for this struggle? What is it about the present state of things that needs changing, and what methods will change it?

During the 21st Conference of the Parties (COP21), tens of thousands of activists and representatives from many front-line communities came to Paris to advance the global climate justice movement. Twelve thousand marched on the day the Paris Agreement was signed (December 12, 2015), after two weeks filled with hundreds of spirited protests and demonstrations around the city. At the Place de la République, around the Louvre, on the Seine, and inside the COP meetings, thousands of brave activists confronted the elite agenda, the carbon polluters, and, inevitably, the police. All these events took place despite a ban imposed by the *état d'urgence* the French state announced after the terror attacks of November 13. By the time the COP21 meetings began, over three hundred climate activists had been arrested. Throughout the meetings, the city was under the microscope; armed military and police were everywhere and mass surveillance was ubiquitous, as were public spaces closures, additional pressure on immigrants and minority groups, and so on. The

---

10   For political purposes, the 2002 Bali statement on Principles of Climate Justice and the 2010 People's Agreement of Cochabamba offer strong starting points to answer these two questions. But they must be extended politically and theoretically, and a nascent social science literature is doing just that by taking up the question of differential inclusion and participation in climate justice movements. See, for example, from political science, Jennifer Hadden, *Networks in Contention: The Divisive Politics of Climate Change*, Cambridge, Cambridge University Press, 2015; from sociology, Richard Widick and John Foran, "Whose Utopia? Our Utopia! Competing Visions of the Future at the UN Climate Talks", *Nature and Culture*, 11, no. 3, 2017, 296–321; and from psychology, Jonas Rees and Sebastian Bamberg, "Climate Protection Needs Societal Change: Determinants of Intention to Participate in Collective Climate Action," *European Journal of Social Psychology* 44, no. 5, 2014, 466–73; Jonas Rees, Sabine Klug, and Sebastian Bamberg, "Guilty Conscience: Motivating Pro-Environmental Behavior by Inducing Negative Moral Emotions," *Climatic Change* 130, no. 3, 2015, 139–52.

demonstrators in Paris should be honored, therefore, not only because they took genuine risks, but because they stood for climate justice and democratic rights (against the *état d'urgence*). This missive from one organizing collective provides a sense of those weeks:

> [O]ur dedication for social and climate justice remains as strong as ever. We are convinced that the geopolitical and economic dynamics that underpin climate chaos are the same as those that feed terrorism. From the oil wars in Iraq to the droughts in Syria caused by ecological collapse, all feed the same inequalities that lead to cycles of violent conflict. We are writing this from a city under a state of emergency. The government has announced that the COP21 negotiations will go on, but all public outdoor demonstrations across France . . . have been banned. We refuse this shadow of the future, we will not bend to the politics of fear that stifle liberties in the name of security. The biggest threat to security, to life in all its forms, is the system that drives the climate disaster.[11]

If climate justice is to be achieved, it will need (among other things) many more statements like this.

Because Paris (not COP21) was the high-water mark for the global movement for climate justice, these events deserve an honest appraisal. Though far smaller than New York's People's march, the protests were higher risk, the stakes greater. There was also greater diversity within the movement (particularly from across Europe), providing a clearer sense of the movement's composition and ideological range.[12] While there were hundreds of events during the meetings, the largest took place the day the Paris Agreement went into effect (December 12, 2015). That day merits some examination, if only because it is understood by many, including many of those present, as a truly decisive moment, one in which popular mobilization was capable of changing the conditions of the political.

Three specific events provide a fascinating juxtaposition. First, early on December 12, a group of Indigenous leaders gathered at Notre Dame without a permit, and attempted to perform a ceremony in front of the cathedral. Our understanding is that the goal was to celebrate Indigenous peoples' persistent anticolonial resistance and to protest the lack of binding recognition of indigenous interests in the agreement.[13] Unlike the other protests on that day,

---

11   "Climate Games Response to Recent Attacks."

12   *Greater* does not mean *sufficient*. In Paris, most activists were from Europe, particularly France and Germany. Spatial-distance decay applies to protesters as much as anything else.

13   Indigenous peoples figured prominently in the events surrounding COP21, but their interests are not reflected in the final text. Aside from references in nonbinding sections, the Paris Agreement uses the word "indigenous" only once: "Parties acknowledge that adaptation action should follow a country-driven, gender-responsive, participatory and fully transparent approach, taking into consideration vulnerable groups, communities and ecosystems, and should be based on and guided by the best available science and, as appropriate, traditional knowledge, knowledge

performed in the familiar style of left political carnival, the Notre Dame event was somber, its message different. Whereas the environmental protests almost all emphasized support for the COP, while calling for a much stronger deal, the Notre Dame event centered on the imperialism that has brought the planet to the brink of ecological disaster. The Indigenous leaders were displaced from the plaza and the historical center of the French Catholic Church, the geographical and symbolic point from which distances are measured in France. Instead, they were forced to conduct their ceremony on a nearby bridge.[14]

The second event that day was a rally called "red lines," coordinated by a coalition of international climate justice organizations. Because of protest restrictions, event plans were uncertain until the afternoon of the previous day, when a message circulated announcing a mass rally along the Avenue de la Grand Armée, west of the Arc de Triomphe.[15] Perhaps 10,000 showed up. Everyone wore something red, and long red banners festooned the perimeter— not to signify socialism, but to draw a red line to symbolize a nonnegotiable point or bottom line. It was a street festival for climate justice, with cheering crowds, red balloons, spirited costumes. But it was a party in a bottle. Entering the "green zone" (police-speak for space where protest is permitted) was straightforward, but exiting was difficult. Hemmed in by police on all sides, we were cut off even from nearby neighborhoods, let alone the delegates at Le Bourget. Moreover, while the performative act of protest was to "draw our red line," it was unclear what we were demanding. What were we claiming was nonnegotiable, that is, what was it we categorically rejected or considered absolutely essential? The COP process? This particular agreement? Capitalism? There were no speakers to articulate possible answers to these questions, only chants, signs, and slogans.

After some time, we and others made our way, accompanied by the police, to the third event: a "Rally on Champ de Mars" coordinated by a coalition of French social-democratic civil society organizations.[16] The rally, separate

---

of indigenous peoples and local knowledge systems, with a view to integrating adaptation into relevant socioeconomic and environmental policies and actions, where appropriate" (Article 7, para. 5, 24). So the one use of "indigenous" in the section of the Paris Agreement text that carries legal weight makes reference to indigenous knowledge, not indigenous rights. There are no statements that would limit the extraction of fossil fuels from unceded indigenous lands. Thus, the struggles of indigenous peoples are made into a resource for capital's adaptation.

14   Around the same time, a creative response to the ban on political protests developed, as protesters moved to geo-referenced points across Paris to hold up illuminated cell phones at a particular moment to spell out "CLIMATE JUSTICE NOW."

15   The text, sent 12.30 pm, read: "#d12 tomorrow: meet on Ave de la Grand Armée between Place de l'Étoile and Porte Maillot at 11:45. Bring something RED." Details were elaborated at a public meeting at the Zone d'action climate.

16   Friends of the Earth France, Attac France, Alternatiba, Action Non-Violente COP21, Bizi, Confédération Paysanne, Coordination de l'Action Non-Violente de l'Arche, Mouvement pour une Alternative Non-Violente, End Ecocide, Collectif National Pas Sans Nous, Emmaüs Lescar Pau, and l'Union Nationale des Étudiants de France.

from the red line, was a result of a split within the coordinating coalition on some questions of permits and audience. The red lines event was organized by international climate justice groups, the Champ de Mars rally by domestic organizations. The latter was permitted, the former was not (although the police relented, allowing a small, rectangular green zone). The "mass citizen gathering" was organized under the slogan, "Declare the State of Climate Emergency!"

> The country greenhouse gas emissions reduction pledges would induce an average global temperature increase of 3°C, which would irreversibly drive us into climate chaos . . . Without radical changes, the COP21 agreement will implicitly allow a global crime against humanity . . . We have to sound the alarm to inform the people of the world on the state and possible outcomes of the climate negotiations . . . [We call] for a massive . . . citizen mobilization in the following years, to relentlessly call on political and economic leaders to push forward true solutions to climate issues . . . We declare the state of climate emergency and call for a mass citizen gathering . . . Saturday, December 12 at 14:00, in the Champ de Mars, under the Eiffel Tower. We are going to form large human chains and carry climate emergency and call to action messages to the people of the world.[17]

A few thousand responded to the call. The rally was subdued and relatively uneventful—a photo opportunity, principally, a crowd set against the backdrop of the Eiffel Tower. As the Paris Agreement was signed at Le Bourget, the speakers on the Champ de Mars exhorted us to push our governments to do more.[18]

In terms of protest planning, international summits like the COP21 present the climate justice movement with the question of whether and how to demonstrate. At the 1999 Seattle protests against the World Trade Organization, the aim was to prevent the WTO ministerial from convening.[19] Demonstrations against the Iraq war targeted state institutions; Occupy Wall Street seized public space. In contrast, most in the climate justice movement did not want to close

---

17   Global Justice Ecology Project, "Call for a Mass Citizen Gathering to Declare the State of Climate Emergency," December 10, 2015, at globaljusticeecology.org.

18   Naomi Klein, the best-known speaker there, backed away from criticizing capitalism; rather, she emphasized the collective psyche. Her speech on the Champs de Mars at the December 12 rally ended with these words:

> We also have to acknowledge the grief, grief that we will not deny nor will we suppress, grief at what we have already lost, for those whom we have already lost. And we acknowledge that there is also rage at those who could have acted long ago but chose not to, and at those who make that same disastrous decision still. But mostly, mostly there is joy. Mostly there is joy and resolve as we witness the next world taking shape before our eyes.

19   We succeeded, for one day (November 30, 1999): Joel Wainwright, "Spaces of Resistance in Seattle and Cancún," in Jamie Peck, Helga Leitner, and Eric Sheppard (eds), *Contesting Neoliberalism: The Urban Frontier*, New York: Guilford, 2006, 179–203.

the UN or COP21 meetings. On the contrary, they wanted to compel them to go further. In that situation, the left protester becomes, if reluctantly or ironically, a cheerleader for elite institutions: less "Shut it Down!" than "Make a Deal!" How should one protest *against* an international forum one wishes was different and more effective, that one would in fact be *for* if it were powerful and radical? This has proven a complicated strategic question for the climate justice movement. This partly explains why we generate more popular traction, and greater solidarity, when targeting concrete things for opposition, like coal mines, pipelines, or (at least in a vague way) Wall Street.

Given the centrality of international negotiations to any plausible plan to tackle climate change, the strategic problem presented by the current institutional regime for climate politics is enormously important. This is really just a broader manifestation of the ambiguities that saturated the red lines demonstrations in Paris. The idea was to tie a critique of the elite climate diplomacy on display in Le Bourget to the notion of planetary limits: beyond our existential "red line" lies death and destruction. But at the same time, those of us at the protest were in fact also vigorously endorsing the very same elite politics. The implicit message was, "Yes to an agreement, just not this one. We will accept the same institutions and politics, if it gives us a different outcome." Although we can certainly follow the logic that leads to it, it must be acknowledged that this is a vague and limited critique of the international climate politics regime. We should not be surprised that the international media portrayals of Paris events of December 12 did not reflect the radical left position. The red lines and climate emergency demonstrations were conflated by the media, hardly discussed but photographed as colorful visual complements to the big story, the signing of the Paris Agreement. The implicit message was that the signing of the Paris Agreement was met with popular *celebration*. (The Indigenous ceremony at Notre Dame was ignored.)[20]

The divisions and limitations of the December 12 demonstrations pose significant and unavoidable challenges for a global climate justice movement. While the media representation of the protests lacked nuance, we who wish to

---

20   The lead story in *The Guardian* on the morning of December 12 made only one reference to the demonstrations: "Peaceful protests are planned by climate activists across Paris. Civil society groups will hand out thousands of red tulips to represent red lines they say should not be crossed, and hold a rally under the Eiffel Tower if and when a deal is reached," the clear implication being a rally to *celebrate* the deal (Suzanne Goldenberg, Lenore Taylor, Adam Vaughan and John Vidal, Saturday 12 December 2015, "Paris Climate Talks: Delegates Reach Agreement on Final Draft Text," theguardian.com). What could have been said instead? "A large group of climate justice activists have come to oppose the COP21 outcomes on anticapitalist grounds. They argue that the Paris Agreement is not going to save the planet, far from it. The commitments to reduce carbon emissions are not binding and, even if they were, would get the world to an average temperature increase of 3–4°C at best. The words 'fossil fuels' are not in the text of the Paris Agreement. We need rapid decarbonization and a transition to a different world, more democratic and no longer organized for profit." Unlikely, to say the least, at least partially because many who share these views nonetheless regard a bad deal as far better than no deal at all.

help create and sustain that movement must not shy away from honest self-criticism. The problem is not that there is a lack of a coherent and unanimous political program—which is something we can hardly expect or perhaps even desire for a movement so diverse—but rather that there is a lack of coherent political positions on absolutely key questions. We are a good way from creating the conditions for the transnational social movement we need. To be sure, the global climate justice movement showed signs of strength and areas of growth. Still, we face enormous challenges in translating ideas and commitments into effective political resistance and global political-economic transformation. Taking the path of Climate X will require a much larger and more radical movement. We should examine some of the fundamental obstacles it faces.

II

The claim that the climate justice movement lacks a coherent political theory or theories that explain its motives, strategy, and tactics demands elaboration. Given the extraordinary energies so many continue to dedicate, and the risks they take in doing so, we want to preface that elaboration with a few clarifications. We are not criticizing friends and allies from a position above and outside the movement, still less to accuse or blame. Rather, our aim is to offer political and theoretical provocation and to stimulate critical reflection. Our motivation is to tackle some of the questions we asked earlier: What do we mean when we say "climate justice movement"? What are we fighting for? In whose name do we speak? What are we trying to change and how? These questions need to be addressed, whatever one's view of the climate justice movement's past, present, and future, and we sense that our answers can and should be much stronger.

The first challenge lies in that there is no such thing as "a" or "the" climate justice movement, at least not in the sense that we could speak of the anti-colonial movement in India in the 1940s, say, or the anti-apartheid movement centered on South Africa in the 1980s. In those cases, diverse social actors and processes, with different conceptions of their political aims, were able to unify and become an effective social-political force. Their internal complexities have not prevented their interpretation as relatively coherent social movements. In both cases, we can identify a fundamental unit of analysis: the territorial nation-state. A significant part of the ideological "cement" that facilitated unity was the same in each instance: nationalism. The unification of these social movements eventually came to focus on transforming the leadership of the state, and both succeeded. These dynamics cannot animate an effective climate justice politics. Nationalism will clearly doom global climate justice (and justice in general, we might add), and while a focus on the leadership of this or that state might enable particular nationally-oriented movements, it will not work to unify a *global* climate justice movement. (The anti-apartheid movement was international, but in a geographical sense that climate justice cannot be, since neither our problem nor its solutions can be contained by territorial boundaries.)

It might be said that focusing on the nation-state or other sub-planetary social units (nations, communities, regions, watersheds, and so forth) makes sense because that is how the world is presently arranged. What good is a spatial politics that targets a scale that does not exist in any meaningful political sense? Hence there will never be *a* climate justice movement or *the* climate justice movement, but an ensemble of different, overlapping, and (hopefully) mutually supportive but more or less distinct movements. From this perspective, the lack of a coherent political theory is not a weakness, but a reflection of our reality; the movement's ethos is pluralist, our diversity is its strength. We should worry less about winning unity and more on winning local battles.

There is a lot of wisdom in this argument. But it can also obscure important and persistent problems, and this, we would argue, was often the case in Paris. Rather than own up to the enormity of the political and ecological challenges of the future—which are colossal, and the Paris Agreement hardly puts a dent in them—we are tempted to rationalize our marginality as an inevitable product of the world in which we are forced to live. This is not to suggest we should instead pretend we live in a different, better world. It is rather to point out that this "realism" can make anything—even the briefest pause in the ticking of a climate time-bomb—seem like great success. Consequently, in place of critical reflection on the current situation, we find ourselves telling each other how awesome our movement is. It is as if we obviously, most certainly, will eventually succeed, however long it takes, when in fact we are cheering our way to catastrophe.

Indeed, if the goal of our movement or movements is to prevent runaway climate change, there is virtual consensus among climate scientists that we have already failed. If the more modest hope is to reframe the debate over the politics of adaptation to a warming world—to emphasize the inequality in who is paying, and will pay, for capital's transformation of the planet with their lives and livelihoods—then we still have a very long way to go and a great deal of work to do. These facts are, to be sure, extremely depressing, but facts they are. It is often said that, in organizing, an emphasis on the negative rarely works—we need a positive vision of change—but we cannot lie to each other or to ourselves. How then can we build resistance and confront our political challenges without lapsing into half-truths or redemptive assurances that it will all work out in the end? Only by bringing many more people into a critical analysis of our challenge, our conjuncture.

Let us try to clarify, for the sake of discussion, what this analysis might entail. If we accept that one way of defining our challenge is to transform the prevailing global political and economic situation so that we can confront climate change in something like a just fashion, then we must create enough

of something—call it a "conception of a just future," a party, or a movement—
to at least temporarily and symbolically generate a unity of our differences in
a way that allows us to coordinate action. We are a long way from this, but
there are some positive signs. For instance, many of us who are committed to
democratic pluralism and diversity nonetheless speak of "the climate justice
movement" in the singular. The Zapatistas have given the international Left a
wonderful metaphor to imagine this form of commonality—the challenge of
unifying social movements while sustaining the basis for diversity and difference within those movements: they speak of it as "a movement of many movements." This is already flowering within the climate justice movement, and
seems to us essential, both tactically and at the theoretical level of grasping
our complex unity. The climate justice movement should be a movement of
many movements.

Still, a movement of many movements can be more or less coherent: some
elements are more likely or more able to align their differences effectively;
others will be more constrained, either by internal or external forces, or both.
This is where leadership and an effective conception of the world are crucial.
The enormous challenge we face is to create the conditions for such a conception and leadership in and through our global diversity. Our political task is in
this sense very different, and arguably far more complex, than that faced by
those who struggled against the British Empire in India or apartheid in South
Africa.

Since 2002, when the Bali statement of principles provided an initial glimpse of
the concept's potential, talk of "climate justice" has multiplied, as have the texts
trying to make sense of it.[21] Rather than review them systematically, it is perhaps
more useful to focus on one well-known text that captures the political-theoret-
ical terrain. In Paris, the book on everyone's lips was Naomi Klein's *This Changes
Everything: Capitalism vs. the Climate*, which offers a historical theory of the
climate crisis and a political theory of immanent climate justice mobilization.[22]
The analysis emphasizes the grip of fossil fuel corporations on capitalist society
and our need to organize "Blockadia" to transform society.[23] Klein was the Left's
star in Paris: her name was everywhere; her events were packed; her excellent

---

21   For the development of the political conception of "climate justice," compare the following
sources: "Bali Principles of Climate Justice," 29 August 2002, accessed at ejnet.org; "Peoples'
Agreement of the World People's Conference on Climate Change and the Rights of Mother Earth,"
April 22, 2010, Cochabamba, Bolivia, available at ienearth.org; Building Bridges Collective, *Space
for Movement?*, 2010, spaceformovement.files.wordpress.com; and the Climate Justice Project
website maintained by John Foran, climatejusticeproject.com.

22   In Paris a blizzard of signs, posters, pamphlets, essays, and books offered competing
interpretations of where we stand and should go. "Climate justice" was the most widely used term
to frame the movement.

23   Naomi Klein, *This Changes Everything: Capitalism vs. the Climate*, New York: Simon &
Schuster, 2014. See also our discussion in Chapter 2.

New Yorker essay framed the climate-justice response to the *état d'urgence*; her reportage from Paris circulated globally.[24] As a defining figure and institutional leader—among other responsibilities, she serves on the board of 350.org, an important international climate change organization—Klein is not merely an important writer but the most well-known leader of the climate justice movement. For this reason, we should think hard about her immensely important contributions. *This Changes Everything* is essential reading, and it has arguably done a great deal to raise the prominence of climate change as a political issue. Its analysis of capitalism, though, is more limited.

The greatest strength of *This Changes Everything* is Klein's insistence that climate change is fundamentally a political problem, a product of capitalism. This is crucial. Her argument as to *why* capitalist societies fail to respond to climate change, however, is not that they are capitalist. Instead, it has to do with the kind of capitalism characterizing those societies: capitalism *could* have developed an adequate response to the challenge of climate change, but did not because its institutions were captured by neoliberalism in the 1980s, just when climate change appeared on the political radar. Climate change is an "epic case of bad timing."[25]

> We have not done the things that are necessary to lower emissions because those things fundamentally conflict with deregulated capitalism, the reigning ideology for the entire period we have been struggling to find a way out of this crisis. We are stuck because the actions that would give us the best chance of averting catastrophe—and would benefit the vast majority—are extremely threatening to an elite minority that has a stranglehold over our economy, our political process, and most of our major media outlets.[26]

At the broadest level, this is surely true—the problem as we see it lies in the qualifier "deregulated." Here and elsewhere in *This Changes Everything*, Klein argues that the world has failed to address climate change specifically because of "deregulated" capitalism. The solution is not the abolition of capitalism, but a regulated, green capitalism not unlike that described in Chapter 5. Whether this is in fact the case is among the key questions upon which the differences in the climate justice movement turn. As elaborated in Chapter 5, our argument too is premised on the claim that capitalism has produced catastrophic climate change, but also that it is incapable of addressing it, and tries to show why this is the case. While we count ourselves among Klein's allies and share her concerns

---

24   Jason Box and Naomi Klein, "Why a Climate Deal Is the Best Hope for Peace," *New Yorker*, November 18, 2015; for Klein's news reports from Paris, see Radio Nation, thenation.com/article/making-the-paris-climate-talks-count.

25   A phrase used in the book and in the title of her speech at the Paris Climate Action Zone, December 11, 2015.

26   Klein, *This Changes Everything*, 18.

regarding the current global trajectory, her analysis of the capitalism question is flawed, both historically and theoretically, and the consequences are potentially grave.

The problem of climate change, Klein writes, "might not have been insurmountable had it presented itself at another point in our history."

> But it is our great collective misfortune that the scientific community made its decisive diagnosis of the climate threat at the precise moment when those elites were enjoying more unfettered political, cultural, and intellectual power than at any point since the 1920s. Indeed, governments and scientists began talking seriously about radical cuts to greenhouse gas emissions in 1988—the exact year that marked the dawning of what came to be called "globalization," with the signing of the agreement representing the world's largest bilateral trade relationship between Canada and the United States, later to be expanded into the North American Free Trade Agreement (NAFTA) with the inclusion of Mexico.[27]

On historical grounds, the claim that capital did not address climate change because the problem was discovered at the "dawn" of globalization in 1988 is difficult to sustain. There is nothing particularly significant about 1988 in either the history of economic policy or climate science. Scientists had understood the physical dynamics driving climate change for decades, and the rise and consolidation of neoliberalism (which Klein has soundly deconstructed in a series of excellent books and articles) was well under way before 1988. Most histories, including Klein's own *Shock Doctrine*, trace it to the 1970s, the decade that began with the collapse of Bretton Woods and ended with the Volcker shock.[28] Moreover, there seems little reason to believe less neoliberal varieties of capitalism would have greened their economies in any meaningful way. The world has by no means been uniformly neoliberal since the discovery of climate change, but capitalist elites have acted basically the same way everywhere.[29] While the neoliberal order continues to wreak havoc on communities

---

27   Ibid., 18–19.

28   See, for example, Klein's *The Shock Doctrine: The Rise of Disaster Capitalism*, New York: Picador, 2007, which dates the emergence of neoliberalism to the early 1970s—a much more defensible periodization. In *This Changes Everything*, Klein summarizes the ideological block to capital's addressing climate in these terms: "[W]hat remained successful were the ideological underpinnings of the entire [neoliberal] project, which was . . . always about using these sweeping [trade] deals, as well as a range of other tools [financial liberalization, for example], to lock in a global policy framework that provided maximum freedom to multinational corporations to produce their goods as cheaply as possible and sell them with as few regulations as possible—while paying as little in taxes as possible. Granting this corporate wish list, we were told, would fuel economic growth, which would trickle down to the rest of us, eventually" (19). Broadly speaking, we endorse Klein's *description* of neoliberalism, but less her *explanation* for it. See Arrighi, *The Long Twentieth Century*; and Harvey, *The Enigma of Capital*.

29   A stronger alternative can be found by contrasting this approach to a critical historicist explanation of capital's ecological crisis, such as we find in the Marxist ecological literature. See especially Andreas Malm, *Fossil Capital: The Rise of Steam Power and the Roots of Global Warming*,

human and non-human around the world, and has accelerated devastating processes unleashed by capitalism, climate change included, we cannot logically or historically hold neoliberalism responsible for the failure to face up to the reality of climate change. Neoliberalism is an historical development in the political economic and social form of capital's hegemony, and it is to this broader process, of which neoliberalism is a crucial moment, on which we must focus. Capitalism did not need to be neoliberal to create the challenges we face.

This Changes Everything is certainly not the only place in the climate justice movement one finds a vague faith in a regulated, green capitalism. For all the reasons elaborated in Chapter 5, this "solution" to climate change is enormously appealing to many, and for lots of good reasons—political, economic, and psychological. If we convince ourselves that a renovated version of what we already have is a solution—or, in a more resigned mood, could have been a solution—then catastrophe seems farther off, even remediable, and its consequences uncertain enough that we can hardly be blamed for our lack of preparation. But the suggestion that the problem is or was neoliberalism, not capitalism, which is what so many of us want to believe even if we know it is not true, is potentially fatal because it consistently leads much of the climate justice movement away from a confrontation with capital, at both the level of political analysis and political practice.

This is a confrontation we cannot avoid any longer. And yet, as more and more people come to this conclusion, we also find that it is much easier to develop an anticapitalist critique of climate change than it is to develop a theoretical and practical vision of postcapitalist social relations that might be adequate to the warmer planet on which we will have no choice but to live. As fervently as we might demand "system change not climate change," we have yet to really elaborate—let alone in a democratic or broad-based manner—what "system change" looks like beyond the absence of fossil fuels. Indeed, most of the time, the tacit assumption is that "system change" means a green, renewables-based capitalism. We find ourselves focused almost entirely on environmental "bad guy" capitalists like mining or petroleum corporations, as if without them things would be mostly acceptable.

Similarly, our contradictory yes-but-no stance regarding global climate politics—structured entirely on the basis of sovereign territorial nation-states, which are taken as the natural and only viable building block for the struggle—has prevented us from taking on the nation-state, both analytically and practically. Of course, movements for climate justice all over the world have bravely confronted particular nation-states' elites and institutions of governance. But the question of the legitimacy and naturalness of the modern nation-state as the

New York: Verso, 2016. In fairness, Malm's book is intended for a narrow audience, and Klein seems to recognize the strengths of his historical approach. In a blurb on the cover of *Fossil Capital*, Klein calls it the "definitive deep history on how our economic system created the climate crisis."

base unit of global political life is rarely raised, at least partly because we too are convinced that (at least at present) interstate "global cooperation" is the only way to sustain a livable planet. Beyond some "realist" argument based in path dependency, however, there is no reason to think so, and many more reasons to suggest that the state is likely one of our biggest obstacles.

Consider once more the omnipresent reactionary state repression in New York and Paris, arguably at absolutely essential moments in the consolidation of a nascent global climate justice movement. Flood Wall Street pushed the limits of the capitalist state's conception of what constitutes a legitimate object of critique. If these large gatherings had demonstrated with the militancy of Flood Wall Street, the state would have shut them down violently and viciously. The protesters in the financial district were intolerable because they seemed to threaten, in however small a way, key components of liberal capitalism's infrastructure, components without which the current hegemonic bloc could not operate. What the reaction to Flood Wall Street said, to those who listened, is that this hegemony does everything in its power to secure the reproduction of the forces driving climate change. Consequently, any attempt to build the sort of broad-based and radical coalition necessary to meet even the preliminary goals of the movement are sure to face concerted opposition from capitalist states in the form of *états d'urgence*, the "exceptional" capitalist state of emergency that has become the norm.

Where does this double deferral to capital and the nation-state leave those working toward climate justice? In a difficult situation, because the struggle over key issues like equality, democracy, and justice takes place on terrain that is for the most part already ceded. The limits to what can be done under such conditions will be familiar to much of the Left since at least the 1970s, when we began the unsteady defensive effort in which we remain engaged today on most fronts. An analysis of the way we debate these issues today reveals the hegemony of liberal common sense, however vociferously many resist or refuse it. If essential aspects of the (neo)liberal capitalist order—capital and the nation-state among them—are understood as effectively unassailable, then our rage at this condition does not undo that hegemony. In other words, the climate justice movement is in some ways not as radical as we often want to believe, despite slogans like "system change not climate change" or occasional courageous radical actions like blockading a pipeline or flooding Wall Street. The vision of many leaders of environmental organizations coordinating the action exhibits a marked unimaginativeness and resigned liberal-ness usually justified as "just being realistic."

This "realistic" political stance is founded in the same logic that underwrites what we call Climate Leviathan: a tacit acceptance of green capitalism and planetary sovereignty as our best or only hope. This is where much of the climate justice movement is tending (especially in the global North), if without a coherent vision or acknowledgement of our aim—perhaps because no small proportion of the movement's participants desperately wish the movement was not necessary. This is why, while at first eyebrow-raising, it actually makes a lot of sense to see the Secretary-General of the United Nations at the head of the People's Climate March, a procession of 300,000 people marching (or at least intending to march) to demonstrate at the gates of his own institution, in the heart of the financial capital of perhaps the one state essential to an emerging Climate Leviathan. The only path with any chance of avoiding catastrophe would appear to lead straight to the doors of the very same powers that got us into this mess. Fortunately, marching in step is not our only option.

8

Climate X

> [For] radical natural-historical thought, everything that exists transforms itself into ruins and fragments.
>
> Theodor Adorno

I

One of the most profound paradoxes of climate justice is that our work is oriented toward an open, just future for those to come, particularly the descendants of the world's less powerful, but this future is so undeniably bleak (and the world's present political arrangements so undemocratic) that any informed, rational response is likely to pull us toward Climate Leviathan, because the further consolidation and expansion of extant power structures would seem to be the only structures of scale, scope, and authority even close to adequate to the challenge of climate change. However dark the future may appear, though, our thought should not shy away from the task of sketching the possible alternative trajectories.

If we begin formulaically, we might say that Climate X is a world that has defeated the emergent Climate Leviathan and its compulsion toward planetary sovereignty, while also transcending capitalism. This is obviously a tall order, to put it mildly. But only in a world that is no longer organized by capitalist value, and in which sovereignty has become so deformed that the political can no longer be defined by the nation-state's sovereign exception, is it possible to imagine a just response to climate change. This general schema gives us some broad sense of direction, and a few indicators by which to identify and measure progress. Support for green Keynesianism, REDD+, climate finance, and the elite politics of adaptation can no longer be priorities. They are distractions, dissipaters of energy for change. The priority must be to organize for a rapid reduction of carbon emissions by collective boycott and strike. Is this utopianism? Possibly, but not necessarily. This is Climate X, and whatever form it takes, it has the extraordinary merit attached to that which is absolutely necessary. We must create something new. More of the same is not an option.

It is tempting to leave Climate X there, if only to acknowledge that we cannot claim to know what form it might take, if any. There is an arrogance to all political prognostication—an arrogance that seems all the worse when history shows so clearly that it is almost always wrong. But there is also duplicity in backing off at precisely the moment when something needs to be said—a duplicity manifesting itself in the desire to avoid saying something refutable and in the hope of appearing wise in retrospect. At times, taking the risk of being very wrong is more productive, and more modest, than maintaining a hesitant silence. We need to work on political visions of a world in which the movement has won—ideas of futures that can guide us in dark times, mobilizations to realize the change—even if those who propose them run the risk of seeming arrogant, of knowing more than can be known.

This challenge or necessity is not new. At the height of the Cold War, when many on the Left had good reason to question the livability of a future dominated by two unacceptable empires with equally apocalyptic destructive capabilities, a similar demand stimulated several attempts to reenergize Marxist political critique. These often took the form of attempts to write a new Manifesto, more adequate to the time. In the weeks after Khrushchev's denunciation of Stalinism in 1956, two of the most prominent Marxist thinkers of the age, Theodor Adorno and Max Horkheimer, made plans to write a new *Communist Manifesto*. They never followed through, but their discussion (which was recorded) of what that document would look like, and what work it might do, is worth thinking about.

> Horkheimer: We cannot leave open the question of what we believe in. The section on work should contain an excursus on the Utopians . . .
> Adorno: The utopians were actually not very utopian at all. But we must not provide a picture of a positive utopia.
> Horkheimer: Especially when one is so close to despair.
> Adorno: I wouldn't say that. I believe that because everything is so obvious a new political authority will emerge . . . The belief that it will come is perhaps a shade too mechanistic. It *can* come; whether it will come or whether it will go to the dogs is terribly hard to predict . . . We have to add that we believe that things can come right in the end . . . How would it be if we were to formulate some guiding political principles today?[1]

We cannot know exactly what was said, but the overriding sense their conversations communicate is the difficulty of the task they are considering. We are hardly better prepared. Clearly, a radical alternative like Climate X is *historically* open to the future in the sense that any form it ultimately takes has no

---

1 Theodor Adorno and Max Horkheimer, 15 March 1956, in *Towards a New Manifesto*, New York; Verso, 2011[1956]), 59–62. The anonymous author of the book's introduction explains that this "unique document is the record, taken down by Gretel Adorno, of discussions over three weeks in the spring of 1956, with a view to the production of—as Adorno puts it—a contemporary version of *The Communist Manifesto*. Although they were speaking barely three weeks after Khrushchev's world-shaking speech, we have no evidence that Adorno and Horkheimer had yet heard about it."

responsibility to fulfill expectations with which we burden it today. But it none-theless seems irresponsible not to heed our own call for ideas of futures that can guide us in dark times, of mobilizations to realize the change, because we are certain these are necessary.

In other words, as Horkheimer says, we cannot leave open the question of what we believe in with the mute hope that it will get worked out as the move-ment progresses. Neither, as Adorno cautions, can we paint a picture of a posi-tive utopia, the unworldliness of which is no more helpful than when Marx and Engels admonished against it in the original manifesto more than a century and a half ago. Adorno suggests that what is required is not an account of a perfect world we can hold in our minds like a dream that can be realized merely because we can dream it, but instead an account of the possible (futures we can come to identify as potential outcomes of our present) in which things *can* (not *will*) "come right in the end." Adorno seems to think this will entail the emergence of a radically new form of political authority, for which we might attempt to "formulate some guiding political principles."

We propose at least three such principles as fundamental to any presently emergent or future Climate X. The first is equality. Sometime in the twentieth century the fundamental claim to the equality of *all* humans (not just members of the white, male, Euro-American "community of the free"), an old proposition on the Left, was hijacked by liberalism; the ransom note says we can have it back, but only if we drop our opposition to capitalism.[2] This we cannot do. Capitalism is a social formation founded on the essential inequality that defines the capital-labor relation, and constantly produces social inequality and the unfreedom of poverty. But this is not the only reason the claim to human equal-ity is necessarily a critique of capital. The planetary ecological crisis illuminates another: if we truly are equal, then we share the Earth. No one can own it. Marx said a long time ago, and it is still true, that "an entire society, a nation, or all co-existing societies taken together, are not owners of the Earth. They are merely its possessors, its usufructuaries, and, as *boni patres familias*, are to bequeath it, improved, to succeeding generations."[3] This wisdom is of course much older than Marx, and can be found in diverse teachings on the appropriate relation-ship between humanity and our common home.[4]

This goes part of the way toward explaining why, as we argued earlier, a critique of capitalism is necessary to an effective climate politics, but not enough

---

2   For a thorough critique of liberalism's "community of the free" (from which we borrow the term), see Domenico Losurdo, *Liberalism: A Counter-History*, New York: Verso, 2011.

3   Karl Marx, *Capital*, Vol. III, New York: Penguin, 1981 [1894], 911.

4   Marxian analyses of "accumulation by dispossession" have been taken to task for their emphasis on the creation of the proletariat and their relative neglect of dispossession. See, for example, Glen Sean Coulthard, *Red Skin, White Masks: Rejecting the Colonial Politics of Recognition*, Minneapolis: University of Minnesota Press, 2014. On Marx's writings on precapitalist societies, see Kevin Anderson, *Marx at the Margins: On Nationalism, Ethnicity, and Non-Western Societies*, Chicago, IL: University of Chicago Press, 2016.

on its own.[5] Many peculiar qualities of climate change as an environmental problem—the importance of climate science for diagnosing the problem; the geographical unevenness and variation in its effects; the apparent urgency of coordinated response; the atmosphere's common pool character; and so on—can neither be explained nor overcome with an analysis limited to the dynamics of capital. Only a radical critique of capitalism *and* sovereignty can orient us today. For many who demand a rapid global response to climate change, the goal is implicitly a planetary form of sovereignty. But that will not be a just world.

This leads to the second guiding political principle: the inclusion and dignity of all. This is a critique of capitalist sovereignty and the thin form of democracy upon which it has come to rely. Democracy is not majority rule and has little to do with the vote. Rather, democracy exists in a society to the extent that anyone and everyone could rule, could shape collective answers to collective questions. No nation-state today meets this criterion. This demands a struggle for inclusion and dignity that can enhance our capacity to transform the politics of rule, a great collective attempt to create conditions for the realization of our self-determination. As Adorno put it, the "single genuine power standing against the principle of Auschwitz is autonomy, if I might use the Kantian expression: the power of reflection, of self-determination, of not cooperating."[6] This dignity is expressed by those climate protesters in Paris who refused "this shadow of the future," who would not "bend to the politics of fear that stifle liberties in the name of security," who identified the greatest threat to security and life in "the system that drives the climate disaster."

The third principle is solidarity in composing a world of many worlds.[7] Against planetary sovereignty, we need a planetary vision without sovereignty, an affirmation of both our common cause and our multiplicity. We could perhaps find some hope for this in the fact that, when Schmitt declared the necessity of the sovereign exception, he explicitly denied the possibility of global sovereignty. But, unsurprisingly, for him it was impossible not because potential planetary solidarity would erode the grounds of sovereignty as the defining

---

5   Dipesh Chakrabarty has made a similar argument:

> climate change may well end up accentuating all the inequities of the capitalist world order . . . Capitalist globalization exists; so should its critiques. But these critiques do not give us an adequate hold on human history once we accept that the crisis of climate change is here with us and may exist as part of this planet for much longer than capitalism or long after capitalism has undergone many more historic mutations . . . While there is no denying that climate change has profoundly to do with the history of capital, a critique that is only a critique of capital is not sufficient for addressing questions relating to human history once the crisis of climate change has been acknowledged and the Anthropocene has begun to loom on the horizon of our present.

Dipesh Chakrabarty, "The Climate of History: Four Theses," *Critical Inquiry* 35, 2009, 212.

6   Theodor Adorno, "Education after Auschwitz", in Rolf Tiedemann (ed.), *Can One Live After Auschwitz: A Philosophical Reader*, Stanford, CA: Stanford University, 2003 [1967], 23.

7   To borrow a Zapatista slogan.

form of the political. On the contrary, he said, global sovereignty is impossible, because universal solidarity is an oxymoron. Any properly political entity, including a state, is irreducibly constituted in enmity; for Schmitt, there is no "us" without a "them."[8]

Given the context in which he wrote (and the terrible alliances he made), it is easy to isolate Schmitt's thought in the particular nationalist, raced, and gendered world he wrote it for and to focus on the human "other" that haunts his understanding of politics. But the "realist" emphasis on exclusion and exception as the basis for political life does not begin with "us" and "them", friend and enemy. Schmitt's division is only possible on a foundation of more fundamental, prior distinctions: between humans and nature (the nonhuman spaces in which territoriality is asserted), between lives and life, humans and humanity, multiplicity and identity—between our collective and individual autonomy, the "single genuine power" Adorno celebrated, and the bounded "universal" abstractions to which Hobbes and Schmitt declare it must sacrificed ("the nation," "the people," "the race," and so on). Paradoxically, perhaps, these distinctions are even more fundamental to the conception of collective planetarity that gives Climate Leviathan much of its "progressive" appeal. Leviathan knows that many ways of life and communities will be lost in the effort to save life on Earth; that is the sacrifice "we" must make. Climate X must reject both the assertion that "planetary" concerns must dominate those of the many communities and peoples who inhabit the planet and the global sovereign that presumes the right to determine those concerns. But does that mean it must oppose all who arrogate to themselves the power to speak on planetary matters? What, if any, form of political life is amenable to a planetarity that does not seem inherently to entail sovereign rule?

Neither these principles (equality, dignity, solidarity) nor these questions descend from an ivory tower. They are, rather, drawn directly from struggles for climate justice coalescing all over the world, and especially among some of the world's most marginal social groups—many of whom, unsurprisingly, are Indigenous communities for whom these principles do not require the radical political renovation they do for much of the settler-colonial and colonizing world. These groups have led the vociferous opposition to the UNFCCC conception of climate politics because they see it as capitalist imperialism's talent show, and, with respect to its capacity to mitigate the impacts of catastrophic climate change, a meaningless liberal piety. These courageous movements—some seemingly little more than quixotic—are the seeds of a Climate X, proof that it is germinating.[9]

The conditions for building this movement reside in the possibilities of the full range of radical developments before us. Some of these take a more or less

---

8   Schmitt, *The Concept of the Political*, 26, 53–54.
9   Patrick Bond, "Climate Capitalism Won at Cancun," *Links: International Journal of Socialist Renewal*, December 12, 2010.

"orthodox" Left form, like economist Minqi Li's anticipated ecological resurgence through communist revolution:

> Hopefully, people throughout the world will engage in a transparent, rational and democratic debate which is open not only to economic and political leaders and expert intellectuals, but also to the broad masses of workers and peasants. Through such a global collective debate, a democratic consensus could emerge that would decide on a path of global social transformation that would in turn lead to climate stabilization ... This may sound too idealistic. But can we really count on the world's existing elites to accomplish climate stabilization while meeting the world population's basic needs? Ultimately, climate stabilization can only be achieved if the great majority of the world's population (not just the elites and the ecologically conscious middle class individuals) understand the implications, relate these implications to their own lives, and actively ... participate in the global effort of stabilization.[10]

The hopeful logic of Li's analysis reflects one attempt to bridge the gap between a "positive utopia" and a vision of a world in which "things *can* come right in the end." But it remains (to quote Adorno) a "shade too mechanistic" (as Li would surely concede). The essential question is how could we create conditions in which these dynamics actually operate? Although time is clearly short, the immediate challenge is one of cultivation, of working the material and ideological ground in which these movements can bloom as rapidly as possible and in their full multiplicity. Cultivation like that requires the kind of radical struggle that proves history wrong. A world revolution for climate justice has no clear historical precedent, which is to say that if Li is right that "climate stabilization can only be achieved if the great majority of the world's population understand the implications, relate these implications to their own lives, and actively and consciously participate in the global effort of stabilization," we have no previous model to go by. We must build the means to render global participation possible while the entire globe is changing, warming, and (potentially) warring. And all this has to happen in a world that is moving fast in the wrong direction.

We noted that challenges to Leviathan in Asia will arise from the numerous social groups at risk from climate change and other political-economic forces. We should expect that those who will suffer the greatest consequences—like the urban poor in Calcutta or Jakarta, or peasant farmers across central Mexico and the Sahel—will find ideological resources where they can, perhaps principally through religion. Any attempt to anticipate the forms these challenges will take must recognize that the prevailing frame of opposition to Western liberalism across much of contemporary Asia is political Islam in various forms.

---

10   Minqi Li, "Capitalism, Climate Change, and the Transition to Sustainability: Alternative Scenarios for the US, China and the World," *Development and Change* 40, 2009, 1058.

Islamist movements could coincide with any of the four squares in our diagram (Figure 2.2) but tend toward what we have called Behemoth, the right half of the four-square, either reaction (upper right) or revolution (bottom right). Where Leviathan calls for planetary management, what we might call "climate al Qaeda" represents an attack on the hubris of liberal aspirations to planetary sovereignty or, more positively, a defense of God's Creation. Take, for example, Osama bin Laden's communiqué of February 10, 2010, on "the way to save the Earth." His memo eviscerates common proposals to address climate change, noting that the "world has been kidnapped" by wealthy people and corporations "who are steering it towards the abyss." He argues that the industrialized countries, especially the United States, are responsible for the climate crisis. Bin Laden is surely correct; and the tactics he suggests—boycotting oil companies and the US dollar—are far from naive.[11] His critique of the West's hypocritical attempt to assume responsibility for managing Creation by expanding its destructive dominance offers a powerful illustration of Behemoth attacking Leviathan.

Although it is not clear to what degree Bin Laden's proposals oppose the hegemony of capital, one might take them—in combination with the militant variety of Islamism to which he subscribed—as one potential version of X. This is certainly not the Climate X we hope to see, but it does raise the question of how this vision might be distinguished from something to which the Left can commit. From our perspective, the principal and decisive difference is that while Bin Laden's vision might perhaps suggest the destruction of earthly sovereignty in some of its more pernicious forms, it is unwaveringly theocratic, and consequently as irremediably bound to a friend-enemy conception of the political as Schmitt's. Bin Laden calls the faithful to the redemption of our "corrupted" world as a means to "save Creation." This is a theological conception of climate "justice" based on the exclusion and domination, perhaps even the erasure, of billions of nonbelievers. Its realization would require the full force of the terror—arguably this kind of virtue's inescapable evil twin—with which Bin Laden is often associated.

This is the likely outcome of all attempts to counter Climate Leviathan in the name of religion, from Hindu fundamentalism to reactionary Christian conservatism. The latter has, for the most part, either adopted the denialism of the US Republican Party or embraced the apocalyptic aspects of the crisis as God's judgment on a sinful world. Pope Francis has taken a different position,

---

11   "We should refuse to do business with the dollar and get rid of it as soon as possible. I know that this action has huge consequences and massive repercussions; but it is an important way to liberate humanity from enslavement and servitude to America and its corporations." Bin Laden adds for an imputed Western audience: "be earnest and take the initiative in boycotting them, in order to save yourselves, your wealth and your children from climate change and in order to live freely and honorably [instead of standing on] the steps of conferences and begging for your lives." Osama bin Laden, "The Way to Save the Earth," February 10, 2010, available at archive.org/stream/Ossama_ihtibas_03/sabil-e_djvu.txt.

but it is precisely his rejection of fundamentalism, and his (cautious) embrace of a universal solidarity, that has simultaneously improved his standing with liberal elites and troubled his status in orthodox (which is to say exclusive) religious communities, including among Roman Catholics. The problem is that even Francis's universalism is ultimately beholden to a Church in which all are supposedly welcome, but to which we are all already supposed subject, whether we understand it or not. It is a house of universality in which all are resident, even the unbelievers, but only by the sovereign grace of God.

The contrast with religion provides an important way to conceptualize the challenge presented by Climate Leviathan, since, for so many, religion is the crucial resource for adapting to a hot and unstable world. X could therefore be seen as an irreligious movement in place of a religious structure. Climate X is worldly and open, and affirms the autonomous dignity of all. It must be a movement of the community of all—including the excluded—that affirms climate justice and popular freedoms against capital and planetary sovereignty. But is that world even imaginable, let alone realizable?

II

One measure of the robustness of a political theory is its acknowledgment of, interest in, and ability to account for its own contradictions. On these grounds, we should be the first to try to identify the limitations of Climate X. Three concerns seem particularly grave, each of which reflects X's relation to one of the other three paths. We must look critically at X from the vantage of each of the other possibilities, or paths, beginning with the hegemonic position of Climate Leviathan.

First, from the vantage of Climate Leviathan, X is impossible by definition. It must be—and indeed at an ideological level, already is—rejected in every way: as illegitimate, impractical, dangerous, fantastical, empty. On the terms of the present geopolitical order, Climate X is not just far weaker than Leviathan, it is not even articulable—a joke no one gets. Consider, for instance, the challenges facing a radical movement toward climate justice in the United States and China. These are not only the planet's two most powerful states and largest emitters. They form a reluctant and unstable "G2," nuclear powers engaged in significant geopolitical conflict (particularly in the Pacific), and capitalist societies locked together (if unhappily) at the heart of the global economy. To bring about a radical reassembly of their relation, to undo the momentum of Leviathan in these societies while overcoming capitalism, would require not only revolutionary events in both nation-states but also forms of radical transnationalism relaying struggles within and between them. We are a long way from this. At best, we have limited forms of solidarity, expressed sporadically and typically filtered through nationalist lenses.

Zapatismo provides some useful lessons for thinking about this kind of struggle. The Zapatista movement has produced a remarkable theory and practice of place-based revolutionary struggle in Chiapas that operates both within and against the nation-state form. Zapatismo has enacted a territorial strategy, one that affirms at once the indigeneity, Mexican-ness, and planetarity of their struggle. Though undeniably anticapitalist, the movement has eschewed a frontal attack on capital in favor of the patient labor of working their way out of capitalist social relations: "*somos anti-capitalistas modestas.*"[12] Rather than attempt to seize control of or unravel the nation-state, they have worked to subtract their communities from it, while producing a novel form of state rooted in rotating, locally appointed "good government." While the Zapatistas are by no means opposed to gestures of international solidarity, their primary external work has been through example. They express a novel radicalism that anticipates many of the qualities we might expect from Climate X. Yet the ongoing siege by the US-backed Mexican state/military, the encirclement of Zapatista communities by a phalanx of military and paramilitary bases and agents, and the limited transnational solidarity supporting the Zapatista struggle indicate and reproduce the geopolitical limitations of their efforts, however blameless they are for their inability to fully overcome them. In other words, to say they still have a long way to go is not to criticize the movement, but to admire and learn from it.

The problem with every attempt to realize particular local instances of Climate X is that, upon reaching a minimal level of viability and visibility, every "X" will be surrounded and attacked by capitalist nation-states and their "privately" organized allies. Unless they are protected by some broader force above or outside (a much-reformed United Nations, for example, working with transnational social movements on the Left), each immanent X will be destroyed or so tightly constrained as to render its full realization virtually impossible. How can we build solidaristic protection "above or beyond" the capitalist state except through some other state-form, ideally a world state? This question could divide the Left—arguably, it already does—and leave many searching for Leviathan, either "progressive" or revolutionary.

This leads to the second limitation to Climate X, from the position of a would-be Climate Mao. Within any climate justice movement that could possibly be effective or radical, we will encounter a deep desire for a planetary sovereign, one capable of the emergency measures needed to save life on Earth. From this vantage, X is too democratic, too antisovereign. There is much to celebrate in the burgeoning worldwide resistance to fossil fuel corporations and the exciting radical challenges to the neoliberal orthodoxy and political pessimism that dominate the ideological landscape.[13] But, in the face of rapid climate change, many on the Left have become convinced that

---

12   "We are modest anti-capitalists."
13   This paragraph reproduces arguments from Geoff Mann, "Who's Afraid of Democracy?" *Capital Nature Socialism* 24, no. 1, 42–48.

something like Climate Leviathan is our only hope. Democracy as we know it (especially its hegemonic liberal variety) seems profoundly inadequate to the problems that lie ahead, and to imagine that democracy in another form is going to fix things takes what many might justifiably see as an increasingly ludicrous leap of faith. Donald Trump is president of the United States; this alone would seem to confirm that there is no reason to believe liberal democracy will help us identify a just and livable way forward simply because it is formally democratic. If, for example, climate policy were placed in the hands of the electorates of the world's dominant, capitalist, liberal democracies, how much would the status quo change? That the obvious answer to this question is "not that much at all" can point toward two radically different conclusions. On one hand, it seems to confirm the need for Climate Leviathan and its technocratic authoritarianism. On the other hand, however, it points not to the futility of democracy, but to the need for a more radical reorganization of political life than simply bringing "the people" into the climate arena through the ballot box. It is a mistake to equate mass politics with radical politics, just as it is spurious to presume that hegemonic elites' fear of the masses and democracy (which we usually feel comfortable criticizing) is driven by a fear of radical ideas "coming true" and realizing social justice.[14]

Third, from the position of behemoth (and disccused in chapter 4), modern liberalism's most powerful internal critique is in fact a liberal effort to ensure that the bourgeoisie do not let self-interest and myopia undermine their privilege and power. Liberals recognize in the multitude only the potential destruction of the social stability they believe keeps chaos at bay. This multitude—the mob, the "rabble"—is a very old specter, and one of its oldest iterations is Behemoth.[15] Fear of its chaos will be one of the main forces that breathes life

---

14   This is a tendency to which Antonio Negri is sometimes prone. Consider, for example, his brilliant critique of Keynesianism. Negri reads the rise of the "planner state" as unconditional evidence of capital's "admission of working-class autonomy," as a recognition that the "problem of repressing the powerful trade union and political movement of the working class" had "extended the revolutionary experience to the whole capitalist world" (Antonio Negri, "Keynes and the Capitalist Theory of the State post-1929," in *Revolution Retrieved: Writings on Marx, Keynes, Capitalist Crisis and New Social Subjects*, London: Red Notes, 1988 [1967], 12, 15). This line of thinking about the masses and democracy takes on a radically different optic if we shift away from the liberal, core-capitalist democracies to, say, openly undemocratic states, especially in the Global South.

15   Fear of it never seems far from left-liberal opposition to capitalism. Consider the response of radicals like Robin Blackburn and Robert Wade to the global economic crisis in 2008. Rather than welcoming the crisis as Marx did the meltdown of 1857 (as he wrote to Engels: "the stock exchange is the only place where my present dullness turns into elasticity and bouncing"), Blackburn and Wade seem mainly interested in stabilizing the system so that unrest does not destroy the whole kit and caboodle (Marx quotation is from Roman Rosdolsky, *The Making of Marx's 'Capital'*, Vol. I, London: Pluto Press, 1977 [1968], 7); Robin Blackburn, "The Subprime Crisis," *New Left Review* II/50, 2008, 63–105; Robin Blackburn, "Crisis 2.0," *New Left Review* II/72, 2011, 33–62; Robert Wade, "Financial Regime Change," *New Left Review* II/53, 2008, 5–21; Robert Wade, "From Global Imbalances to Global Reorganizations," *Cambridge Journal of Economics* 33, 2009, 539–62.

into Leviathan. For while liberalism has little fear of climate change *per se,* it dreads the mob, the rabble, the climate refugee. These figures threaten to destroy not only the bourgeoisie, but the entire order it understands as "civilization." Recall the liberal dystopian fantasy of Oreskes and Conway with which we opened Chapter 6: warming shatters West Antarctica, flooding lets loose the masses, refugees spill across the planet, and Western Civilization is destroyed. The stories may be new, but their eschatology is ancient.

Some may find the contradictions of X discussed above to be so fundamental that they constitute a basis for siding with Leviathan or Mao. Yet these contradictions do not prevent us either from conceptualizing X as a left political strategy or from laboring to realize X in revolutionary practice. Still, there remains the theoretical task of illuminating possible paths through apparently impossible problems. Putting aside the false solution of urging others on in the name of a mandatory liberal "optimism," we see two intertwined but distinct genuine openings for left praxis, each reflecting a distinct tradition of thought.

The first opening might find inspiration in the categorical refusal that underwrites Marx's critique of sovereignty and of communism. Although he coauthored the manifesto of the Communist Party, which many read as a work of prophesy, Marx wrote almost nothing about the future, and even less about what a future communism will look like. His clearest statement on the matter is a refusal of the possibility that revolutionary thought can "know" in a definitive manner where revolutionary activity is going. Communism, he wrote, is

> not a *state of affairs* which is to be established, an *ideal* to which reality [will] have to adjust itself. We call communism the *real* movement which abolishes the present state of things, the conditions of this movement result from the premises now in existence.[16]

The second opening might be grounded in Benjamin's call for politically resolute witness to crisis, a stance that finds affirmation in Agamben's appeal to a "coming community" and "destituent" power. We wager we need to say yes and yes, affirming both positions at once. In this view, Climate X is at once a means, a regulative ideal, and, perhaps, a necessary condition for climate justice. This is the logical result of the equal necessity of politicizing the present and incessantly questioning the future: a rejection of utopian blueprints, of nostalgia for a lost past, and of futile mourning over missed opportunities.

What would this look like in action? Much can be learned from grassroots climate justice movements across the planet; so too can wisdom be gained from unlikely sources. After the Paris meetings, ecologist Miguel Altieri circulated a

---

16   Karl Marx and Friedrich Engels, *The German Ideology,* in *Karl Marx and Friedrich Engels, Collected Works,* Vol. 5, New York: International Publishers, 1976, 49.

text celebrating "the most important . . . message for humanity in 2015: Pope Francis's ecological encyclical *Laudato Si'*."[17] His enthusiasm is understandable. Assailing a "global problem with grave implications," Francis emphasizes the essential political-economic injustice of climate change: the product of the world's richest societies, the poor pay the greatest price. They "have no other financial activities or resources which can enable them to adapt to climate change or to face natural disasters, and their access to social services and protection is very limited." Without these resources, we are already witness to "a tragic rise in the number of migrants seeking to flee from the growing poverty caused by environmental degradation," refugees who "are not recognized by international conventions as refugees; they bear the loss of the lives they have left behind, without enjoying any legal protection whatsoever." Their plight is no fault of their own, and yet

> there is widespread indifference to such suffering, which is even now taking place throughout our world. Our lack of response to these tragedies involving our brothers and sisters points to the loss of that sense of responsibility for our fellow men and women upon which all civil society is founded.[18]

Francis names the source of this indifference unflinchingly—on the same ethical basis as his recognition that Donald Trump is not a Christian—the privileges of wealth and power. Those "who possess more resources and economic or political power seem mostly to be concerned with masking the problems or concealing their symptoms, simply making efforts to reduce some of the negative impacts of climate change."[19] The duplicity of the powerful is revealed when "this attitude exists side by side with a 'green' rhetoric" that arrogates to the very same elites the power to determine the planet's future. Against this, "we have to realize that a true ecological approach always becomes a social approach; it must integrate questions of justice in debates on the environment, so as to hear both the cry of the earth and the cry of the poor."[20] The conclusion is radical: the refusal to center our political analysis of climate crisis on the poor and powerless helps explain why the "solutions" proposed are false and why international leadership to reduce carbon emissions has been so pathetic.

> We lack leadership capable of striking out on new paths and meeting the needs of the present with concern for all and without prejudice towards coming generations.

---

17   Pope Francis I, "Encyclical Letter Laudato Si' of the Holy Father Francis on Care for Our Common Home," 2015, w2.vatican.va.

18   Ibid. Francis's "civil society" is not the bourgeois social formation that has obsessed European political theory for centuries. He uses the term to describe a society founded in civility—what once might have been unhesitatingly called "civilization." Avoiding the latter term, the Pope is indicating an awareness of at least some of civilization's troubling legacies.

19   Pope Francis, "Laudato Si'," §26.

20   Ibid., §49.

The establishment of a legal framework which can set clear boundaries and ensure the protection of ecosystems has become indispensable; otherwise, the new power structures based on the techno-economic paradigm may overwhelm not only our politics but also freedom and justice . . . It is remarkable how weak international political responses have been. The failure of global summits on the environment make it plain that our politics are subject to technology and finance. There are too many special interests, and economic interests easily end up trumping the common good and manipulating information so that their own plans will not be affected . . . The alliance between the economy and technology ends up sidelining anything unrelated to its immediate interests. Consequently the most one can expect is superficial rhetoric, sporadic acts of philanthropy and perfunctory expressions of concern for the environment . . .[21]

More forcefully than any other world leader, Francis has called upon political leaders to act, exploiting his position to make gestures of solidarity with climate activists.[22] Indeed, an argument could be made that the Pope's climate politics offers a more precise set of commitments than that of many in the climate justice movement. The most direct, coherent, radical statement of principles to address climate change we read in Paris came from Francis. During COP21 we walked to Sacré-Coeur, a cathedral built by a reactionary Church on the ruins of the Paris Commune of 1871, a church the Left loves to hate.[23] Inside was a display explaining the Pope's encyclical, emphasizing his call for a new planetary arrangement based on solidarity, dignity, and equality of all. The values of 1871, inscribed inside Sacré-Coeur! It was as though the Commune had broken through the marble floor, its ideas germinating a century and a half later than planned.

But we are not Catholics and have not joined the Church, at least not yet. The problem is not that there is some hidden reactionary message beneath Francis's discourse on climate. The problem with the Franciscan approach lies instead in its theological and institutional commitments, a problem that limits all religious approaches to planetary environmental issues. The clarity of the Pope's encyclical should put the Church on the side of the Indigenous radical critics who attempted to perform their ceremony at its steps. Unfortunately, the boundaries between religions remain intact, as does their unforgiving attachment to those divisions, to who is included and who is excluded from the faithful—symbolized here by the closed doors of Notre Dame and the police defending its plaza. If the unexpected radical words inside Sacré-Coeur give us some hope for the role of religion in the face of the climate crisis, it must be tempered

---

21   Ibid., §§53–54.

22   In the run-up to the Paris meetings, for instance, the Pope placed his shoes in the Place de la République in solidarity with the banned climate march.

23   See David Harvey, "Monument and Myth," *Annals of the Association of American Geographers* 69 no. 3, 1979, 362–81.

if not extinguished by the inhospitable rejection of the Indigenous leaders outside the gates of Notre Dame.

To some extent, modern religions' institutional rigidities have been finessed by suitably ecumenical "interfaith" movements to enrich and unify religious perspectives on environmental change. But even when these movements transcend the ostensible solidarity of an airport chapel, the theological frame is no less limiting because it is built upon the essential structure and political imaginary of sovereign authority ("theology" is literally the word of God). This is a complex matter to which we cannot do justice here, but on our terms, it concerns the ambiguous relation between X and the capitalist millenarianism of Behemoth, which would appear to be strictly divided by their radically opposed attitudes to capital. Francis's widespread appeal to progressives and the Left undoubtedly reflects a latent potential for X, and his position concerning the climate emergency reflects a critique of capitalism. Parallel illustrations may be found from every religious tradition.

Yet, like all religious calls to transcend the present order, it leaves the question of rule radically open. Our point is not that Francis is surreptitiously laying the groundwork for some sort of "ecological theocracy." Rather, the point is that theocracy is unavoidably a constitutive ideal in a theological worldview. If one accepts the absolute authority of the word of God as Truth and Wisdom, then the rule of God (or His or Her earthly representatives) is a logical and unconditional, if idealized, objective. If God could rule, why would humanity stand in the way? As radically progressive as Francis's position on climate might seem, this proposition is inseparable from it. What is needed instead is what Benjamin calls the "real state of emergency," in which sovereign supremacy in its theocratic or secular forms—and hence the links that might appear to tie Behemoth and X together—are broken.[24]

III

Over the last twenty years, the Italian communist philosopher Antonio Negri has turned often to the biblical figure of Job—the very same figure whose powerlessness God taunted with the Leviathan—as a metaphor for "our" present condition:

> [the] reality of our wretchedness is that of Job, the questions and the answers that we pose to the world are the same as Job's. We express ourselves with the same desperation, uttering the same blasphemous phrases. We have known riches and hope, we have tempted God with reason—we are left with dust and inanity.[25]

24   Walter Benjamin, "Theses on the Philosophy of History," in *Illuminations*, New York: Schocken Books, 1969, 258.

25   Antonio Negri, *The Labor of Job: The Biblical Text as a Parable of Human Labor*, Durham, NC: Duke University Press, 2009, 15.

There may indeed be something to this. Those who struggle for climate justice in the age of Trump are like Job. Trump is not God, of course, but taunts the desperate "reason" that underwrites so much of the argument for climate action.

But this is not why this book is structured by figures from the Book of Job (Leviathan and Behemoth). The debate on the politics of climate change turns, like Job's with God, on sovereignty. Capital is also a fulcrum, but it seems that the Left's arguments concerning it—that capital's ceaseless expansionist imperative drives carbon emissions; that the capitalist nation-state constrains effective responses to climate change—are relatively uncontroversial. This says something important about the contemporary climate change discourse. Until recently, only a few radical political ecologists, in various shades of red and green, contended that planetary environmental change was a logical consequence of capitalism. No longer. Today even some of capital's best-known champions—Paul Krugman, Joseph Stiglitz, Christine Lagarde, and others—have drawn the connection between the relentless logic of accumulation and climate change.[26] Theirs is not the liberal common sense shaping state policy, but it is a noteworthy development. If nothing else, it is now possible to openly discuss the failures of capitalism to deal with climate change (if only as "market failure"). By contrast, the engagement with the political, the problems raised by climate change for sovereignty, are only beginning to be grasped, even on the Left.

While our description of Leviathan as a definite social formation may therefore be a contingent abstraction and may prove to be wrong, the specter of Leviathan is no less real. The hopeful subjects of Climate Leviathan will be seeking something in particular, a desire for more than abstract "change." The mass mobilizations for a meaningful international agreement from Copenhagen to Paris, however quixotic, are no aberration. On the contrary, they are desperately sincere, driven by a palpable urgency. This logic must be respected, and we expect it to become more popular (and not only on the Left). The shrill calls emanating from elites demanding a global finance-sovereign are the precipitate of similar reasoning: the problem is identified as arising from gaps in sovereignty, and their solution is a rule without such gaps—a single, decisive monolith; a sovereign fit for a capitalist world.[27] This is closely tied to why Climate Mao appeals so strongly to some anticapitalists. Refusing capitalism, they call no less energetically for a sovereign supreme to save us all—and punish those who have brought us to the precipice. We can understand this urge, but it must be rejected. For, if it seems clear to many on the Left that a planetary sovereign

26 Christine Lagarde "Ten Myths about Climate Change," n.d., imf.org/external/np/fad/environ/pdf/011215.pdf.

27 Elite calls for an omniscient global finance-sovereign—in the form of "radical" reregulation by (among others) the International Monetary Fund, the Bank of International Settlements, and the Basel banking accords—were ubiquitous in the immediate aftermath of the financial meltdown of 2007–2008.

is the only way to save life on Earth, it is crucial to consider what exactly we would be saving.

It would not, obviously, be a world of many worlds, built in solidarity—the third principle of Climate X. Leviathan and Mao both require a categorical rejection of that principle, whereas for any realizable Climate X it is nonnegotiable. Indeed, it is essential to emphasize both the false universality of the call for Climate Leviathan (necessary to save "us")—unmasking the privileged "we" is partly what must define Climate X—but also the nonidentity of Climate X. Emancipatory opposition to Climate Leviathan is founded on a rejection of the promise of planetary sovereignty. The reasons for that rejection must not be homogenized into an ultimately universalizing "we" that experiences a common "wretchedness." As we have been at pains to emphasize throughout the preceding pages, the subjects of capitalist rule that bear the brunt of ecological disasters are not an undifferentiated "we," and the forms X might take will be shaped by the diversity of the histories and communities in which they take shape.

In other words, in the formulation of Climate X as one of a set of ideas of the future that, as we said, can guide us in dark times, we must avoid falling victim to the universalizing claims of subjectivity that, for example, Hardt and Negri attribute to "Empire." Climate X is definitively *not* "the set of all the exploited and the subjugated, a multitude that is directly opposed to Empire, with no mediation between them."[28] We might, generously, take this to mean that anticolonial nationalism and communist militancy no longer monopolize the mediation of subaltern resistance, and we should not be nostalgic in the face of this development. But the "set of all" in which the multitude experiences "our wretchedness" is a myth, and an antisolidaristic myth at that. In that sense, it is not unlike the Anthropocene, the era that now puts all humans on the same geological page.[29] The world's peoples live in a multitude of geo-ecological times despite our planetary "simultaneity," and the forces that have helped shape those worlds are not reducible to "humanity" in general, but to particular natural-historical social formations.

Capital and the nation-state have been fundamental to many of these formations, always in vastly uneven ways that must be understood on the terms of the social formations they transformed. For instance, if the Anthropocene is defined as a planetary and historical regime shaped in irreversible ways by "humanity" or "man," then Indigenous peoples in the Americas have been

28   Michael Hardt and Antonio Negri, *Empire*, Cambridge, MA: Harvard University Press, 2000, 393.

29   Against the false universalism of the Anthropocene, some alternatives have been proposed: capitalocene, plantationocene, "great derangement;" others will surely follow. See Donna Haraway, "Anthropocene, Capitalocene, Plantationocene, Chthulucene: Making Kin," *Environmental Humanities* 6, 159–65; Jason Moore (ed.), *Anthropocene or Capitalocene? Nature, History, and the Crisis of Capitalism*, Oakland, CA, PM Press, 2016; Amitav Ghosh, *The Great Derangement: Climate Change and the Unthinkable*, Chicago, University of Chicago Press, 2016; Benjamin Kunkel, "The Capitalocene", *London Review of Book*, 39, no. 5, 2017, 22–28.

surviving the damnation of the Anthropocene for more than 500 years. (How else could we describe the so-called "Columbian Exchange" of disease and invasive species, in combination with capitalist property relations and state-supported dispossession?) If the more recent periodization is defended because the concept is supposed to name the moment when humanity as a *species* fundamentally altered Earth's systems—as opposed to a moment like the colonization of the Americas, in which only some groups undid a world or community of worlds—well, that is patently false. "We" clearly did not all contribute equally to the planet's and its residents' predicament.

All of which is to say that just as there is not one "set of all" that is the "multitude," there is no one Climate X. Some of the political formations that help consolidate the movement for climate justice will not understand themselves as standing in opposition to Climate Leviathan, or even necessarily understand Climate Leviathan as structurally different from the mode of capitalist sovereignty they have historically experienced. If Leviathan is partly defined by the arrogation of the authority to declare the exception, save "humanity," and determine whose lives will be sacrificed in the universal interest, then that form of sovereignty is hardly new to Indigenous and colonized peoples; neither environmental injustice nor the Anthropocene mark a new historical beginning for them.

There are, we might say, two broad but distinct trajectories that might lead to Climate X. The first is a radical analysis and practice based in an open embrace of the tradition of the anticapitalist Left, sprung from Marxist roots. While by no means a panacea for emancipatory political struggle, the diverse and creative ways that Marxian ideas have inspired movements across the planet testifies to their fertility. Even when it has been radically reinvented or taken to task (for example in the community economies work associated with J.K. Gibson-Graham), it nonetheless provides a foundation and counterpoint to efforts to think how things could be otherwise and how to get there.

The second trajectory gets its momentum from very different sources: the knowledge and lifeways of peoples who have long historical experience with ways of being that are not overdetermined by capital and the sovereign state. It is no accident that Indigenous and colonized peoples are at the frontlines in the struggles sowing the seeds of any realizable Climate X. While these groups have, of course, been subject to capital and state power, to generalize, their present strategies do not emphasize forging internationalist solidarity for a revolutionary communist or socialist future. Their point, rather, is to ensure that the full multiplicity of those lifeways has a vital and dignified future—and, in some cases, to communicate to those willing to listen what they might learn from it.

The challenge that defines Climate X is bringing these two trajectories together; not to merge them, or subordinate one to the other, but to find some means by which they support each other, give each other energy and momentum. This is not impossible, although a left turn toward Leviathan or Mao will almost certainly undo the potential for synergy. This is another reason for Climate X—movements for climate justice that reject both capital and sovereign rule—because to fall back on Leviathan or Mao is to reject the first and second principles as well, equality and dignity for all. Both sovereign paths oppose those principles by definition. Adorno said of a potentially radical, new form of authority, "It *could* come." What would it be? The answer can only be a democracy so radical it is contrary to sovereignty. Indeed, it must be said that real democracy can only be nonsovereign, because there cannot be a principle of rule, or a territorial closure, that is so sacrosanct it cannot be otherwise.

Adorno is no doubt building on the early Marx, but this thinking has more than one source. To understand what he is trying to articulate, and thus what the radical Left trajectory can bring to the struggle, we can return to Hegel's analysis of sovereignty, which Schmitt came to celebrate in light of the "failure" of Hobbes's *Leviathan*.[30] Marx struggled with the same material in the 1840s. Throughout his notes on Hegel's *Philosophy of Right*, Marx subjects to tireless criticism the very feature of Hegel's state which arguably appealed to Schmitt— its "logical pantheistic mysticism":

> If Hegel had set out from real subjects as the bases of the state he would not have found it necessary to transform the state in a mystical fashion into a subject. "In its truth, however," says Hegel, "subjectivity exists only as *subject*, personality only as *person*." This too is a piece of mystification. Subjectivity is a characteristic of the subject, personality a characteristic of the person. Instead of conceiving them as predicates of their subjects, Hegel gives the predicates an independent existence and subsequently transforms them in a mystical fashion into their subjects.[31]

Marx's critique of Hegel anticipates the essential problem we face with Climate Leviathan, which is nothing but a form of sovereignty in search of a subject. In both its capitalist and noncapitalist forms, the mysticism of the would-be planetary sovereign resides in what Marx calls "the actual regulation of the parts by the idea of the whole."[32]

Today, despite the rise of abhorrent racist nationalisms and their concerted efforts to derail climate action and global cooperation of any sort, among both elites and progressives the Idea of planetary governance as *the* response to

---

30   Carl Schmitt, *The Leviathan in the State Theory of Thomas Hobbes: Meaning and Failure of a Political Symbol*, Chicago, IL: University of Chicago Press, 2008 [1938], 85, 100; Carl Schmitt, *Political Theology II: The Myth of the Closure of Any Political Theology*, Chicago, IL: University of Chicago Press, 2008 [1970], 32.

31   Karl Marx, "Contribution to the Critique of Hegel's Philosophy of Law," in *Marx-Engels Collected Works*, Vol. III, New York: International Publishers, 1973 [1843], 6, 23, emphasis in original.

32   Ibid., 24.

climate change is unfolding like a caricature of Hegelian necessity. It moves toward the ultimate end of sovereignty, the coming into being of sovereignty's global *telos*, a Notion mystically realizing itself. Planetary sovereignty stands, as in some ways it always has, as the completion of modernity. Though it presents itself as a defense of life and civilization, planetary governance cannot countenance democracy. This is not a contradiction or a paradox; democracy and sovereignty have never been allies. For Hegel, they are antinomies:

> But the usual sense in which the term "popular sovereignty" has begun to be used in recent times is to denote *the opposite of that sovereignty which exists in the monarch.* In this oppositional sense, popular sovereignty is one of those confused thoughts which are based on a *garbled* notion of the *people. Without* its monarch and that *articulation* of the whole which is necessarily and immediately associated with monarchy, *the* people is a formless mass.[33]

Marx, at least at this stage in his thinking, was outraged by Hegel's dismissal of radical democracy. Hegel, he wrote, thinks of the monarch as

> political consciousness in the flesh; in consequence, therefore, all other people are excluded from this sovereignty . . . But if he is sovereign inasmuch as he represents the unity of the nation, then he himself is only the representative, the symbol, of national sovereignty. National sovereignty does not exist by virtue of him, but he on the contrary exists by virtue of it.[34]

Here, the young Marx's "Rhenish liberalism," while constraining his efforts to break free of the state, did not prevent him from grasping what was at stake for Hegel in this situation: in the modern world, democracy can serve neither as a mode of sovereignty nor as a means thereto.[35] It is, rather, sovereignty's negation. This is perhaps why Schmitt abandoned Hobbes for Hegel in the late 1930s. Hegel posits sovereignty in the monarchical manner he does because for him, democracy cannot constitute sovereignty, by definition. Instead, the monarch or sovereign is "political consciousness in the flesh" because the sovereign decision—the constitution of sovereignty as such—defines the substance of the rational state and thereby determines the terrain of the political.[36] Likewise for Schmitt, for whom sovereignty is also constituted in the act of decision. On these grounds, the political cannot pre-exist sovereignty; a world without sovereignty is no world at all.[37]

---

33   G. W. F. Hegel, *The Philosophy of Right*, Cambridge: Cambridge University Press, 1991 [1821], §279, emphasis in original.

34   Marx, "Contribution to the Critique of Hegel's Philosophy of Law," 26, 28.

35   Stathis Kouvelakis, *Philosophy and Revolution: From Marx to Kant*, London: Verso, 2003, 235.

36   Hegel, *Philosophy of Right*, §§278–79.

37   Schmitt, *The Concept of the Political*, 43–45; Schmitt, *Political Theology II*, 45.

These are not idle matters trawled from the past. On the contrary, from the perspective of the tradition of the radical Left, they magnify precisely what is at stake today in realizing this crucial dimension of Climate X. At bottom we face the old question: must we have sovereignty? Is a nonsovereign entity impossible? Even if it is a utopian gesture, the answer must be no. This is the essential utopianism of Climate X, the polar opposite of Climate Leviathan's "realism."[38] Marx identified the limits of our inherited conception of sovereignty as cause for great hope; in the juxtaposition of sovereignty of the people and monarchical sovereignty "we are not discussing *one and the same sovereignty* with its existence in two spheres, but two *wholly opposed conceptions of sovereignty . . .* One of the two must be false, even though an existing falsehood."[39] Hegel and Schmitt are right—democracy undoes the very possibility of rule. For them this is democracy's great failure; for Marx and us, however, it is its great promise. If the coming climate transition is to be just, there can be nothing left of sovereignty in the Hegelian-Schmittian sense. Another way to put this is to say X exposes and refuses the mysticism of the Idea of planetary rule, a sovereignty in search of a global subject.[40]

Much of the distinctiveness of climate politics comes down to temporality—the distressing urgency, the dreadful waiting, that we feel today. We can only grasp this present by coming to grips with these contingent historical dynamics that make it necessarily what it is. Only then can we glance, tentatively, into the future. This history is not without hope, but our efforts to rally it to our current conjuncture are inevitably fraught. There is certainly no reason to

---

38   See Mick Smith, *Against Ecological Sovereignty*, Minneapolis: University of Minnesota Press, 2011. One of the many provocative theses Smith advances is that sovereignty is essentially "an antiecological . . . principle" (xiii), since it emerges from a conception of the world as a space of resources for human use, hence in need of a sovereign to govern. While arguably correct, to claim that ecology is antisovereignty displaces the puzzles we face into a special region of the political (treating environmentalism as more radical because it is about nature). The Marxist tradition offers other (nonecological) ways through by treating a future communist democracy as something essentially different than sovereignty. Smith argues:

What if sovereign powers take it upon themselves to decide that there is, after all, an ecological threat to people and state sufficient to warrant the definition "crisis"? Isn't there now a real . . . possibility that the idea of an ecological crisis . . . will find itself recuperated by the very powers implicated in bringing that crisis about, as the latest and most comprehensive justification for a political state of emergency . . .? (xvi).

In that case, Smith writes, we would "find that the global war on terror will segue . . . into the crisis of global warming" (xvi). What Smith describes here as a "real . . . possibility" is Leviathan's fraught hegemony, and his propositional warning ("isn't there now . . .?") is not paranoid conspiracy theory. To the extent that Smith can describe this development as "real," that is, historically discernible, Leviathan is already present.

39   Marx, "Contribution to the Critique of Hegel's Philosophy of Law," 86, emphasis in original.

40   This is what Benjamin means by "divine violence": a form of transformation that, rather than smashing the existing sovereign/law and replacing it with another, disables sovereignty altogether. This is the source of inspiration for Agamben's destituent power.

expect that Climate X will ever consolidate at this or that scale, which means that even if it is to ultimately realize itself, it will almost certainly never be a unified phenomenon, a consolidated order or mode of organization. We might expect it to emerge as a ragtag collection of the many, but we cannot really say anything definitive. X, after all, is a variable. This does not mean, however, that anyone can choose what it should be:

> [My standpoint, in which] the development of the economic formation of society is viewed as a process of natural history, can less than any other make the individual responsible for relations whose creature he remains, socially speaking, however much he may subjectively raise himself above them.[41]

If the political is not a matter of individuals' responsibility and subjective decisions, then what? To say that it is a question of natural history may sound deterministic, but our conception of natural history follows upon Gramsci's radical critique of materialism and aligns, in the end, with Adorno, who also placed his final bet on a critical conception of natural history. Adorno's argument for natural history is not only to signal that nature has become historical (socially mediated), but also to turn our attention to *how* this mediation operates in capitalist society so that we may someday overcome it. We have insisted throughout that this is not only a problem of capital. As Marx and Adorno argued, the mystification of society in Hegel's *Philosophy of Right* results in making something (sovereignty) "divine and enduring and above the sphere of that which is produced," resulting in "absolut[e] domination . . . projected . . . on to Being itself."[42] Today, this historical process is bringing into being planetary sovereignty, an emerging form of domination that is changing nature, including human nature, anew. In calling our attention to this possibility, Adorno's intention was not to call for a romantic return to unmediated, "true" nature, or to transcend our own naturalness. Both strategies, persistent temptations for environmentalists of different stripes, are misguided. Instead, Adorno expressed an admittedly utopian hope for a potential reconvergence of nature and history. But this reconvergence cannot happen just anywhere, and it cannot be willed. It is not a matter of simply renaming our time the Anthropocene. It requires living differently, radically differently, than we do now. And this—the question of living radically differently than "we" do now—is arguably a question that Marxism has never been very good at answering. The radical Left has

---

41   Karl Marx, *Capital*, Vol. I, New York: Penguin, 1976 [1867], xx, 92.

42   Adorno, *Negative Dialectics*, 1966, 356–57, cited in Deborah Cook, *Adorno on Nature*, Durham, Acumen Press, 2011, 15. Cook's study of Adorno is a major contribution to the task of reclaiming Adorno's thought for political-ecological thinking. See Adorno's essay "The Idea of Natural History," in Robert Hullot-Kentor, *Things Beyond Resemblance: Collected Essays on Theodor W. Adorno*, New York: Columbia University Press, 2006, 252–70, and Fredric Jameson's commentary on Adorno's conception of natural history in *Late Marxism: Adorno, or, The Persistence of the Dialectic*, New York: Verso, 2007, 94–110.

justifiably always rejected the false nostalgia for a "return" to nature, or a rolling back of history to some time that probably never was. It has equally justifiably remained skeptical of no less illusory utopian futures. But Marxism's materialist embrace of history means that the futures to which it aspires have more often than not looked like freer, nonexploitative variations on the world in which we live. Indeed, prior to the emergence of eco-socialism and other "green radicalisms," the communist future was for the most part understood as an industrial paradise, a highly developed economy stripped of its disequalizing and repressive capitalist domination. Eco-socialist visions are not all that different. They almost always include a full suite of "green" technologies in combination with a more just form of governance and distribution—usually, so that we could continue to live as we do, at least in the material sense, but more justly and "sustainably." These proposals rarely posit a clear conception of living radically differently, and while they are clearly offered in the interests of democracy, they virtually never question the principle of sovereignty.

Some of the richest resources we have access to for thinking about what it would mean and require to live radically differently are to be found in the engagement and flourishing of the second trajectory that can constitute Climate X: the modes of life of many Indigenous and colonized peoples. Radical Indigenous thinkers have grounded a powerful critique of sovereignty and our relation with the planet and its environments in the experience of dispossession—an experience, one might expect, that would tend to lead those from whom land was stolen to reassert the centrality of sovereignty, and that is indeed where a substantial part of Indigenous political energy has been understandably directed. And yet, against that urge—and often working on terrain first tilled by earlier Indigenous and anticolonial struggles like that of the Zapatistas—writers like Taiaiake Alfred, Glen Coulthard, Aileen Moreton-Robinson, Patricia Monture, and Audra Simpson have attempted not merely to undo the sovereign claims of colonial powers, but to go further, challenging the very form and nature of sovereignty.[43] In the words of Alfred, "the actual history

43   See, for example, Patricia Monture-Angus, *Journeying Forward: Dreaming First Nations' Independence*, Halifax, Fernwood Publishing, 1999; Taiaiake Alfred, "Sovereignty," in Joanne Barker (ed.), *Sovereignty Matters: Locations of Contestation and Possibility in Indigenous Struggles for Self-determination*, Lincoln, NE: University of Nebraska Press. 2005; Aileen Moreton-Robinson, *Sovereign Subjects: Indigenous Sovereignty Matters*, Sydney: Allen and Unwin, 2007; Coulthard, *Red Skin, White Masks*; and Audra Simpson, *Mohawk Interruptus: Political Life Across the Borders of Settler States*, Durham, NC: Duke University Press, 2014. It is worth noting that these scholars come from territories now claimed by former British colonies and OECD countries (Canada mainly). There are deep traditions of Indigenous struggle and thought the world over, of course, and often they revolve around precisely these concerns—reciprocity, land, and a way out of the liberal-colonial sovereign mode. Among others, we can turn to the remarkable efforts of the Mapuche in the southern Andes, or to the (Indigenous and non-Indigenous) people of Oaxaca—who have brought together anticapitalist class-based and Indigenous struggles—for courageous and critical examples from which to learn. See John Severino, "The Mapuche's Struggle for the

of our plural existence has been erased by the narrow fictions of a single sovereignty"; "sovereignty" has become a big part of the problem: it has "limited the ways [Indigenous peoples] are able to think, suggesting always a conceptual and definitional problem centered on the accommodation of indigenous peoples within a 'legitimate' framework of settler state governance." His bracing conclusion: "'sovereignty' is inappropriate as a political objective for indigenous peoples":[44]

> One of the main obstacles to achieving peaceful coexistence is of course the uncritical acceptance of the classic notion of sovereignty as the framework for discussions of political relations between peoples. The discourse of sovereignty has effectively stilled any potential resolution of the issue that respects Indigenous values and perspectives. Even "traditional" indigenous nationhood is commonly defined relationally, in contrast to the dominant formulation of the state: there is no absolute authority, no coercive enforcement of decisions, no hierarchy, and no separate ruling entity.[45]

But, if anticolonists are not fighting for *sovereignty*, for a better position as "full" participants in the prevailing, nation-state based politics of recognition, then for what do they struggle?

One political strategy that seeks to realize these commitments is to multiply political practices of "disruptive *countersovereignty*," in Coulthard's words.[46] The really difficult question is how countersovereignty could articulate the struggles for what appear standard liberal goods: land, autonomy, and the authority and capacity to found alternative modes of governing.[47] How can the fight against capitalist imperialism—not to mention the material struggle for *land*—escape the clutches of sovereign governmentality and help move us all toward climate

---

Land," *Counterpunch*, November 2013, available at counterpunch.org; A. S. Dillingham, "Mexico's Classroom Wars: An Interview with René González Pizzaro," *Jacobin*, June 2016, jacobinmag. com; and Amy Goodman's interview with Gustavo Esteva, "Struggling for Our Lives," Democracy Now, June 22, 2016, democracynow.org.

44   Alfred, "Sovereignty," 34–35, 38.

45   Ibid., 41–42.

46   Discussing the widespread Indigenous blockading in Canada in the late 1980s, which (in the eyes of many) culminated in the summer of 1990 at Kanehsatà:ke and Kahnewà:ke (the "Oka Crisis," outside of Montréal), Coulthard remarks:

> If settler-state stability and authority is required to ensure "certainty" over Indigenous lands and resources to create an investment climate friendly for expanded capital accumulation, then the barrage of Indigenous practices of disruptive *countersovereignty* that emerged with increased frequency in the 1980s was an embarrassing demonstration that Canada no longer had its shit together with respect to managing the so-called "Indian Problem".

Coulthard, *Red Skin, White Masks*, 118, emphasis added.

47   See for example ibid., 122; on standard liberal goods, see also Charles Taylor, *Sources of the Self: The Making of Modern Identity*, Cambridge: Cambridge University Press, 1989.

justice? For Coulthard, the answer is straightforward, though not simple, and points us in a direction that much of Climate X—at least in its present, inchoate forms—is moving:

> Indigenous struggles against capitalist imperialism are best understood as struggles oriented around the question of *land*—struggles not only *for* land, but also deeply *informed* by what the land as a mode of reciprocal *relationship* (which is itself informed by place-based practices and associated forms of knowledge) ought to teach us about living our lives in relation to one another and our surroundings in a respectful, nondominating and nonexploitative way.[48]

The principle distinction between an orthodox conception of sovereignty and this framework—indeed, the dynamic that gives it a "countering" sense of active refusal or reversal—is the centrality of reciprocity.[49] Within any given territory, sovereignty is a non-reciprocal relation, by definition. Whether one understands it as constituted in the Schmittian "decider" who arrogates the power of exception, or in the adoption of subjection by the many before the authority of the one, or even in a more collective-democratic mode, sovereignty is, at root, all about rule.

This is a challenge not only to specifically colonial forms of sovereignty, but to any and all forms of sovereignty that can be logically or historically paired with the modifier "colonial"—which is all liberal-capitalist forms.[50] What is at issue is not captured by the idea of a struggle *over* sovereignty; rather, the dynamic construction of countersovereignty is best understood as an attempt to claim "the right to be responsible," individually and collectively: to have power, to have meaning, to understand oneself, one's communities, and one's histories as not only inseparable but also ineliminable from reciprocity and the land. This is not land that individuals or states own in the liberal, capitalist sense, as state-space (territory) and property (commodity), but land of which one is a fundamental part.[51] Insofar as Indigenous modes of life are not about "settling" the land—colonizing it, making it property—but rather about the continuity of

---

48   Coulthard, *Red Skin, White Masks*, 60, emphasis in original.

49   These paragraphs draw on Geoff Mann, "From Countersoevereignty to Counterpossession?" *Historical Materialism* 24, no. 3, 2016, 45–61.

50   The place of what Audra Simpson (in *Mohawk Interruptus*, 2014) calls "nested sovereignties" remains uncertain in the face of Coulthard's "countersovereignty."

51   In the context of British Columbia, sovereignty is taken to be "crystallized" by European settlement. In the landmark 1997 decision in *Delgamuukw v. British Columbia*, the Supreme Court of Canada maintained that "Aboriginal title crystallized at the time sovereignty was asserted," as if it were a kind of legal antimatter: *Delgamuukw v. British Columbia* [1997] 3 S. C. R. 1010, at 1017. Precolonial Indigenous "occupation" of British Columbia was deemed *eo ipso* "pre-sovereignty"; sovereignty is defined as an event in (past) time: "if, *at the time of sovereignty*, an aboriginal society had laws in relation to land, those laws would be relevant to establishing the occupation of lands which are the subject of a claim for aboriginal title": ibid., 1101–2.) With the closure of pathways for the articulation of Indigenous demands except for those constructed by the colonial state and its modes of "doing law" (courts, tribunals, contract law, and so on), Indigenous claims to a variation on national sovereignty have emerged as a "default" politics (Coulthard, *Red Skin, White Masks*, 53).

living together within and upon it, they show the poverty of the liberal concept of sovereignty, which "designates less a content that can be replaced" and more "a process of compulsory relation, one predicated on the supposedly unquestionable fact of national territorial boundaries."[52] Hence, as we witness the gathering of Indigenous leaders in opposition to a colonial climate injustice, in Paris or Standing Rock, it is a grave mistake to assume "that what indigenous peoples are seeking in recognition of their nationhood is at its core the same as that which countries like Canada and the United States possess now."[53]

Is it really fanciful to anticipate that these two trajectories, movements inspired by either one or some combination of these fundamental traditions of critical thought and practice, might (in Adorno's words, following the lead of Benjamin) "intersect in the moment of transience," a transience experienced as both crisis and opportunity?[54] Benjamin's model for a political strategy to achieve this transience was the general strike, the collective decision to cease our ceaseless production and consumption and form something different. Even if that moment is an event we can never fully grasp, this possibility must be cultivated in the openness of Climate X. This is one of the reasons it is Climate X: it must be able to become and include what it needs to be to point us toward (at least the beginnings of) a solution. Bundle together the most radical strategies of the climate justice movement—mass boycott, divestment, strike, blockade, reciprocity—and you will glimpse Benjamin's vision of another world, where natural history and human history "intersect in the moment of transience."

This glimpse may seem too imprecise a way to close this account. However, because the account is in fact not closing, but only just opening, we prefer to see it as a politically and analytically responsible gesture in radically uncertain times. The planetary crisis is, among other things, a crisis of the imagination, a crisis of ideology, the result of an inability to conceive any alternative to walls, guns, and finance as tools to address the problems that loom on the horizon. Our task is to see the ruins and fragments of our natural-historical moment for what they truly are; not to draw up blueprints of an emancipated world, but to reject Leviathan, Mao, and Behemoth, while affirming other possibilities. What remains? All we have and all we have ever had: X to solve for, a world to win.

---

52   Mark Rifkin, "Indigenizing Agamben: Rethinking Sovereignty in Light of the 'Peculiar' Status of Native Peoples," *Cultural Critique* 73, 2009, 105.

53   Alfred, "Sovereignty," 42.

54   Adorno, 359, in Cook, *Adorno on Nature*, 17.

Index